Dispatches from Ray's Planet

Caitlin Press Inc.
8100 Alderwood Road,
Halfmoon Bay, BC V0N 1Y1
www.caitlin-press.com

Text and cover design by Vici Johnstone
Edited by Betsy Warland

Printed in Canada

Caitlin Press Inc. acknowledges financial support from the Government of Canada and the Canada Council for the Arts, and the Province of British Columbia through the British Columbia Arts Council and the Book Publisher's Tax Credit.

Library and Archives Canada Cataloguing in Publication

Dispatches from Ray's planet : a journey through autism / by Claire Finlayson.

Finlayson, Claire, 1957- author.
Canadiana 20200222783 | ISBN 9781773860305 (softcover)
LCSH: Finlayson, Ray. | LCSH: Finlayson, Claire. | LCSH: Finlayson, Ray—Family. | LCSH:
　　　Finlayson, Claire, 1957-—Family. | LCSH: Autistic people—Canada—Biography. | LCSH: Autistic people—Family relationships—Canada. | LCGFT: Biographies.
LCC RC553.A88 F56 2020 | DDC 616.85/8820092—dc23

Dispatches from Ray's Planet

A Journey through Autism

Claire Finlayson

CAITLIN PRESS 2020

For Writing Man

CONTENTS

PREFACE

I grew up in a large family and only found out later in life that one of my brothers is on the autism spectrum. This is my account of our mutual struggle to understand—or should I say, try to understand—each other. I had no formal knowledge of Asperger's syndrome (as it was once called) or autism spectrum disorder (as it is presently called) when I began writing this book. I had no idea that I was considered "neurotypical," or indeed that other neurotypes existed; my ways of thinking and behaving were simply the "correct" ways. Ray just had to stop treating everyone to his unfiltered observations. He needed to be more sensitive to the feelings of others—for their sakes and his—and I offered my well-meaning help in that regard.

I have since come to believe that I was torturing him.

I love my brother. I have stopped trying to remake him in my own image. I do not censor him, and I will not apologize for him. He has suffered enough for his unwitting social sins already. He and I both hope that his difficult journey and his raw and eloquent account of it on these pages will smooth the way, just a little bit, for the next generation of neurodivergents and those who love them.

Maybe one day nobody will have to dream of a world somewhere out there on the edge of the galaxy where they can safely be themselves. Maybe one day this will be everybody's planet.

THE QUEST

Could a greater miracle take place than for us to look through each other's eyes for an instant?
— Henry David Thoreau

Ray was at it again. We were sitting in the high school cafeteria one day during lunch hour, and he was expounding loudly on the treacherous games people play and how he loathed them. "On *my* planet," he said, gesturing skyward with what remained of his peanut butter and jam sandwich, "sugar-coating the truth is an insult. Do I have spinach in my teeth? Thanks for letting me know! Did something I said offend you? Oops! Sorry about that! Glad to have the feedback; how else would I do better next time?" He tossed the crust into his brown paper lunch bag, crumpled it with both hands and pushed it toward the middle of the table.

I'd heard this speech one too many times.

I was fairly certain that my older brother was the child of earthling parents just like me and our four younger siblings, and I was sick of hearing how much better things were on *his* planet. I rolled my eyes and sighed.

Decades have gone by since that day, but in spite of all the things I've forgotten along the way, I still remember exactly what I said to him: "You know what, Ray? I swear I'm going to find out what planet you come from."

It would be thirty more years before I would make good on that vow.

THE GAME

Goongbalong. That is the word Ray invented to describe the game that humans play among themselves. It's the game of tact, social niceties, subtle hints, little white lies, polite chit-chat—manoeuvres that have eluded him all his life. To him, those things amount to a lot of people working very hard to *not* say what they mean.

It's not only master manipulators who play the game—we all do. Anyone who says, "Are you *sure* you can't stay for dinner?" when she's grateful you're leaving and hopes never to see you again is making a nice Goongbalong pass. Anyone who pretends he doesn't notice the wart on your nose or your "lazy eye" is playing just a little.

The rules of Goongbalong—or "The Rules," as Ray calls them, always with air quotes for emphasis—are unwritten, and yet somehow everybody else seems to know them. The consequences of flouting them are swift and severe. Ray spells it out to me in an email:

> There is a certain kind of person—a woman, usually—who can come to hate me so much that they seem to be on the brink of insanity. It would be a Great Moment in my life if I could come to understand why this happens. This hatred can, on occasion, blossom almost instantaneously. I commit some Goongbalong foul that seems to entail absolute and permanent expulsion from that person's social circle. It can happen anywhere, anytime, which is why I'm in a state of constant terror when I'm around other people.

Constant terror? Ray's use of such a potent phrase takes me aback. We grew up in the same house, and I, only sixteen months his junior, have never detected a mote of fear in him. I always thought of him as, if anything, a little overconfident.

"Surely you're just being paranoid, Ray," I write back. "It can't be that bad!"

But Ray, who insists on using my long-obsolete childhood nickname, assures me that it is:

> Yes, Babs, it's that bad. Some of them have erupted in spitting, stuttering, purple-faced rage. One example was my dentist's receptionist back in West Van. I only saw her once every six months—and that was at the beginning and end of my appointments. For the love of God! How much did we have to do with each other?? What on earth could one say to a receptionist to piss her off to such a degree?

Ray answers his own question:

> I didn't really "do" anything; I just emit the wrong magnetic field or something. I'm mostly always terrified and maybe people can smell fear the way a dog can. Maybe fear smells like arrogance.

And unfortunately, there's no opting out:

> You are not permitted to sit out the game—you *are* playing all the time, whether you like it or not.

Goongbalong. It doesn't roll easily off the tongue. And that's just the way Ray wants it: it's hard to say because it's hard to play. "Every time someone has to pronounce my word," he tells me, "they are forced to do something unnatural and counterintuitive. That's my life. My word is my revenge."

Ray just couldn't seem to learn The Rules—even though they came factory installed in the rest of us. As he grew into a teenager, many people concluded that he was simply too arrogant to toe the line. They said that a guy as smart as he is could easily fall into step with the rest of us if he wanted to, but he preferred to make some sort of "statement" by thumbing his nose at accepted standards of behaviour, always looking for a way to distinguish himself from the herd. "Well, that's Raymond, isn't it, dear?" said our Aunt Nell when he turned up at a family party in greasy coveralls with grime under his nails. "He just *has* to be different." And maybe there's some truth to that: Ray is not interested in blending in. But given what I now believe to be the case, it seems to me that he never had as much choice in the matter as everyone thought. Including him.

Ray has always known he's different, but at sixty-three years of age, he certainly doesn't believe he needs to be cured. According to him, the world would be vastly improved if everybody thought and behaved the way he does. He embraces the fact that he's eccentric. But being eccentric, he says, is not the same as being defective. "We don't say someone *has* eccentricity," he tells me. "We simply say he's eccentric. It's not a disease." He vigorously resists the idea that he needs to be fixed because, as he would say, on *his* planet he ain't broken.

Despite sharing a given name with the autistic savant portrayed in the movie *Rain Man*, which brought autism into the popular consciousness, Ray has no single massive talent set against a backdrop of disability. And he doesn't look or act much like the autistic characters that are played—one might say "parodied"—on popular shows today. Those characters usually live in nice apartments, surrounded by well-dressed, indulgent, neurotypical friends. They possess prodigious intellects, and their awkwardness is played for laughs. A favourite plot device is to put the science geek in a room with an attractive neurotypical woman in a low-cut top and watch the fun. It's always just enough to make autists somehow endearing despite their rough edges. Sure, Ray can talk intelligently on many topics, but he's no genius, and he cannot entertain and amaze the crowds with any particular super-ability. Lacking any such schtick to hide behind, he writes, with a note of melancholy:

> It is bitterest gall to me that I'm not some sort of savant. It would at least compensate for all the rest.

Although he grudgingly admits at this late date that he meets certain criteria that *might perhaps possibly* earn him a place on the autism spectrum, he's wary of being formally diagnosed with anything, and thus far, like many of his generation, he hasn't been. "Why," he asks me, "do we need a *syndrome* to describe people who say what they mean?"

The fact that he remains undiagnosed is not for a lack of trying on my part. But no sooner had I discovered that there was a plausible explanation for his puzzling combination of intellectual gifts and social deficits, and that it is called Asperger's syndrome, than the shrinks went and rewrote their book (the *Diagnostic and Statistical Manual of Mental Disorders*, or DSM), eliminating it as a diagnosis. The correct term as of May 2013 is "autism spectrum disorder." I was still trying to sell Ray on the fact that he was an "Aspergian" when he heard the news and called me up. "Hey," he said gleefully, "I hear I'm being delisted!"

Brainy nerds like Ray no longer have their own clubhouse; they're now part of a vast continuum ranging from the highly gifted but "mostly always terrified" to the severely incapacitated, from the loquacious to the nonverbal, the highly focused to the fixated.

Ray is not happy about the change. Over time he has become more or less reconciled to having Asperger's syndrome even though, as he has made abundantly clear, he's never going to be entirely comfortable sporting this or any other label. But if forced to pick a name for his "disorder"—sorry, Ray, that's what they call it—he'd rather not "have" autism spectrum disorder. He feels no kinship with deeply autistic people: they seem determined *not* to communicate with others, when he was born to do precisely that.

Here, for the record, are his feelings on the matter, delivered with smashing political incorrectness:

> I shouldn't say this, but I hate being referred to as "autistic." Asperger's I can handle. Even if you want to advocate for "the spectrum," it seems wrong to use "autistic." It just paints the wrong image in the mind; I think Asperger's is more descriptively accurate. I know I probably shouldn't worry about it.

Actually, he probably should. There is no longer any such diagnosis. Even if there was, would he be comfortable wearing the name of such a controversial figure? Dr. Hans Asperger, the pediatrician for whom the syndrome is named, was until recently hailed as patron saint and saviour of the unique subset of autistic people who bore his name. He has often been quoted as saying, "For success in science or art, a dash of autism is essential. [It imparts] an ability to turn away from the everyday world, from the simply practical, and to rethink a subject with originality so as to create in new untrodden ways." A "dash of autism"—I've always loved that. But Asperger has been posthumously accused of cherry-picking "high functioning" autistics to study while tacitly surrendering the more "defective" children to the mercies of the Nazi eugenics program. Autistic people are renouncing his name in droves.

But Ray is not quick to jump aboard the bandwagon demonizing Asperger (or any other bandwagon, for that matter). In this email, he goes on a proper rant about historical revisionism:

> It is the fashion these days to try to remove everyone from history who has been accused of some violation of our current politically correct norms. The Americans will tear down the Washington Monument one day because Washington was a slave owner. Martin Luther King was known to attend orgies, JFK was a womanizer, Tchaikovsky was a pedophile, Jefferson had a black mistress. Werner von Braun was a Nazi, but he put a man on the moon.

> Many people who did bad things would not have done them had the situation been different. Hans A. did not ask to be born when and where he was born. Even if he did some bad stuff, we will never know if he enjoyed it and we will never know what we would have done in the same situation and I think we should give him some charity. We still call it the Gregorian calendar even if we have since discovered that Pope Gregory was not a very nice man. Can we only name things after nice people? If we discover that Amerigo Vespucci beat his wife, will we be renaming North, South and Central America?

It's Asperger's syndrome, damn it.

And for the record I don't want to be labelled autistic.
I don't sit in a corner all day banging my head on the
floor. The "spectrum" is not something I want to be on.

Ray can take that up with the proper authorities. Until the dust
settles, I will use the terms "Autism Spectrum Disorder" (ASD) and
"Asperger syndrome" (AS) interchangeably, as the latter term is still in
common use, despite Dr. Asperger's latter-day fall from grace.

The DSM-5 is a behemoth compared to its earlier incarnations.
It contains many new diagnoses, including Social Communication
Disorder, with symptoms and behaviours that overlap those seen in
Autism Spectrum Disorder. Ray's a shoo-in for that one. He'd happily admit to having a galloping case of Social Anxiety Disorder, too
(around since the DSM-4), and maybe we could throw in Avoidant Per-
sonality Disorder from the DSM-3 for good measure.

Ray likes to point out that "social anxiety" used to be called shyness, which is not a disease—or it wasn't until the shrinks invented
"social anxiety disorder" and started medicating it. "Oh no!" he says,
eyes wide and fingers fanned out beside his face in mock horror, "Call
an ambulance! My child has *shyness*!"

To further illustrate the absurdity of our rush to medicalize normal human behaviour, he indicates our brother-in-law, Mike, who
has invited a bunch of us over for dinner and is busy cooking it while
we lounge about in his living room with our pre-dinner drinks. "Does
Mike have 'jerk syndrome'?" asks Ray theatrically, waving his beer in
Mike's direction. "No! We simply say, 'Mike is a jerk.'"

My brother is deeply ambivalent about the whole autism/As-
perger's thing. On the one hand, he acknowledges that an official
diagnosis could be a lifesaver in sticky situations; on the other hand,
he doesn't want his experiences and his way of thinking arbitrari-
ly boxed up and labelled so that everyone can presume, based on a
five-minute Google search, to know precisely who and what he is.
Can you blame him?

But Ray has also made it clear that he would not elect to be a garden-variety neurotypical like me for any money. He told me not long

ago, "I don't have the slightest desire to be normal. I may be a freak, but I don't want anyone to change me."

The truth is, I cannot imagine any other version of my brother than the one I have. But when I tell him I don't need him to be "normal"—whatever that is—he isn't buying it.

"I believe you believe yourself," he scoffs. "But the entire world is a conformity hammer. As a round peg, you slide through the round hole with barely a tap of the hammer. The square peg in the round hole has an entirely different view of things."

Ray wears his sharp corners with pride, even though it means he will continue to feel the bash of the mallet all his life. He bears his loneliness with proud stoicism—that is, until someone like me comes along with a sanding block and a sheet of 60-grit sandpaper and offers to lovingly smooth off those edges. Then just watch his hackles go up.

People sometimes ask me if I can tell when Ray is just being difficult and when his behaviour can be excused by his—ahem—"condition." How I wish I knew the answer! I think his intentions are almost always good, but he's just a man, after all, and a wounded one at that, so any answer I might give would be a complicated one.

He is always thinking up novel ways to do things. "Standard procedure" is nothing more than a challenge to his ingenuity, a gauntlet thrown down.

There are times—though I bet he'd deny this—when he does things just to be contrary. He enjoys his status as a nonconformist and looks for ways to distinguish himself from the herd. Oh sure, he does that without even trying, but he's after the bonus points. If "we" do it *this* way, Ray will do it *that* way.

Even his cellphone's voice mail message shows his contrary streak:

> Ray Andrews here. Please wait a few minutes for me
> to call you back before you leave a message. Voice
> mail is by far the worst possible way of getting a hold
> of me. *Beeeep.*

I grow incrementally more exasperated each time I hear that message telling me not to leave a message. "Just text me!" Ray says when I suggest with some impatience that he check his voice mail like a normal person. "Text me! Way better!" Not way better for *me*, though, especially back in the early days of cellphones when I had an old flip-top model like his, requiring several ulcer-inducing minutes of pecking and poking to get a simple message out.

A family friend named Steven was making the trip by ferry from Vancouver to our home here in Gibsons on British Columbia's Sunshine Coast. Steven is a humble and diffident man for whom Goongbalong is an exercise in agony. I was making a nice dinner for him and tried calling to invite Ray. I listened to that infernal message several times, but he didn't call back as advertised. I finally resorted to leaving a voice mail—"by far the worst possible way" of getting a hold of him. I later followed up by getting in my car and driving to his place—honestly, it was faster than texting—to invite him in person. "Oh, sure, love to," he said. "Just text me when you know what ferry Steve's on." So I did. I texted him three times, starting mid-afternoon. The last time was during dinner: *Ray, Steve is here—where r u?*

Ray was a no-show. I tried to brush it off, but the next morning I woke up feeling uneasy. He is usually reliable and punctual. What could have happened that would cause him to pass up good company and a roast beef dinner with all the trimmings? My phone call to him again went unanswered: "Ray Andrews here. Please wait a few minutes for me to ..." I snapped my phone shut. One of my sisters said she was going out and would check on him. A short while later, I received a text message from her that said, *All well. Ray says you didn't email him.*

Speaking of email, he even refuses to do that like everyone else does. Instead of writing replies above my messages where his cursor is obligingly blinking at him, he'll scroll down and stick his reply below mine. Worse yet, when he and I are having an involved email discussion and it's his turn, he "tidies up" our correspondence by copying and pasting dismembered bits of text into a fresh new email, wedging his comments between those sentence fragments instead of letting the conversational thread unspool in a nice long stream.

When I complain or entreat him to humour me by doing it my way, just this once, just for me, pretty please, he offers to come over and install his obscure email program on my computer so that all replies will automatically indent with an ever-increasing number of chevrons the way his do. One must count chevrons to figure out how many times a given line of text has shuttled back and forth.

I once spent a whole evening copying and pasting swaths of text from dozens of emails, patiently reconstructing the flow of our conversation. I used colour-coding and italics to show who was "speaking." Satisfied that it all made sense at last, I sent the reworked version to Ray. He did not appreciate my efforts. He asked me to cease and desist:

> Babs, would you please correspond using the "indent" style? As I see this, it is a mishmash of different fonts and colours that is very difficult to read. It might be an Aspie thing, but I find the overuse of fonts, colours, sizes, italics, etc. to be not only unhelpful but positively disturbing.

His singular style extends into every corner of his life. He has an assortment of cheap drugstore reading glasses, the kind that come with peel-off stickers on the lenses stating the strength of the magnification. He uses different powers for different tasks, and he likes the stickers right where they are, thank you very much—it's easier than squinting at the teensy numbers inside the arms. Almost every single person, upon first noticing one of these stickers, will helpfully try to peel it off, assuming he's just forgotten to do so himself. It startles Ray to have people—sometimes perfect strangers—reaching for his face. I've seen him jerk his head away, hands flying up to protect himself from their darting fingers, but he's sticking with the stickers.

Almost everything Ray owns he has either built himself or modified in some way. A few years ago he started teaching himself to play the cello. One evening my phone rang. The call display indicated that it was him, but he didn't respond to my hellos. Just as I was about to hang up, I heard a scraping sound, followed by an unearthly series of quavering squawks. It took me a minute to realize that I was being treated to a screechy rendition of "The Swan" from Saint-Saëns's *Carnival of the Animals*. I found myself blinking back tears, touched that he had chosen to favour me with his amateur performance—but also because it was so sweetly, ear-splittingly awful.

Ray has done some after-market modifications to his cello to make it work more efficiently:

> I replaced the Stone Age wooden tuning pegs with modern mechanical string winders, like on a guitar. This makes tuning much easier and narrows the head, which makes it possible to rest it on my shoulder.

What that means is that the cello now has ugly chrome bolts sticking Frankenstein-like out of its neck.

Ray goes on to explain his rationale for butchering the beautiful instrument:

> It is now braced much more solidly, and it becomes possible to play "thumb over" across the whole length of the fingerboard. Also, the lower and more sloped holding position means that the forearm is more perpendicular to the fingerboard, which strikes me as much more natural. Besides, that way it's possible to see the fingerboard while playing, which of course invited me to draw frets on it so that I know where my fingers should go. This would no doubt make any normal cellist retch. Oh, and I'm on the verge of drilling a few discreet holes in it to control resonance. Now if I could just learn to play the damn thing ...

"And didn't you cut its pretty head off, too?"

> Alas, the scroll interfered with the winders; there was no avoiding it.

"Well, I think you'll burn for that."

Ray is fatalistic:

> I'll burn for so many things before that even comes up on my charge sheet that it will hardly make a difference.

Regardless of what Ray "has" or doesn't "have," the fact is that placing computers between him and me causes his social deficits to magically disappear. That I don't have to deal with his atrocious handwriting and that there is a spell-checker to catch and correct most of his spelling mistakes—these are mere fringe benefits.

When Ray composes his thoughts on a keyboard, he hits the pause button on the Goongbalong action. The players are mercifully frozen in place while he calmly plans his next move. He can rewind the tape and play it again in slo-mo. He doesn't make the verbal gaffes that have caused him—and those around him—so much pain. Over the years of our email correspondence, I have come to think of these two aspects of Ray, the speaking version and the emailing version, as almost separate individuals, and I have given them capitals: *Writing Man* and *Speaking Man*. Ray's gone along with it, although he sometimes refers to Writing Man as Thinking Man, Inner Man or Silent Man—so we use those terms interchangeably. After five decades of misunderstandings, we have finally found a sturdy bridge between ourselves—the written word.

Writing Man, unlike his jittery spokesman, will tackle any issue, answer any question willingly and with astonishing fluency. His thoughts are honed and perfectly polished before they are sent out. When my brother places his fingers on the keyboard, the inner, voiceless man shimmers into view. Respond by email and you will find yourself in conversation with Writing Man. The real Ray.

If Ray can turn his dentist's receptionist into a homicidal maniac during a routine visit, you'd think he would be terrified of strangers, but that is not the case.

> Fact is, I can chat with a stranger in a lineup as well as the next guy. I even tend to be a bit of a joker.

Yes, Ray can perform this common ritual like a pro—I've seen him do it. His proficiency in talking to strangers may seem surprising given his sometimes paralyzing social anxiety but think about it: there is always a "topic" during these brief exchanges; no mind-reading is required, and there is little, if any, emotional reciprocity expected. And though Ray can't avoid seeing his dentist's receptionist at least once or twice a year, he will probably never see the stranger in the lineup again, so there's nothing to lose.

It's a different story when he walks into a social gathering where he must interact with people he knows superficially. Every one of these people—who are neither trusted friends nor strangers—represents a clear and present danger to Ray. In fact, they are the most intimidating demographic on the planet. He explains:

> The trouble is with folks I *half* know. With a stranger, nothing much is expected beyond simple politeness, and with family, well, they know what to expect. But with the Halfers, the rituals of Goongbalong are at their most intense. You go through a sort of act of pretending to be very close friends when you aren't.

The minute Ray comes eyeball to eyeball with a Halfer, a macabre dance begins. An elaborate series of Goongbalong manoeuvres must be performed—and performed *correctly*. If the Halfer is a loud, chattering woman wearing a big smile that shows most of her teeth, it is safe to assume that Ray will be petrified. If, in addition to having her volume set at maximum, she is showing a lot of cleavage, wearing garish makeup or displaying any other prominent features that attract Speaking Man's attention, he's doomed, and he knows it. With no topic of mutual interest queued up and the Halfer bearing down on his position, his brain sends the distress signal: *"Warning! Chit-Chat Ahead!"* He fights a rising dread as he scans for the nearest exit.

"You have no idea how unpleasant it is for me," he says of navigating a room full of casual acquaintances. "Nobody does." Halfers always appear warm and friendly—this is a primary doctrine of Goongbalong—but he knows they are furtively totting up his infractions on their scorecards without ever breaking their smiles. He hugs the wall and prays no one will approach him. When that fails—and it always does—he makes a desperate gambit to steer the conversation somewhere safe and solid, away from the dangerous, swirling eddies of "Nice-to-see-you-again-you're-looking-well-how've-you-been?" and the unwritten but mandatory responses to those vacuous inquiries that so utterly elude him and upon which his acceptability as a human being is graded. The clock is ticking, it's his move, and Speaking Man, in his terror, blurts out something he fervently hopes is appropriate. Thinking Man assumes the crash position and covers his ears.

Honesty, Ray adds, doesn't pay in a neurotypical world:

> When I try to make small talk with a Halfer, I will intend to say something like, "You are looking very well today," but I end up making some honest observation about how the person looks—and that is always a mistake.

It was a long time before the awful truth finally sank in:

> I find it very easy to talk about pretty much any subject, but almost impossible to talk about nothing. "Normal" people find talking about nothing to be very important. Sometimes I just tune it out. Seagulls express their "matedness" by squawking and babbling. People do that too. I don't mind it. I just can't do it. I was probably in my thirties before I realized that when someone comes up to me and says, "How are you?" they are not actually asking a question. You say, "I'm fine, how are you?" But you're not asking a real question either ...

Ray is never going to be able to approach a knot of neurotypicals and ooze right in with easy grace and charm. He knows his only chance of getting through the ordeal unscathed involves playing a socially acceptable version of himself, but he has a tough time with the necessary charades. It is undignified, he says, to be required to ape the behaviour of neurotypicals to gain their acceptance. Besides, it makes for a thin disguise, one that can slip at any moment, revealing him as an impostor. But in he goes, talking about nothing as though his life depended on it. Because in a way it does.

This is Goongbalong, and oh, how he resents having to play the despicable game. On his planet, it's a capital offence.

WHIPLASH

Dad was a real estate developer in West Vancouver when much of it was still under virgin forest. In the late 1950s, he cleared a patch of land at the base of Black Mountain and created a new subdivision with a curving main street that he called Cranley Drive.

We lived in a whole lot of those houses, some more than once, as Dad juggled rentals and real estate deals. Our youngest sister, Trish, was even born in one of them, after Mum realized she wasn't going to make it to the hospital in time for the arrival of baby number six. So we do not locate our childhoods to any specific house. To this day, as soon as any one of us turns up Cranley Drive, we are home.

In those days, kids spent most of their summers outside, only coming in when mothers hollered from kitchen doors that supper was ready. We were masters of our domain, free to roam the unspoiled evergreen forests and mountains just beyond our backyards. Mum was far too busy with her two youngest children to worry about where her first four were and what we were doing. We climbed trees, rode bikes, caught tadpoles in jars and fished for rock cod off the dock at Fisherman's Cove. In summer we practically lived at Eagle Harbour beach. Occasionally we would lug heavy flannel sleeping bags up Black Mountain and camp on mossy granite outcroppings—usually under a lean-to fashioned out of cedar boughs by an enterprising young Ray. I always felt safe with him. The worst that ever happened was the lean-to collapsing on us once in the cold light of dawn when one of us—he says it was me; I say it was him—accidentally kicked out a supporting post. I woke abruptly to find a corner of my sleeping bag in the ashes of our fire and my long hair frozen to the rock. We were home in time for breakfast. Mum checked us over for ticks and carried on with her housework.

Perhaps best of all, we had our own creek. Nelson Creek tumbles down Black Mountain and follows Cranley Drive, running along the back edges of the lots on the west side of the street before joining the ocean. We played the length of it, from the top of Cranley to the bottom. Ray delighted in re-engineering the watercourse. He would roll the smooth, heavy rocks around to make dams, and I'd fill the pools behind them with minnows and water skeeters I caught in my hands. I discovered caddisfly larvae—aquatic bugs that create their own body armour out of gravel, twigs and bits of leaf matter—so perfectly disguised that I didn't even know they were there until I realized that bits of the creek bed were trundling around on spindly black legs. I spent hours kneeling, bum up and nose almost touching the water, lost in fascination as the creatures of the creek bed went about their business. Meanwhile, Ray made stepping stones across the creek.

Was he a "normal" kid back then? He says he was. I ask him to cast his mind back fifty or so years and tell me about his early days.

"Why?" he asks a little warily. "You were there."

The question is too broad, he says, too vague. But when I pose a few specific questions by email—What did you like to do? Who did you do it with?—he answers without hesitation, drawing from a library of crystal-clear recollections. It quickly becomes obvious from his reply that most of his memories are happy ones:

> All in all, I'd say I had a fine childhood. We did all the normal things—ride bikes, swim, explore the woods. Me and my friends spent a great deal of time in the bush, and we more or less owned the Ridge.
>
> Woody and Dave were my best buddies. We spent a lot of time on or near the water. Sailing with Dave was always fun. And he and I loved to draw. We'd spend endless hours drawing racing boats and insulting each other's work by saying, "Yours is a pleasure barge."

I dimly recall Ray getting into some mischief as a boy, so I ask him about it, and he cheerfully comes clean about his elementary school criminal career:

> Woody and me, we used to break into houses on
> Cranley. We'd never do any damage, of course, but
> we'd always steal one thing as a souvenir. Only got
> caught once. And we did burn down a cabin in the
> woods. It was derelict but used as a clubhouse by the
> Eagle Harbour Gang, who were the other tribe.

Even as a preteen, he was confident of his physical, emotional and intellectual prowess:

> Although I was smaller and more sensitive than
> my buddies, I was usually the leader—I knew I was
> smarter than them. Braver, too. I was the first to face
> the nameless horrors that awaited anyone going past
> the sign to Whyte Lake.

"Good heavens! Whyte Lake? You were just a little boy! What were you doing way up there?" I ask, retroactively questioning our mother's fitness as a parent. "And what sign?"

> The sign said, WATERSHED: KEEP OUT. We didn't
> know what a "watershed" was or what might happen
> to us if we were caught in one. It was pretty ominous.
> But I led the way past that sign, and we swam in the
> lake, and we all lived to tell the tale. I was also the
> first to walk across the train trestle and swim under
> the raft and jump off the Parthenon.

The Parthenon was a replica Greek temple on private waterfront property, perched on a granite cliff a fifteen-minute swim across the harbour from our beach. The more intrepid kids would swim over in groups and clamber up the rock face till they stood at the top, their backs to those gleaming white marble columns, contemplating the abyss below. Only girls of rare valour would take the plunge—but the boys would have to jump lest they be outed as cowards in the presence of those bikini-clad females. As I recall, it was at least ten thousand feet down at high tide. Ray was fearless; he has my undying respect for his Parthenon jump record, but I never did summon the courage myself. I remained rooted to the rock, transfixed, as the sun bored into my skin. Finally my braver comrades, tired of treading water and shouting up encouragements, would swim back to the beach while I picked my way down the rocks in ignominious defeat and swam back alone.

So I was a coward, then as now. But not Ray. He was no loner, either. There were always other boys around him. Come to think of it, he may have gotten a little extra respect from his friends because he happened to have a bunch of sisters coming up right behind him.

Ray was fascinated with science and often got chemistry sets for Christmas. When he was eleven and deep into his Mad Scientist phase—mind you, he says he's never left it—Dad built him his own bench in the basement, where he conducted experiments. I have a picture of him holding a test tube up to his lips as though he's about to drink a Jekyll and Hyde potion, while his friend Dale looks on in mock horror.

Ray had many other interests too, and we heard about them *all* in great detail. For a number of years he collected rocks, eventually lining his bedroom walls with shelves holding egg cartons full of specimens. *Igneous, metamorphic, sedimentary*—he tossed off the primary classifications with ease. Indeed, he could speak at length and with great confidence on any subject that interested him. Our parents were proud of their precocious child scientist. He was clearly destined for greatness.

It never occurred to any of us to think there was anything wrong with him. On the contrary, I felt a trifle superior bathed in the glow of his intellect. After all, nobody else's big brother was reading the *Encyclopaedia Britannica* for fun.

Maybe if we had just stayed in our natural habitat, things would have been different. But life was about to get a lot more complicated—and Ray got a lot less "normal."

In 1967, the year Ray would turn eleven, we relocated to Alberta, where Dad had taken a job as the project manager on the construction of a hospital. There were no backyard mountains by which to orient ourselves, just an endless patchwork of flat fields that were muddy in spring, golden in summer, stubbly brown in fall and white in winter. We had two new schools to deal with, one after another, as Dad moved us from somewhere out in the prairies to the suburbs of Edmonton. I would have no idea how hard this was on Ray until we were adults; certainly, his demeanour did not suggest the inner turmoil he was experiencing.

But in 1969 things changed again, this time even more drastically. Dad landed a job with CIDA—the Canadian International Development Agency—managing a variety of construction projects scattered throughout the Caribbean islands. His first overseas posting was to Barbados. He went ahead of us to get established and find a place to live. Months later, Mum and we six kids stepped from the plane onto a tropical island made of bleached coral and smelling of blacktop and burnt sugar. Heat waves undulated off the tarmac. Ray was thirteen. As far as he was concerned, we might as well have landed on another planet. "Culture shock" does not begin to describe it.

Dad wanted only the best school for his clever son, so Ray was enrolled in Harrison College, a boys' grammar school that still smacked of its British colonial origins. His school uniform included khaki shorts, matching shirt with epaulettes, a tie and tan knee socks with brown lace-up dress shoes. Discipline was strict, almost military. Students were required to stand respectfully when a teacher entered the classroom as well as any time they answered questions in class. Insubordination was punished by lashes with a rattan cane.

Ray was lost. He couldn't make sense of the rigid social structure that was so apparent to everyone else—though he knew he would be swiftly punished for violating it. His fears were not unfounded: a mouthy young white boy who did not understand the pecking order would have made a pretty tempting target for a teacher itching to prove a point. Ray lived for a year like a hunted animal. Some mornings he sat slumped over the breakfast table, sobbing into the crook of his arm, begging our parents not to make him go. "Where is the love?" he wailed one day, lifting his head to look wild-eyed at Dad, who was haunted to the end of his life by his son's anguished plaint.

It was here, Ray tells me, that it all began to go sideways for him:

> It was mostly the trauma of Harrison College. Not
> only was I a fish out of water, but there was the terror
> of knowing that the slightest mistake could very pos-
> sibly end up with me getting caned. I had one friend,
> a black kid named White, ironically. He was the only
> person I felt safe talking to.

Ray honestly believes to this day that he was just a normal kid who
got pushed past his breaking point. He identifies that year in Barbados as the beginning of his undoing. I am ashamed to say that I didn't
know how much he suffered until almost forty years later. I was only
twelve when we moved there, and I guess I was caught up learning the
ropes myself. I was kitted out in a white shirt, blue tunic and cap, and
sent to Queen's College, an all-girls' school that was as foreign to me as
Ray's was to him. In no time I had figured out how things worked, but
Ray never did.

Was there any single event that broke him?

> No single event, just an accumulation of traumas. I
> am what you get when you take an emotionally frag-
> ile, sensitive kid and tear him to bits over and over
> again. Eventually the pieces can't re-form.

Now that I can look back and apply insights that were unavailable
to me at the time, I am inclined to think that Ray is what you get when
you take an emotionally fragile, sensitive *autistic* kid and plunge him re-
peatedly into jarring new situations, expecting him to quickly read and
adapt to unfamiliar cultural landscapes one after the other. After all, everything was new to me too, but the only thing I caught that year was an
acute awareness of the muscle-bound black boys at the beaches where
we hung out after school. We swam and snorkelled almost every day or
bodysurfed the big waves when the black flags were up and the tourists
stayed away. Ray was always first in and last out. If not for the reprieve of
that salty turquoise water, I don't think he would have survived.

Things did not improve for him when we returned to Canada.
High school in BC starts in Grade 8, and it's a nerve-wracking adjustment for most kids even when they are making the transition with a

peer group that includes their pals from elementary school, but we knew almost no one. I started Grade 8 and Ray Grade 9 at West Vancouver Secondary. The other kids in his grade had already had a year to settle into their various cliques and castes. He was the new kid, stiff and awkward, sporting a military-style haircut. I'm sure they smelled fear on him.

His narrative continues:

> Then there was the whiplash of being sent back to West Van, where I was called "Barbados" and put the whole class into hysterics when I stood up before talking to a teacher.

I was experiencing some whiplash of my own. The boy whose locker was beside mine had tousled black shoulder-length hair and wore a fringed leather jacket. He reeked of testosterone and tobacco. To me he was part monster, part god. I tried not to stare. The art teacher—Mr. Evans to me but Mike to most of my peers—wore striped hipster bell-bottoms and *smoked cigarettes*. Sometimes in the *smoke pit*. With *students*. These sins would have been punishable by firing squad in the Caribbean. We were agog.

There was no time for Ray to acclimatize to any of this. We had been in Canada less than a year before Dad received another Caribbean posting, this time to the island of St. Lucia, where we would live for the next two years. It was now 1971. Ray was fifteen and I was almost fourteen. We were the only white kids in our new school—so different from our peers that Ray's extra differentness hardly registered. The school was a converted army barracks made of hewn stone and brick, perched high on a hill called Morne Fortune, the site of many bloody battles in the 1700s between the British and the French. On our lunch breaks we wandered through the cemetery, looking at the names and ages of the young soldiers who had died there two centuries earlier. Nutmeg-scented trade winds cooled us as we ate our sandwiches while sitting on cannons overlooking Castries Harbour.

With that earlier year in Barbados under our belts, we were better prepared for life in the tropics this time, but it wasn't all smooth sailing. We cocky Canadian kids found ourselves the class dunces—we were the only ones who didn't know our times tables up to twelve, and we couldn't conjugate even the most basic Spanish and Latin verbs. My penmanship, until then a source of vanity, was found to be not up to par and vigorously corrected. Ray's handwriting was illegible, and no amount of practice seemed to improve it. His spelling was hopeless; English grammar lessons were torture, and the syntax of the other languages eluded him completely. My writing style was altered for life, but Ray just couldn't fix his. He ended up inventing his own phonetically based written language—which he still uses today when he doesn't have a computer handy.

The hems of girls' uniforms were required to touch the ground when they knelt. The most audacious student I ever saw during our schooling in St. Lucia was a girl named Rosemarie Payne, who rolled up the waistband of her skirt so that her knees showed—and dared to walk around like that. Insubordination was punished by strapping—girls on the palms, boys on the buttocks. The crack of that strap and Rosemarie's yelping in the headmaster's office instilled in me a profound reverence for authority—and in Ray, sheer terror.

He was floundering at school despite his obvious intelligence, and no one could figure out why. Dad hired a dynamic young Peace Corps teacher named Jim Verhoff as a private tutor. Mr. Verhoff would come by on Saturdays after Ray had endured a week's worth of slings and arrows at Morne Fortune.

Ray recalls those days almost as if he had dreamed them:

> I could ask Mr. Verhoff anything on any subject. Anything! He opened my eyes to so much. It was kind of like flying. Together we flew through knowledge.
>
> Sometimes we'd go up to the school, open up the chemistry lab and do experiments. It was ALL THERE and ALL MINE. It's hard to describe how it felt, really. Something like the "kid in a candy shop" feeling, but the "candy" for me was knowledge.

He tries hard to make me understand the healing nature of those long-ago interludes:

> Labs and classrooms are usually full of noise. But after school, those spaces have what I can only describe as "un-noise." It is more and better than just quiet; it seems to wash the noise pollution all away.

Soothed by the quiet and allowed to go wherever his curiosity beckoned, Ray was in heaven.

After two years we left St. Lucia and found ourselves plunged once again into the Canadian educational system. It was 1973, the year I would turn sixteen and Ray seventeen. He and I had been only dimly aware of the social upheavals in the western world while we were coming of age in the shelter of those little sugar-cane islands, but North America's mad evolution had only gathered steam in our absence. I recall having to almost physically lean into those first days back in the halls of West Van High the way one might lean into a gale force wind. The height of rebellion for me in St. Lucia had been wearing bell-bottoms and listening to the Jackson 5 on AM radio. My girl classmates and I had swooned over Jermaine Jackson singing "I'll Be There" with his little brother, Michael, but it was all about Jermaine for us; Michael had moves, but he was just a child back then and not a suitable subject for our torrid imaginings.

Now my siblings and I didn't know the right music; we weren't wearing the right clothes. The school counsellors decided that Ray, disoriented and drowning in all the changes, would have an easier time if he resumed high school a year back, and that is why, even though he was smarter than me, we ended up doing Grades 11 and 12 together. I quickly found my bearings and reverted to North American high school protocol; Ray did not. Incredibly, he repeated an earlier mistake that had earned him widespread derision after our return from Barbados: the first time he was called upon to answer a question in class, he rose smartly to his feet and addressed the teacher as "Ma'am," thus broadcasting his status as a weirdo. The cool kids wordlessly backed away as though he were radioactive.

Ray's differentness was now impossible to ignore, and his social missteps began to cost him dearly. His peers were no longer impressed with his verbal monologues and his formidable collection of encyclo-pedia factoids. They had evolved into complicated creatures who in-teracted on a sophisticated level, one that Ray couldn't hope to com-prehend. He knew something was going on between them, but he couldn't catch them at it. It was too swift, too subtle. It appeared to be some sort of new game they had all learned while we were away. There was this magical understanding flashing and flickering back and forth, some sort of group telepathy he could not tune into. This ability to hear and navigate by social sonar had been growing in the rest of us along with the maturing of our physical bodies. But Ray heard noth-ing. He was confused and frightened, walking into invisible walls that everyone else nimbly sidestepped. That's when he came up with the name to describe what he saw as an insidious game of secrets and lies. *Goongbalong.*

His childish exuberance stiffened into defensiveness. He tried to get out of sticky situations the only way he knew how: by comman-deering conversations and steering them toward areas in which he was knowledgeable—but his strategy often backfired. He came off as a know-it-all, talking his way into trouble not just with fellow students but with teachers and other authority figures. Now that there was no fear of corporal punishment holding him back, he did not hesitate to challenge a teacher in class. In fact, he looked for opportunities to en-gage in this way in order to prove himself intellectually worthy.

He did find companions at school: other kids who were barred from the members-only clubs and circles that form the intricate hi-erarchies of high school. These teenage anomalies clustered together at the darkened ends of hallways and in empty classrooms, and I tried to keep watch over my brother by integrating myself among them. My attempt to keep one foot in Ray's world and one in the geek-free zone didn't really work. I only succeeded in telegraphing to my peers my own status as a semi-outcast. I spent the last two years of high school in a sort of no man's land. I had a small circle of "outsider" friends I shared with Ray, including my best friend Cori, a girl with whom he would end up falling in love. When I wasn't hiding in the sewing room working on my projects, I was with them.

When Ray started heading into enemy territory, I'd step into the space between him and whomever he was provoking and try to draw their attention my way. In the animal kingdom, this risky business is called a "distraction display," and I used it all the time. Ray would be holding court among his friends when the apex predators of West Van High, sensing an easy kill, would begin to circle. Seeing a danger-ous situation developing, I would laugh gaily and say something that I hoped was witty, trying to take the heat off him before some high school jock could make a meal of him.

I didn't know it at the time, of course, but Ray had no idea what I was doing. He badly misinterpreted my interventions, viewing me as anything but his protector. What he saw was a ruthless social climber, a cunning Goongbalong player who pretended to be on his team and then laughed with her friends and pointed at him as he ran the wrong way with the ball. He watched me doing my little routine a hundred times, believing that I was betraying him in a heartless attempt to boost my own popularity at his expense.

Ray finally found sanctuary in the persona of Mr. Spock, a character from the original *Star Trek* TV series. The Starship *Enterprise* was crewed by creatures from various galaxies in their glorious 1960s hokeyness. Spock's father was from the planet Vulcan, but his mother was an Earthling. This made Spock an interstellar oddity, as Vulcans didn't generally interbreed with other races. The highly evolved Vul-cans had long ago gained mastery over their emotions and looked with some contempt upon the humans, who continued to be governed by their base urges and impulses. Vulcans were not unfeeling; on the con-trary, their emotions were powerful—but always tightly reined. Spock had been raised on his father's planet, but despite the best efforts of his teachers to drum the human out of him with discipline and training, he had not quite been able to rid himself of the taint of his mother's race, and every once in a while, his emotional control would slip. For this he had been cruelly taunted by his Vulcan peers, while the hu-mans sneered at him for the ice water that seemed to run in his veins. I wonder to this day if Gene Roddenberry, the creator of *Star Trek*, had an autistic relative upon whom he modelled the Spock character, so completely does he evoke the outsider's puzzled perspective on humanity.

Young Ray identified instantly and deeply with Spock. He admired the Vulcan's intelligence and clarity of thought, and above all his seeming immunity to emotional pain. He lived and breathed the character, hoping to find protection from his own emotional pain—and some respect, if not acceptance, from his peers. It was around this time that he began prefacing everything with, "On *my* planet ... " followed by a litany of things that needed to be changed on this one.

I am grateful for *Star Trek*. Mr. Spock provided good cover for my brother, who soon found that he could walk around right under the noses of the bullies, impervious to danger in his Vulcan guise. Most kids came to accept his weirdness because it was actually kind of cool having their very own Vulcan on campus. In fact, Ray came to enjoy a bit of a cult following. Students would silently raise their right hands as they passed him in the hallways, giving the traditional Vulcan salute that Trekkies know so well. Ray was not displeased. He knew who the superior race was.

INTO THE ABYSS

Ray and I graduated from high school in 1975. We had to share a grad yearbook—with four other kids in school, Mum thought it too extravagant to buy us each our own copy. Our black and white photos, *Claire Andrews, Ray Andrews*, are side by side on the first page with the other "A" names. My blurb says I spent a lot of time in the sewing room "turning out coats and such." Ray's says "Logical, logical, logical, a debater, always gets the last word." One of his friends had scrawled on the page, "Error! Error! Error! Does not compute!" This was a reference to the robot from *Lost in Space*, another 1960s TV series, in which the robot—which had a stereotypically "robotic" voice—was dazzlingly futuristic back then but looks to me now like it was built with spare parts from an air conditioning unit, a popcorn maker and a slide projector. I made my own dress for grad and was escorted to the ceremony by one of Ray's eccentric friends who had somehow summoned up the guts to ask me to be his date for the evening. I've never seen the boy since. Ray went with Cori.

After that, Ray and I went our separate ways. I took an office job in Vancouver. At seventeen, I fell in love with Ian Finlayson (inconveniently, he has the same first name as my younger brother, Ian Andrews) and married him when I was twenty. Ray became a letter carrier for Canada Post. It was a strange career choice for a bright young man who was designing airships and steam engines in his spare time. Dad thought it a shameful waste of a fine intellect and often said as much to Ray.

"Are we to do nothing with our lives?" Dad challenged. "Were we not put on this earth to make something of ourselves?"

"We have brought nothing into the world," Ray replied, reciting the Bible to Dad, "and neither can we carry anything out. Having sustenance and covering, we shall be content with these things. The love of money is the root of all evil."

Dad, whose first language was French, almost always called his son by his full name, Raymond, but when he shortened it in conversation, it came out *Rem*. "Listen to me, Rem," Dad said, exasperated, "if I had been content with sustenance and covering ..."

And that's how it went. The debates between the two of them were painful and protracted, and neither gave an inch. Ray was very anti-establishment in those days; the last thing he aspired to be was a dog-eat-dog businessman like his father. Besides, delivering mail must have seemed like a relatively safe bet after his long, forced march through high school, where only his Vulcan camouflage had kept the wolves at bay. Working as a postman would require occasional brief ceremonial exchanges with the householders, but he knew how those went: *How are you? Fine, how are you?* Throw in a comment about the weather and you're done. Nothing to it. Other than the pleasantries, people pretty much leave a mailman to go about his rounds.

Unfortunately, the end of high school meant the end of Ray's quasi-celebrity as a Vulcan. Without his Spock persona, he was just an impudent young man again, at the mercy of his mouth.

At nineteen, he signed up for flying lessons. These begin, of course, with classroom instruction before students are deemed ready to climb into the cockpit. During one class he challenged the young female flight instructor on some esoteric point of avionics. She waffled on the answer, and despite her mounting distress he persisted, pressing the point until she ran crying from the room. This information came to me by way of a friend who was in the same class. "What an asshole!" he said of my brother.

Ray remembers the incident. He realized the instructor was getting rattled when he wouldn't let the matter drop. It was a long time ago, he says now, but it might have been something about radio navigation. And he was *right,* damn it. Doesn't that count for anything?

> The fact is she couldn't answer my question, but she tried to pretend she could, and it became apparent that she was guessing. I keep forgetting that people on your planet aren't really interested in the correct answer; they are interested in maintaining their status. It's so primitive. On my planet, status—if we

even *had* status—would come not from what you
know, but from how open you are to new knowledge
and how well you impart knowledge to others.

Ray may have humiliated his flying instructor in front of her class,
but he was a fine student once he got behind the controls of a plane.
He got his pilot's licence and "slipped the surly bonds of earth" many
times in a single-engine Cessna. "It's nothing romantic," he said at the
time, brushing aside my admiration at his derring-do. "Cessnas are the
Toyotas of the sky. They're noisy and inelegant." But his first solo was
still a thrill. "There's no one to help you land the plane," he told me.
"It's land or crash." That was a risk Ray gladly accepted. He felt confident in his new skills and knew that the gauges and dials on the little
plane's dashboard would give him all the information he needed to
make sound decisions.

Here on the ground, though, Ray was still getting incorrect social
signals—or none at all. He continued to miss warning signs, blunder-
ing into taboo topics and crashing through social barriers he could not
see. So when he wasn't delivering mail, he'd head for the hills, far from
the Goongbalong arenas.

Flying was an expensive pastime, but climbing required only
brawn, a bit of technical know-how and the right gear. Lucky for Ray,
the part of the world where we live is ringed by mountains and nestled
against the sea; in any direction you travel, you will encounter one or
the other. He knew a number of other avid climbers, and they trusted
each other with their lives. So instead of flying over the mountains, he
was more often scrambling up and rappelling down their sides. They
became Ray's places of asylum.

He always took his camera and over the years accumulated a su-
perb collection of slides. He dusted them off recently and did a little
slide show. Most of the pictures were of stunning snow-white peaks,
glacier-fed lakes in those crazily incandescent blues and greens, or
views of the spreading vistas below. A few, obviously taken by his
climbing buddies, were of Ray dangling off a precipice or posing regal-
ly on some crag high above the clouds, ice axe in hand. I had forgotten
how handsome he was then, and how bold.

I popped up in a few pictures too, on hikes we had done together, my braided pigtails disappearing into a 1970s-style puffy, fluorescent-orange ski jacket. I felt a pang of nostalgia.

The day after the slide show, I emailed him to tell him how much I had enjoyed the evening and how surprised I was at his exploits: "I didn't realize you were such a serious climber!"

> Yes, I was a pretty competent mountaineer. I've been on top of almost every notable peak around these parts.

"What was your most dangerous climb?" I asked.

He corrected my question before answering it:

> The highest was Telescope Peak in California—but the idea of "most dangerous" doesn't amount to much; you could be killed on a "safe" mountain or survive a "dangerous" one. "Most difficult" is more objective. That would be Shuksan or Slesse, both of which were also the most exhilarating—maybe with Alpha thrown in.
>
> Why climb a mountain? Well, because it's there, of course. Because it challenges you. Because it's magnificent and pristine.

And maybe because up there everybody leaves you the hell alone.

Ray is a respectable astronomer; he knows his way around the night sky and can pick out most of the constellations of the northern hemisphere. On summer nights he can often be found with a cluster of young stargazers congregated around him, some way past their bedtimes, craning their necks upward, spellbound, as he tells the stories of the gods and goddesses, witches and warriors, maidens and monsters of ancient myth whose names adorn the constellations overhead.

For him, there is no more perfect experience than one involving the sea and the stars at the same time. Swimming at night, there are no bright lights around to dampen the celestial display. The Milky Way looks like a fat white brushstroke across the sky.

If Ray experiences something sublime, he wants to share it. When a high summer tide combines with a new moon, he will sometimes gather small groups of swimmers at the beach late at night and lead them out into deep water for what he calls "astronomy swims." Once they're far enough away from the shore, the swimmers flip over onto their backs, and as they float together in the darkness, they get an animated lesson on the architecture of the heavens. Most of these kids now know the major features of our sky and can easily negotiate their way from Ursa Major up to Polaris, the North Star, and over to Cassiopeia, queen of the autumn constellations, who, as legend has it, was punished for boasting of her unrivalled beauty.

Night swimming can bring unexpected benefits. Sometimes in late summer, the ocean off the coast of British Columbia blooms with living sparkles that can only be seen at night. This phenomenon—called phosphorescence by most people around here—is created by tiny bioluminescent creatures that absorb the sun's energy during the day. At night, wherever the water is agitated, they give off brief pulses of light, like undersea fireflies. Ray and the more fearless of his young companions will dive into the darkness below and pirouette upward, sweeping their arms to create whirlwinds of little comets around themselves as they ascend. I have watched from the beach in the dark and seen the silhouettes of my daughters and their friends emerging from the water, laughing with delight at the little sparks caught in their long hair or sliding down their legs. Vain Cassiopeia could never match such a sight.

Ray once told me about a time on a family houseboat vacation on Shuswap Lake when he achieved a kind of nirvana. The boat was tied up at a remote beach for the night, her bowline tethered to the rocky shore. A bunch of us had stayed up late, lolling in the on-board hot tub, drinking wine and staring up at the velvet sky. It was a new moon, with no ambient light save that from the stars. Ray was in fine form, a regular tour guide to the galaxy, pointing out all the major "skymarks," including a dim fuzzball rising in the east that turned out to be the Andromeda Nebula. We took turns squinting at it through his portable scope.

When everyone else trailed off to bed, Ray slipped naked into the lake and swam out into the dark heart of it. There he floated on his back, suspended between heaven and earth. There was no separation between the blackness of the water and the blackness of the sky, and no separation between himself and the swaddling darkness that enveloped him. The experience was transcendent; he says it will remain in a holy place in his memory until he dies.

Ray's always been happiest in water, and apart from that miserable stretch in Alberta when he was a preteen, he has never been far from the ocean. He is able to swim right out of whatever ails him. He says, "All my problems leave me when I'm in the water."

He is a strong swimmer, chugging along for miles without seeming to tire. He prefers to swim in the nude and will do so whenever he can without scandalizing the locals. Still, the sight of a naked man swimming along a quarter mile from shore, past rowboats, kayaks and windsurfers, his unsunned buttocks luminous just beneath the water's surface, has undoubtedly caused a raised eyebrow or two.

Ray was in his twenties when he discovered that if he swam straight *down*, there came a point at which he experienced both elation and a rare feeling of tranquility. And the deeper he went, the longer that feeling lasted. He had discovered free diving.

After that first thrilling experience, whenever he got a chance, he'd ride his motorbike to one of his favourite secluded beaches, don a wetsuit and weight belt, fins and a mask, and swim out into deep water. He'd fill his lungs to capacity and slip beneath the surface, stroking his way powerfully downward into the cold, quiet world below. He wore no breathing apparatus. As he descended, his natural buoyancy was replaced by an increasing heaviness. He allowed himself to free-fall, always mindful of the precise amount of time and effort required to make it back to the surface.

"The deeper you go," he tells me one day after a dive, "the more the black abyss sucks you down. It's very spooky. Takes some getting used to."

"But how do you know how far down you can go before you have to turn around?" I am trying to stifle my panic at the possible consequences of even the slightest miscalculation.

"Well, experience, of course," he answers matter-of-factly, "and a basic understanding of human physiology. The limit isn't *time*. It's the fact that the human larynx doesn't compress, and we run out of air to equalize our ears. At a hundred metres, your lungs have completely collapsed. When the pressure is such that it's squeezing the larynx, you're as deep as you can go."

My hand goes slowly to my throat.

"Seals have compressible larynxes," he adds, as though this fact will somehow make me feel better about the ocean wrapping its icy fingers around his throat and squeezing until his windpipe collapses and his eardrums explode.

"But if you—"

Ray has already anticipated my question. "I carry enough weight to pull me down quite fast—but it's not more than I can fight against going back up. And control of ascent isn't really an issue. Below, say, a hundred feet, you're sinking like a rock, so you need to swim against that on the way up."

My mind effortlessly conjures my brother's frenzied bid for the surface and his lifeless body falling gracefully to its final, frigid repose on the ocean floor.

"You have to be very careful not to get too self-confident," he says, sounding briefly sensible. "But within about twenty feet of the surface your buoyancy is back, and you just float up the rest of the way. Besides, in all cases where you intend to push your limits, you have a buddy right there who can rescue you if you black out on the way up."

Ray can read my dismay.

"Believe it or not, this isn't such a big deal," he continues by way of reassurance. "If you're going to pass out, it's almost always near the surface. That's because at depth, the pressure forces oxygen into your blood. As you ascend, your blood gives it all back to your lungs and you conk out. Your buddy just helps you to the surface and holds your head out of the water till you come 'round."

He makes it sound so simple, so safe. But I know he hasn't always been able to rustle up buddies for these excursions, and sometimes his need to dive means he dives alone. We wouldn't even know where to look for him ...

"It's never happened to me," he adds hastily. "When you are diving recreationally, the rule is that you never go anywhere near your limits."

But of course there are times he *does* intend to push those limits, and for those dives his preparations are meticulous. He ties one end of a rope to a makeshift buoy and the other end to a rock or brick of appropriate weight. He swims this rig out a suitable distance and drops the weighted end. Then, after a series of carefully calibrated deep breaths, he inverts himself, "walking" down the rope hand over hand until gravity takes over and, like some upside-down Icarus, he is flying toward the centre of the earth. He counts the rings of coloured tape he has placed at intervals along the rope so he can identify his target depth and linger there for as long as his lungs will allow.

One day he made it to twenty metres. He was euphoric. Not long after that, he made twenty-five, and all he wanted was to go deeper, stay longer. The cold ocean felt sweet and calming pressing against his body. Ecstasy suffused him as he hung suspended in the water. His jangly nerves quieted; his heartbeat slowed and steadied.

"Free diving is about the only sport where peak performance is related to serenity and a deliberate slowing down of oneself," he says. "For me, it's not just recreation; it's a very spiritual thing. It's hard to explain, but I feel closer to God in the water than anywhere else."

Perhaps my brother is not really from another planet after all. Maybe he belongs to some rare, undiscovered branch of the human family tree, *Homo aquaticus*—water-based humans who took a terrible wrong turn coming up to live among us here on dry land. Maybe he has some primal memory of the womb as the only place he ever experienced perfect peace and serenity. Or maybe it's just that he has found his way to a hushed realm where Goongbalong cannot follow him.

Flying, climbing, swimming, diving. Now that I can put things in context, I see that his choices of recreation have all been designed to get him as far as possible from the exhausting complexities of society. Instinct has guided him to places and pursuits where any comrades who join him share a oneness of purpose, a common goal. This is parallel play at its finest. For Ray, mountains, ocean and sky are elements against which he can test his mettle unencumbered by any rules but those he clearly understands.

COURTING TROUBLE

Ray has many fond memories of his years delivering mail in leafy West Vancouver. He had cordial relations with most of the homeowners on his route, despite a somewhat unconventional approach to the job. "It was one of the beauties of being a letter carrier," he tells me. "So long as you got your route done without overtime, no one cared very much about the details. Supervisors tended to worry about problems on their desks, and stopping for coffee with a customer didn't create any such problem. I loved the job for that."

He'd occasionally put his satchel down to do various side jobs along the way. His specialty was tree work. People on his route got used to seeing their mailman up a tree with a homeowner's chainsaw or swinging an axe. He chopped and stacked wood for an elderly widow and accepted only a piece of pie and a cup of coffee as payment. I asked him if he did much pro bono work like that. "Mostly paid," he replied, "though I did the odd freebee. The burghers of West Van were rarely poorer than me."

I'm not so sure these extracurricular activities on company time—or "details," as Ray calls them—were actually condoned by management, but as far as I know, Ray flew under the Canada Post radar most of the time. But once in a while, he walked right into trouble.

"There was this one lady," he remembers, "all I ever did was say, 'Good morning, ma'am,' and 'Nice day.' Stuff like that. Well, she phoned the post office and told them she refused to allow me on her property ever again. My supervisor called me into his office and asked me, 'Ray, what on earth did you *do*?' I had no idea. I have no idea to this day."

I have no idea either. But I can picture Ray taking the most efficient route to the next house by cutting through the lady's yard, trampling her tulips with a nod and a cheery, "Morning, ma'am!" He would have been oblivious to her escalating distress signals as she glowered at him from her doorstep day after day, hands fisted into her waist. Everything about her would have said, "Don't you see what you're doing to my flower beds, you horrible man?" But Ray didn't see.

Hostile householders were not the only occupational hazard Ray faced while making his rounds for Canada Post. There were dogs—all kinds of dogs of varying shapes and sizes and temperaments. Some were docile, some yappy but harmless—and yet others would explode into rabid frenzy at the sight of Ray striding up to the front door. One dog might stare menacingly through a living room window, muscles twitching. Another might hurl itself at the door or yip maniacally at the slot as the daily mail was poked through, hoping to pull a whole postman in by the fingertips—and failing that, to reduce the bills and flyers sullied by his scent to spittle-covered shreds. Then there were the *outside* dogs, the tethered ones who strained at their chains, teeth bared, throttling themselves in their lust to eat my brother for breakfast. Worse still, there were loose dogs who came roaring toward their uniformed prey, challenging his every step with sharp warning barks and pinned-back ears.

Many posties develop a deep mistrust of man's best friend after being chomped a few times, and Ray was no exception. "I've been bitten at least a dozen times," he told me matter-of-factly. "Usually it's little dogs, like Yorkies. You can just kind of punt those ones over the hedge, but I've been attacked by a few big dogs, too. There was this shepherd that came at me once. By the time you see it, you've got maybe two seconds to react. It's funny how fast you think in those two seconds. You weigh your options. It's either run for your life, climb up on something like a car, or kick the thing in the chest—and you've only got one chance to get it right. Anyway, I walked into the yard and this shepherd came at me like a bat out of hell. I started to run. I didn't think I was going to make it. Fortunately, the dog was on a rope, and it pulled up short at the last second. It took me the rest of the day to settle down."

Although Ray has been bitten and barked at, he was only ever sued by one dog. "It was a Kerry Blue Terrier," he told me, "the most hysterical of all dog breeds. The owner, Mr. Lawson, was one of those people who supplement their incomes by suing large corporations in hopes of a nuisance payoff—so he let his dog loose on me. Naturally I defended myself. He sued, of course, but he somehow managed to get Misty's name on the lawsuit."

"The *dog* sued Canada Post?" I asked, incredulous.

"Yup," said Ray. "Probably has never happened before or since."

Finding out that Misty was a male, I wondered out loud if he was extra aggressive in an attempt to overcome his dreadfully unmacho name. Ray ignored me.

"Lawson deliberately opened his gate to let the dog attack—he looked right at me when he did it. Those dogs are pure muscle, like steel. I knew I couldn't outrun it, so I booted it in the throat. I didn't hurt it at all—just gave it something to think about—but a year later it developed hip trouble and Lawson tried to blame that on me. By that time he wanted twenty grand. At court he was drunk and raving. He literally wanted to put the dog on the stand to identify me."

Lawson had tried to enlist his neighbour, a retired judge, to act as his lawyer, confiding to him that he planned on making a bundle with this latest lawsuit. The retired judge declined to participate in the scheme and warned Ray of Lawson's intentions—on the condition that Ray not reveal him as the source of the damning information. The old judge didn't much care for Lawson, but he understandably wished to avoid being the target of his hostilities.

Unfortunately, Ray is no good at keeping secrets—especially when he's on the hot seat. "On the stand," he said, "I let it slip that I knew someone Lawson had confessed his intentions to. The presiding judge pounced on me. I told her that I had given my word not to reveal my source, but she insisted. I still wasn't going to back down and tell her how I knew about Lawson's plot, but our lawyer called a recess and twisted my arm, so I had to tell the judge about the whole thing."

It was in the nick of time, too. Ray can come off as quite cavalier, even when—no, *especially* when—he's nervous. And the more nervous he gets, the more he talks. But the judge had lost patience with the smart-aleck mailman who seemed to be treating the whole trial like a game.

"The Goongbalong played in court has particularly strict rules," Ray told me gravely, "and fouls normally mean that you lose the case. I don't know why, but judges take an instant dislike to me almost every time, and this one was no exception. But since the suit was against the

PO and not against me individually, she had no choice but to grant us the victory. She couldn't give the decision to that jerk just to hurt me—though I bet she'd have liked to. Anyway, she threw Lawson out of court. The bottom line was that he never got home mail delivery again."

So the case ended well for Canada Post and the Brave Little Letter Carrier they had spent untold thousands of dollars defending against Misty and his scheming owner, but Ray had come within a hair's breadth of being found in contempt of court. Only his opponent's outrageous behaviour and bald-faced greed had saved my brother from becoming the focus of the trial judge's ire.

For Ray, court proceedings hold all the appeal of playing hopscotch on a minefield. He once went to civil claims court in a dispute over a fender-bender. Mum and I went to support him. He won—but he didn't seem to know when it was over. The judge kept saying, "Mr. Andrews, will you sit down? You are out of order! Please sit *down*, Mr. Andrews, or I will find you in contempt!" He avoided jail that time by the skin of his teeth, but none of us would be surprised if he went to court to dispute a parking ticket and ended up in the slammer. He's not out of the woods yet. Ray's never out of the woods.

The next time he went up against the law, he wouldn't be so lucky.

Ray was bombing down I-5 in a Volkswagen camper van with three women on board: Mum, our sister Anita and our cousin Dorothy. Final destination: Arizona's Grand Canyon. They were making good time on the way to their first night's stop, a KOA campground on the far side of Seattle, when Ray decided to make a pit stop at a sporting goods store in the city to pick up some last-minute supplies. "Wait for me," he said as he parked the van and jumped out. "I won't be long."

The better part of an hour crawled by. Cousin Dorothy, an avid outdoorswoman, eventually decided she might as well wander up and down the aisles and feast her eyes on all that camping and hiking gear, so she went into the store. Mum and Anita sat in the van and steamed in the late afternoon sun. Finally, they too decided to go in to see what had become of Ray. They walked through the doors just in time to see him being led past them in handcuffs.

"Follow me!" he yelled over his shoulder.

"Where?" they yelled back, but the officers, with their hands clamped around his biceps, were not about to allow him to stop and chat. They hustled him out the door, stuffed him into a police cruiser and drove him away.

All this may have taken place more than thirty-five years ago, but Ray remembers the whole fiasco in lurid detail. Everything was fine, he says, until he made that one last impulse purchase, a T-shirt to take home for our younger brother, Ian.

"I still remember it," Ray tells me. "It said: *You're one in a million!* Ian and I are about the same size, so of course I tried it on. It fit perfectly. I never took it off before going through the checkout. The tag was still on it. The clerk was going to charge it along with the other items I'd put on the counter, but a security guard had told him ahead of time not to. It was a setup."

It's a bit of a recurring theme for Ray, this idea that he's being set up, framed, sabotaged.

I'm trying to piece together the events of that long-ago summer day in 1980. "But why would a store want to frame their own customer, Ray? And why would you assume the clerk would ring in the shirt you were wearing? Why didn't you just tell him to make sure he put it on the bill?"

"I spread my arms out," Ray replied patiently, as though I was slow to pick up on the obvious, "so he could see the tag hanging from the sleeve. I knew he'd seen it. But the security guard had followed me around the store, and he told the clerk before I got to the checkout not to charge it unless I declared it. It was all preplanned. I suspect the store dick was having a slow day and needed a kill to justify his hire. I got nabbed right there at the till and taken to the store's holding cell."

Why had Ray not just explained the misunderstanding, paid for the shirt and gone on his merry way?

"They weren't interested in my story. They were only interested in bagging a kill. Same with the cops. I assumed that when they showed up, I'd get to tell my side. Nope, I was cuffed and led off with hardly a word spoken."

My brother is no thief, and I can only imagine how agitated he must have felt at being treated like one. But when Ray's agitated, he talks. And apparently, in this case, he talked a blue streak.

Cousin Dorothy was at the scene of the crime. "Yes, I remember it. He tried on this T-shirt right over top of his clothes," she told me. "Now, you know Raymo—why would he carry it when it was more efficient to just wear it? I was right there when he said to the clerk, 'Don't forget to charge me for this,' or words to that effect, and he held both arms out wide to make sure the guy saw the tag."

"Wait, are you sure?" I interject. "Ray says he didn't say anything to the clerk!"

"No, no, he very definitely said he wanted to pay for the shirt. But there was this eager beaver security guard right there watching the whole thing. He pounced, and well, of course Raymo started to argue. I think he might have called the security guy a moron or something. I could still hear him even after they took him away."

Calling a self-important young security guard a moron with staff and customers around would have been like waving a red flag in front of a bull. But regardless of whose account is correct, the whole thing should never have escalated the way it did.

Ray argued himself all the way into a holding cell in Seattle's King County Jail.

Anita picks up the story. "Mum and Dorothy and I vaulted back into the van and tried to tail the police cruiser, but we lost them almost right away. For the next eternity we drove around attempting to get from this side of the freeway to that side, find an off-ramp, figure out where they had taken Ray. We finally found a pay phone, and we were flipping through the Yellow Pages. It was pretty surreal. I mean, what do you look under? *Prisons*?"

It was near dawn when Ray's frazzled companions finally found him. Mum wrote a cheque to spring her son. She can't remember the amount; whatever it was, she didn't have it. "To tell you the truth," she said, "I think they were just happy to get rid of your brother. We got out of there as fast as we could."

"So what happened in the end?" I ask Ray.

"They dropped the charge" he says. "Otherwise I'd have a criminal record in the States. I told them to instruct their security people to give their customers the benefit of the doubt in future."

The Great T-Shirt Heist is something of a legend in my family, and as with all legends, the facts subtly reshape themselves with each telling. There's one version wherein Ray ends up languishing in a Mexican prison—but that was a different trip, and it only went as far as the Manzanillo police station.

Did Ray learn anything from his ordeal? It seems not.

Anita writes:

> It amazes me that he has since done the same thing. A few weeks ago, I was at the Dollar Tree waiting for Ray. He was two people back in the lineup for the cashier, and darned if he didn't grab a chocolate bar from the rack, rip off the wrapper and eat it in a large way, mentioning to anyone and everyone how hungry he was and why wait, the wrapper was all they needed. It was weird because he doesn't eat chocolate bars, and I happen to know he wasn't at all hungry. It's a thing he does, like a testing. It *should* be okay.

Maybe on Ray's planet, it *is* okay. But Anita's aside gets me thinking: Was he testing the system that day in Seattle?

To this day, my brother remains indignant at the store for their wrongful accusation and the way he was manhandled. He says he briefly considered suing them but, in the end, decided it wasn't worth his time. He let them off with a warning.

CASTLES IN THE SAND

Ray started building castles when he was a little kid squatting in the sand at Eagle Harbour beach. It wasn't long before his creations were outshining the bucket molds of the other little boys and girls, and unlike them, he never stopped. As he got older, he became ever more ambitious. His physical strength and creativity probably reached their zenith in the early 1980s, by which time he was winning honours at sandcastle competitions around BC.

His teams were assembled from among family and friends who mistakenly thought that building a sandcastle would be a collaborative effort. I served on his crew for two or three big competitions and was instrumental in recruiting some of the strapping young men we'd need to get the preliminary shovel work done; it was biceps we were after, not brains. A lot of the organizing fell to me—it's not Ray's thing—but once we hit the beach, he was the acknowledged master, and the rest of us did precisely as we were told. This usually involved shovelling a ton of wet sand and hauling water as Ray demanded it. His homemade sheet metal forms were stacked one tier upon the other in successively smaller sizes, like a giant aluminum wedding cake. Each was filled with sand that was thoroughly watered in and tamped—air pockets spell calamity in critical structures made of sand. I recall being heavily pregnant on two of our builds, but I received no concessions, nor did I expect any. We girls did our share, staggering up the beach with heavy, sloshing trash cans full of water between us, while our contingent of brawny lads in 1980s short shorts shovelled furiously. Glory was within our reach if we could beat the clock and the incoming tide.

Once we had achieved our target height, maybe seven or eight feet above sea level, we began to sculpt our way down from the top, the forms being peeled away in the reverse order that they had been placed. The shovel boys were then reassigned to the pump sprayers that would keep the structure from drying out in the midday sun. A few of us were permitted to assist the master, the way Leonardo da Vinci's students might have been allowed to paint backgrounds, but we all knew these were *Ray's* creations. Like everyone else on those projects, I was in his thrall and hoping to be noticed for my devoted servitude. I doubt he appreciated how hard his pregnant sidekick worked; had I gone into labour on the job, he would have found it most inconvenient. "Babs, how long is that going to take?" he would have said. "I need some arrow loops cut into this tower."

We won many honours for our castles with their gothic turrets, arches and flying buttresses. One year we were the best in the world in our division at the prestigious Canadian Open Sandcastle Competition held in White Rock, BC. In pictures of that glorious day, I am pear-shaped, my red team T-shirt stretched over my swollen belly. My knees are a matching bright red, the skin pumiced away from hours of kneeling in damp sand. Ray looks vaguely exotic in long pants, a long shirt, sunglasses and a hat, like he's going on safari. He stands proudly in front of his masterpiece, holding a large trophy, with his exhausted but exultant drones all around him, blue ribbons pinned to our sandy and sweat-stained T-shirts.

I have forgotten so much—like what I did with my first baby while I was building sandcastles pregnant with my second, and what happened to the prize money—but I remember a specific moment from that day. It is perfectly preserved in my mind, as though I am looking at it through a little circle of clear glass spit-polished into the time-etched window of my memory. Ray and I are working under a clear blue sky, putting the finishing touches on the highest tower of the castle while the rest of the team toils at landscaping the mound spreading out below us. He points to a featureless area about halfway down. "I'm going to put a bridge there." He pauses for a moment, carving tool poised in his hand. "You know," he says, almost to himself, "I can already see this castle perfectly. I can walk around it in my mind. I can even see it from above, like I'm flying over it."

What sort of person, I wondered, could soar in his imagination over a great heap of wet sand and look down on a finished project? Ray was not an architect, not a sculptor. He was a mailman with a Grade 12 education, recreating a castle he had already built in his head.

LIGHTNING
STRIKES TWICE

On several episodes of *Star Trek*, Mr. Spock found it necessary to perform a "Vulcan mind meld," fully uniting his mind with the mind of another being. This procedure broke through the strict emotional restraint that all Vulcans cultivated and was therefore used only as a last resort, when vital information could be obtained by no other means. The powerful onslaught of another creature's emotions into a brain ordered by logic was potentially lethal to a Vulcan, and the intensity of suppressed Vulcan emotions flooding unchecked into a more fragile life form could likewise have catastrophic results.

For Ray, falling in love bore all the risks of a mind meld.

His first serious relationship began, as I mentioned, while he was still in high school, when he was maybe seventeen or eighteen. Cori was a couple of years younger than he was. She had come from a background of abuse and dysfunction that was quite beyond what we could have comprehended at the time. Once introduced into our nuclear family of six kids and two parents, she wove herself in seamlessly. I don't think Dad even noticed his tall, strawberry blonde seventh "child" in the mix. Cori and I would listen to Joni Mitchell records while braiding each other's hair and painting our nails. Then I would watch her effortlessly switch gears, talking science and philosophy for hours with Ray, listening raptly as he spoke of the things closest to his heart. It was heady stuff for a boy in search of a mind mate.

In retrospect I can see that for Cori this highly rational Vulcan and his entourage looked like the perfect escape from the alcoholic maelstrom that was her home, and things between her and Ray got serious pretty quickly before she realized a few months in that he expected nothing less than a lifetime commitment and exclusive devotion. I don't know if she was seventeen yet when she panicked, abruptly dumping him. He, of course, had no idea why. He was in ruins, face down on his bed, wracked for hours with sobs so violent that each one almost levitated him. I watched somberly from across the room, knowing he could not be comforted by any means at my disposal. Four decades later, Ray still says Cori scarred him for life.

He spent the next eight years putting himself back together and was not anxious to repeat the experience. But fool that he was, he allowed love to strike again. Yvette was another young refugee from a turbulent childhood, bereft of a father and looking for a safe harbour. She idolized Ray, steadfastly ignoring all evidence that he might not be capable of slaking her enormous insecurity. Like Cori before her, she folded herself into our family without a ripple, and we all loved her. Still do.

We threw a bridal shower for Yvette a few weeks before the wedding. I remember Mum's sister, Aunty Rene, taking a long draw from her cigarette and blowing the smoke out in a straight stream, her eyes coolly appraising the girl, who was working her way through a pile of presents while I taped ribbons and bows to the obligatory paper plate hat. "You're sure you don't want to change your mind, dear? It's not too late." Aunty Rene's mouth smiled when she said that, but her eyes didn't. I couldn't tell if it was a good-natured joke or a warning. We all laughed, some of us perhaps a little too heartily.

Yvette did not change her mind. If she had any doubts about her upcoming marriage, we were not aware of them. She did all the work, organizing a big wedding and dressing both herself and Ray in white, like cake-top figurines. It was May 15, 1982. Yvette was eighteen and Ray twenty-six. In the wedding pictures, the bride looks beautiful—triumphant, even—the groom, dashing but dazed.

Married life was not what Yvette had dreamt it would be. Ray was up for work at 4:00 a.m. and had a nap every day after he got home from his rounds. He was in bed by 7:00 each evening. He left her a daily roster of chores that he expected her to perform, along with the length of time it should take her to accomplish each one. And he didn't seem to need or even want the emotional connection she craved. He had already told her that he loved her, and he had demonstrated it by marrying her; there was no point in constantly reiterating the obvious.

"He just left me by myself every night," Yvette explained when I tracked her down twenty-five years later. "I hung out with your mum a lot at first, but then I started going to the gym. Ray was always scared I'd get fat—he used to make me do sit-ups every day—so the gym seemed like the thing to do, right? Of course, there were all these guys there pumping iron. I started flirting with one of them, and pretty soon things got heavy. I told Ray about it. I guess I wanted him to be jealous or something, you know? To fight for me? But it was so weird ... there was nothing ... no reaction, just a blank."

How could Ray understand that his wife's dalliance with another man was a desperate bid for his attention? The marriage was not two years old when Yvette committed adultery to escape it. Ray divorced her. Barely out of her teens, self-esteem in tatters, she dove headlong into a life of wild partying, drinking and drugging. "I just wanted to disappear," she says. "I wanted your family to forget me."

She got a job as a waitress. "What else?" she says now with a wry laugh. "Ray always told me I was trailer trash, and I guess in a way I was. He taught me a lot, though; I'll give him that. Taught me about music. I remember once he was playing his classical music, and I was so thrilled because I actually recognized it—it was *The Moldau* by Smetana. I said, 'Oh, I love that song!' He was all disgusted. He says, 'It's not a *song*, it's a *piece of music*.'" Yvette enunciated the words and looked down her nose as she said them. "And you know what? It's still my favourite *piece of music*." She laughs again. I detect no trace of bitterness.

She eventually remarried and had a family but remained haunted by the failure of her first marriage.

As for Ray, under that "blank" exterior was a heart in unimaginable pain. He now saw all women as treacherous creatures. They might be beautiful on the outside, but he knew for certain it was just a façade, masking the evil that lay within. He came to fear them as the mariners of Greek mythology feared the sirens, those dangerous and devious creatures that beguiled sailors onto the rocks with their sweet songs.

In spite of his often fraught relationships with women, he has always had plenty of them in his life. After his marriage ended, he moved in with Mum's sister Nell. In 1964 Aunt Nell, who had been widowed a heartbreaking six days after giving birth to her only child, bought one of the original houses Dad had built on Cranley Drive, and while Dad moved his growing family up and down that street like chess pieces, she had stayed put for fifty years. Mum and all six of us kids lived with her on and off, returning to spend summers at her house when we were based in Alberta, and descending on her quiet home between stints in the Caribbean. So Ray headed back to that most familiar landmark of our childhood and rented a room from her. It was to be a mutually beneficial arrangement: Aunt Nell could use the extra income to supplement her pension, and Ray needed taking care of.

Aunt Nell relinquished the master bedroom to Ray and took a smaller one, and for the next fifteen years the two of them lived in a sort of uneasy détente. She cooked all his meals, made his bed and did his laundry in exchange for what he considered to be a handsome rent and some home maintenance chores—plumbing, electrical and the like—many of which he performed in his own unorthodox way, whether she liked it or not and sometimes over her voluble protests.

One such chore illustrates the frequent friction between the two of them. A few winters back, Aunt Nell tells me, heavy rains undermined the banks of Nelson Creek, causing an old hemlock tree to list precariously across it from the opposite side. Ray decided he'd better cut it down. The municipality of West Vancouver rigorously protects its waterways with stringent bylaws, so, aware of the trouble she could get into if Ray proceeded with his self-appointed task, she followed him across the lawn in her housecoat and slippers, imploring, "Raymond, for God's sake, *no!*" But it was for her own good, he said—kids could be playing down there, and there was no telling when that tree might topple over and kill one of them. He hopped from rock to rock across the creek and fired up his chainsaw. It was early on a Sunday morning, Aunt Nell recalls—so not only was Ray trespassing, he was also contravening the Water Act by "interfering with a fish-bearing stream and its vegetated streamside," and violating West Vancouver's noise bylaws into the bargain. The neighbours heard the whine of the chainsaw and called the authorities. The tree crashed across the creek. While Ray was bucking it up, Aunt Nell received a visit from a uniformed bylaw officer and was issued the first and only fine of her long and law-abiding life.

This happened a long time ago. In the interests of fairness, I asked Ray for his version of the story. The way he tells it, his actions make a whole lot of sense:

> It was a mid-sized hemlock from the far side of the creek that was hung up on some trees on "this" side. It was just a matter of time till it fell completely, so I figured it may as well be dropped safely and under control. Some bylaw person did show up, but after some discussion I was allowed to continue so long as I was careful not to let any sawdust enter the water—we couldn't have that now, could we!

He permits himself some resentful commentary on the aftermath of his good deed:

> Had this tree been left to rot, and had someone been injured by its inevitable fall, no doubt Aunty would have been liable, so I did the right thing. I knew perfectly well what awaited me—Aunty always found a way to make anything I did for her into a fine subject for a bellowing. I cut up the tree for firewood, but according to Aunty it smelled funny and gave off no heat and would never burn properly.

In my first draft of this chapter, I wrote about this incident just the way Aunt Nell had told it to me. It seemed a prime example of Ray's crazy hijinks and insensitivity to the wishes of others—or in this case, the explicit "cease and desist" order of his landlady, who clearly outranked him in matters pertaining to her property. But imagine how hurt Ray would have been to see himself portrayed as a scofflaw with a chainsaw when his intentions were honourable—and his hard work netted Aunt Nell a winter's worth of split and stacked wood for her fireplace.

"Hmm," I wrote, chastened after reading Ray's account, "glad I asked. There are two sides to every story, aren't there?"

His next comments showed that Aunt Nell's feelings were not the only ones hurt:

> Even on the first face of it, folks should ask themselves what I had to gain by risking my own ass dropping a very dangerous hanging tree. What was in it

for me? Absolutely nothing. It's one thing not to be
thanked when you do someone a service, it's another
to have your service turned on its head so that you
are made to look like the villain of the piece.

But villain he was to Aunt Nell, who seethed with anger and humiliation as she continued to serve him three meals a day, make his
bed and do his laundry. She might have set his coffee mug down just
a little harder on the table those next few mornings to signal that she
was still upset about Ray's actions on that fateful Sunday, but I'll bet he
never figured out what her problem was.

MAN IN THE RHINE

Ray was shop steward of his postal union by this time. His job involved negotiating with management, filing grievances on behalf of workers and sitting in on disciplinary hearings to see to it that they were properly defended. He was making pretty good money, so he could well afford to travel. Now that he was single again, he could go where he wanted, the way he wanted. He covered a lot of ground in the early post-Yvette years and is quite daunted by my belated request to boil it all down to a few memorable sights. I have to goad him a bit for details, but he soon warms to the challenge.

> I travel hard and try to see as much as possible. The best things were probably the Parthenon and the cathedral at Amiens.

Ray doesn't content himself with lining up and following the crowds through the front doors of major attractions.

> At Amiens Cathedral, the resident English eccentric guide (all French cathedrals have resident English eccentrics who give tours) was so delighted by my questions about the architecture that he gave me the "unofficial tour" after the tourists had left. I got to go up above the vaulting and into the towers where only hunchbacks and bats normally get to go.

Many of Ray's highlights, like this one, are not so much places as accomplishments. He got to help carve a gargoyle, he tells me with pride, for Cologne Cathedral in Germany. I picture him hanging off a grotesque stone monster 150 metres in the air with a chisel in his free hand, but it turns out there are masonry workshops attached to all the major gothic cathedrals in Europe. On the ground.

How did he manage to infiltrate such an off-limits area?

> I was poking my nose where I'm not allowed to go and generally making a pest of myself. I found the mason's workshop and managed to wheedle my way in. I just sorta said how much I'd love to carve a gargoyle and before you can say "Verboten!" I was hacking away at a chunk of basalt. It was "real" carving, but I had to stay inside the lines. I also got myself into the stained-glass workshop and found a few shards of coloured glass on the floor, which I still have, so I can truthfully say that I have a piece of Cologne Cathedral.

Ray pities neurotic over-organizers like me. He doesn't believe in planning his itineraries down to the last detail, preferring to improvise as he goes along. But his penchant for leaving the beaten path and striking out toward the unknown has led to a few—as he delicately calls them—"situations."

If Ray doesn't have an ocean handy, he'll improvise with the nearest body of water, and in Germany, at least two of his "situations" involved rivers. At my prompting, he tells me about them, playfully sprinkling his emails with his word of the day: *verboten.*

> I did a few verboten things in Germany—which is verboten! I swam across both the Rhine and the Danube.

As it happens, a friend from work, Olav, was going to be visiting his mother in his hometown of Kempen while Ray was in Germany, and Olav invited him to spend a few days there. Olav introduced Ray to a friend named Charly, and when Olav had business to attend to, Charly gallantly offered to show Ray around, unaware that he was on a mission to swim the Rhine—naked.

Here is Ray's lyrical account of what happened:

> The Rhine is as busy as a highway, so swimming across is sorta like jaywalking. I had to time it just right crossing the "down" lane where the boats are

moving very fast, tread water while a barge went by in the "up" lane, then race across before the next barge drowned me.

When I got to shore, I was at least half a mile downstream. Charly had my clothes. He had to take a ferry across from where I had jumped in so he could meet me on the other side. I crawled along the shore to the ferry dock and got there before he did, *but* I assumed he had already arrived and had gone looking for me. I ended up walking to the nearest phone booth wearing a piece of garbage bag. He eventually found me, so I wasn't lost for too long.

Poor Charly, clutching Ray's clothes in a ball under his arm, probably thought the crazy Canadian had been swept out to the North Sea on his watch. But other than dropping Ray's underwear somewhere along the riverbank during his frantic search, Charly was able to deliver Ray back to Olav's house not only alive and well but rather pleased with himself.

Ray had no idea that Charly was a musician until an autographed CD arrived in the mail after he had returned home to Canada. Charly had written a song called "Man in the Rhine." It contains the following lyrics:

There was a man swimming across the River Rhine

It was cold and windy, but he said that he was fine

He was waving at the captains of the riverboats

Right in the middle of the stream—*man, that was not allowed!*

If Charly had been writing in his native German, he might have said that Ray's stunt was *verboten.*

Ray doesn't always travel alone. In his younger days, he had a ready supply of mates for excursions closer to home. I still run into them from time to time. When I mention I am working on a book about

Ray, they get strange gleams in their eyes. All want to ply me with stories. There's Michael, now a mature man with thinning grey hair, who tells of taking his new bride on a cross-country skiing excursion along with his brother Peter—and Ray. The four of them set out on a glorious morning along the backcountry trails of Tetrahedron Provincial Park on the Sunshine Coast. Not long into the trek, Ray decided that skiing naked would be a wonderful enhancement to the experience and stopped to take off his clothes. Peter bashfully followed suit. The two of them finished the circuit wearing only boots, skis and backpacks. As Michael is telling me the story, his wife is interjecting with details of her own, undimmed in her memory after thirty years. I think that trip qualified as a "situation"—but only for her.

On a day climb in BC's Tantalus Range, Ray arranged to meet friends at a cable car spanning a glacier-fed river. The plan was to leave his car there at the terminus of the route. They'd pick him up in a second car, and together they would drive to the local airport, where a chopper would be waiting to deliver them to the base of Mount Alpha. Sure of the directions to the rendezvous point, Ray turned off the main highway onto a dirt road and drove until it was no longer drivable. Perplexed, he parked and started to walk. He could hear the river, so he knew it must be close—the cable car was supposed to be only a few metres downstream from the parking area. And it *would* have been if he had been on the right road, but he had overshot the turnoff and was some distance upstream from where he reckoned he was.

The path degenerated into a game trail, then petered out altogether. But Ray soldiered on.

> I often have trouble realizing when I need to turn back. The river didn't seem to be getting any nearer, but it became a matter of principle—it *had* to be in front of me. I ended up on my hands and knees pushing through brambles and brush.

Scratched and bleeding, Ray finally reached the river.

> The river course has many deep "S" bends, and I had crawled up the middle of a long thin "peninsula"

with the river only a few metres away to the left and the right, but hundreds of metres "ahead"—which is why I could hear it "everywhere." When I finally got to it, I faced another problem: it was in flood, and the water was well up into the brush—walking along the bank was impossible. It would take me hours to go back the way I had come, and I was already late.

The only thing to do was to jump in and swim down to the cable car. It *should* have been just around the bend.

So Ray stripped down, stuffed his clothes and climbing gear into his backpack and waded into the icy river.

Unfortunately, as I found out later, I was at least a kilometre upstream from the cable car. I was in the water for some time before I got to where I was going. I was so cold I could hardly get out.

Imagine his companions seeing a naked and hypothermic Ray being washed down the swollen river toward them with a backpack held over his head. Once he had thawed out and gotten dressed, they sorted out the car conundrum and made their way to the airport, where they boarded the waiting helicopter and were deposited at Alpha's base camp.

The climb, Ray says, was spectacular.

UNCLE RAY

By 1985 Ian and I had three preschool children, so I was preoccupied with the little earthlings in my own house and wasn't in close touch with Ray. But as our kids grew into interesting people, he began to come around a bit more. Young children don't frighten him the way adults do. Guileless and easy to read, they are as yet unskilled in the ways of Goongbalong. My sisters and friends were also busy producing playmates for him during those years, and Uncle Ray became very fond of his nieces and nephews. The feeling was mutual.

He considered the cultural education of the children to be his privilege and responsibility. There was so much to teach them about art, architecture, music and poetry! Ray believes all kids should learn poetry by heart, and at any opportunity he would patiently guide them through one of his favourite poems. Eventually these ad hoc sessions took on a bit more structure, with a core group of devotees gathering for the sole purpose of memorizing poetry. They called themselves the Dead Poets Society after the 1989 movie starring Robin Williams—unoriginal, yes, but in Ray's version, there were no criteria for inclusion besides a willingness to try; all comers, young or old, were welcome to participate. I eventually screwed up my courage and joined in, finding myself exercising long-dormant memorizing muscles. Ray would go line by line, stanza by stanza, and we'd have to repeat his words, going around the room. Anyone plucky enough to take a shot at Robert Service's epic ballad, "The Cremation of Sam McGee," was okay in Ray's book. We'd slog away until our brains hurt and we could not absorb another word, then Ray would dazzle us all by taking a giant lungful of air and reciting the whole damn thing at top speed on a single breath, a feat doubtless made possible only by his years of training as a free diver.

Ray becomes reverent when he speaks of his favourite poems; they are, he says, "greater than the sum of the words from which they are made." He has his top ten—or maybe it would be more accurate to say his top twenty or thirty. He's happy to reel them off for the asking. There's "The Tyger," by William Blake—"the best thing ever written about God," he says. This is one of the poems he often starts first-timers on, along with the classic "If," by Rudyard Kipling. He is deeply moved by Shelley's "Ozymandias," "fourteen lines that say everything that needs to be said about human grandiosity." He adores "High Flight": "A young man tearing up the sky in a Spitfire—what could be better?" Included are many of Shakespeare's sonnets about love, but he also appreciates poems about social justice ("Jerusalem"), fate ("Two Roads") and duty ("Oh Captain! My Captain!"). It's hard for him to pick a favourite, but if pushed, he might choose the grim and resolute "Invictus." He says that one's about "facing it with style."

"It matters not how strait the gate," goes the last verse, "How charged with punishments the scroll/I am the master of my fate/I am the captain of my soul." There are no truer words to describe Ray's personal credo. Lord knows, the gate has been "strait," and the Goongbalong score sheet is thickly inscribed with punishments, and yet he remains "bloody, but unbowed."

I wasn't the only grown-up getting in on the poetry action, and Ray was happy to have us, but it was the younger attendees that gave him the most joy. His encouragement at their progress, however halting, spurred them on. Ray never speaks down to kids—perhaps because he is incapable of gauging their developmental levels and adjusting his expectations accordingly, but they feel dignified. Everyone goes the extra mile to earn a "well done" from Uncle Ray.

As with his favourite poems, classical music sometimes enters the realm of the divine for my brother. There are a few pieces that he calls "the sacraments," including Camille Saint-Saëns's massive *Organ Symphony* and violin concertos by Max Bruch and Felix Mendelssohn. These are to be savoured, he says, not more than once every couple of years. He enters a sort of trance when he listens to them.

My friend Cody once invited Ray and me over to his basement suite to check out his killer sound system—possibly the most valuable thing he owned at the time. We brought the *Organ Symphony*. "Okay," Ray said as he swung his feet up onto the coffee table and closed his eyes. "Let's see what this baby can do." After a few false starts—"Nope, we need more bass," and "Wait, the balance isn't quite right," and

"Hold it, hold it! Way too much reverb!"—Ray pronounced the sound acceptable. We settled down and let the music wash over us. Cody's speakers performed admirably. Finally, the last gigantic notes of the cathedral-sized organ crescendo thundered in our chests, then echoed away, leaving a vacuum of silence. Ray did not stir. Slumped on the sofa, he appeared to be fast asleep. Cody and I waited a respectful amount of time, then I took our tea mugs to the kitchen and rattled around a bit. I came back into the living room and sat down. We looked at each other and shrugged, our mutual thought unspoken. *Asleep? Through that? How is it even possible?* Eventually I prodded Ray in the arm, and his hand shot up in the universal "Wait!" gesture. Perhaps he was being melodramatic, but I believe he just wasn't ready to come back from where the music had taken him.

We sometimes have music nights at my house, with Ray as the master of ceremonies. My husband flees for the nearest hockey game or superhero movie. ("No soul" is Ray's sorrowful diagnosis.) I do the arranging, inviting, wine pouring, candle lighting and appy serving. I try to make sure I don't ask anyone to these gatherings who might run out of the room crying if my brother makes a faux pas.

Ray likes to start the evening off by pointing out the inadequacies of my husband's sound system and fiddling with the knobs and dials. We have been overly concerned with aesthetics, it seems, tucking our stereo speakers away on shelves among books and plants. Sometimes Ray will find it necessary to jam my pretty toss cushions in around the speakers to dampen annoying vibrations. If that doesn't work, he drags the speakers across the floor, trailing dust bunnies and wires. He will push things around until he's satisfied that the acoustics are as good as they're going to get. A few simple baffles hung from the ceiling, he tells me, would reduce the noise pollution in our living room and make all the difference to the sound quality.

Once we have dispensed with the preambles, we settle down to the listening, and though we take that very seriously, it's not a formal thing; some get pillows and comforters from the bedrooms and hit the floor, others drape themselves on the couches. Sometimes a teenager or two will skulk by, trying to be inconspicuous. Ray will draw the reluctant kid in with a challenge: "Here's a loonie for the first person who can tell me when the French horn comes in," or, with index finger upraised, "Listen carefully! What instrument is that?" Such is the power of Ray's charisma that many of the skulkers have ended up lingering despite their initial suspicions that being caught at such events might play havoc with their coolness quotients.

Most of those teenagers eventually turned their noses up at classical music nights and stopped showing up for Dead Poets—there were much more exciting things to do than memorize Sam McGee or listen to Beethoven with old Uncle Ray—but many of them left with a love of classical music and an ear for poetry that has lived on.

Mum underwent a serious surgery in 2005. One evening during visiting hours, Ray stopped in at the hospital, where she lay in a four-bed intensive care unit, tubes and wires sprouting grotesquely from her nose, neck, chest and arms.

"He came bounding into the room in his postie uniform," Mum tells me later. "To my amazement, he bent down and kissed me on the only patch of face that wasn't covered with tape or wires. He had never done anything like that before in his life."

I am moved, astonished at my brother's uncharacteristic display of tenderness.

"Then," continues Mum, "in a voice loud enough for all the other patients to hear, he said 'Wow, you look like Frankenstein's monster.'"

Ray's not a hugger or a kisser. Never has been. He wishes it were otherwise, but as he told me once, "It's hard to let go of the stiffness." His low tolerance for touch had always been a source of heartache for our dad. "Raymond would not accept any affection from me," Dad said, still pained at this fact to his dying day.

He once told me about an incident that happened when Ray was twelve or thirteen.

"I remember it vividly," he said. "We were all at a restaurant when we lived in Barbados. I got up to go pay the bill, and I passed behind his chair while he was still seated at the table. I put my hands on his shoulders and gave them a gentle squeeze. He suddenly spun around in his chair and said, 'Don't *ever* touch me!'" Dad paused for a moment, remembering the scene. "And I never did again."

Dad was seared by his son's seeming rejection. Knowing what I know now, I'm willing to bet that Ray was not so much rejecting his father's innocent gesture of affection as he was reacting to a surprise attack from behind. His rebuke might have had more to do with a hypersensitive startle reflex than anything else—but Dad could never have been expected to guess that. For him, the wound inflicted by his son's words was deeply personal and lifelong.

When I asked Ray why he doesn't like being hugged, he told me that I had it all wrong—he loves hugs and kisses. That was news to me; I've never seen that side of him. But maybe he wasn't just playing the devil's advocate, the way he often does with me. There are probably "conditions" that make some hugs okay and some intolerable. But there are other ways of showing affection that don't involve physical contact, and in these Ray is unstinting. He is a man of action. If he sees someone in need of assistance, he'll jump right in. Need your old fridge taken to the dump? That dangerous tree taken down? Your oil changed? Is your faucet leaking? Do you need a hand putting up that new fence? Ray's your man.

One fall, he drove Mum and Dad to Whistler Village along with some other family members to hear the Vancouver Symphony Orchestra play a free outdoor concert, including Tchaikovsky's bombastic *1812 Overture*, one of Dad's favourites. They set up their lawn chairs in the big field near the bandstand. Dad was ninety, and there wasn't a lot of meat left on his bones. Not long into the programme, Ray noticed him shivering uncontrollably. He disappeared, picking his way between folding chairs and groups of people lolling on the grass and came back with an armload of blankets—no one is sure where he got them—which he draped without a word over the old man's shoulders. Mum's voice wavered when she told me this.

My brother is by no means rich, but he is generous—especially so where young people are concerned. He has paid for music lessons and school instruments and gone to the resulting concerts, basking in the accomplishments of his protégés. When my son, Simon, still in elementary school, expressed an interest in playing an instrument with the local community orchestra, Ray showed up with an old French horn that he had rustled up from somewhere and refurbished, its big brass bell polished to a gleam. Simon ended up as second horn in Prokofiev's *Peter and the Wolf*, playing the wolf's recurring theme. Uncle Ray could not have been prouder when the boy, not much bigger than the instrument he carried, took his final bow.

Ray doesn't only show up for glorious moments like that one. He appreciates the small triumphs too. He once took the forty-minute ferry ride from his home in Gibsons, BC, then drove forty-five kilometres to buy something he didn't need from a grocery store in Squamish—just so he could go through the checkout where our then-sixteen-year-old niece, Emily, was bagging groceries at her first job.

He has reclaimed discarded trikes and bikes, made them new again and left them in the driveways of deserving children. He has built forts and lean-tos in the woods and given very young boys very sharp knives, to the muffled horror of their mothers. He takes kids hiking (too far), diving (too deep) and climbing (too high)—all of it deliciously unauthorized. They love it. But sometimes their parents don't.

I heard about one mother causing a fuss when she found out that Ray had coaxed her young son to swim with him across Ruby Lake without her knowledge or permission, but he waxed philosophical about it in an email to me:

> I reserve the right to have a tiny slice of life as I would live it. I do "bad" things all the time, but I try to be discreet so as not to upset the natives. Win a few, lose a few.

You can never stop Uncle Ray once he has the bit between his teeth and a clutch of eager young accomplices. His projects gain a momentum that other people's objections just ricochet off. He once built a tree fort with our sister Lisa's three boys in the backyard of their rented house. Lisa and her husband, Dave, didn't want this fort— much less the sheaf of bills from the building supply store that were handed to them during its construction. But as per the rules of Goong- balong, they didn't come right out and *say* so, and soon Ray was back- ing his old Chevy pickup truck up the driveway, disgorging purchased, poached and pilfered parts onto their lawn. The yard was full of kids and lumber and hammers and saws. Eventually a fine behemoth of a tree fort took shape in the forest canopy. It was the envy of every kid for miles around, and most of them managed to spend time in it, despite being forbidden to do so by their parents.

Not long after the fort was completed, Dave and Lisa bought a home of their own, but before they moved, their landlord, who had never been happy about having this major safety hazard on his property, insisted they dismantle it. When Ray offered to move it to the new place, Lisa gently tried to make it clear that they didn't want it, though she made her husband out to be the spoilsport: "Despite my many attempts to hint that Dave *really* didn't want the fort, Ray continued to argue his case that every boy needs a tree house. He was hurt, and I felt so bad for him!"

So the massive structure was moved in sections. Ray chose a perfect new perch between two towering cedar trees in the woods at the back of Dave and Lisa's property—well, the trees were technically *outside* their property line on municipal land, but Ray's not one for such subtleties. Dave and Lisa were distraught when heavy branches started crashing to the ground, but they could not bring themselves to cross the Goongbalong line: their subtle hints and desperately polite innuendoes were drowned out by the roar of the chainsaw.

The main structure was reassembled on the ground, then hoisted with a system of pulleys and securely fastened in its lofty new home. Lisa watched it all from her kitchen window with horror-stricken fascination. Here is her email account, capital letters and exclamation marks faithfully reproduced:

> During the construction period, I wasn't able to pull myself away. I was terrified that one or more of the kids would be crushed, hung or paralyzed. Ray had them swinging on ropes, holding onto pulleys that would lift them way into the air! I HATED THAT BLOODY TREE FORT and couldn't sleep at night worrying that my kids—or worse, the neighbours' kids!—would fall!! We should have put up a huge sign saying PRIVATE PROPERTY! NO TRESPASSING! to offset the lawsuit we would surely be slapped with when someone's kid became a paraplegic!

How high was that treehouse? I emailed all three of Lisa's boys, now grown men, to ask for their best guesses.

"Oh, it was a good forty feet up there," says Nick.

"Twenty-five, thirty feet, I'd say," is Justin's reply.

"About forty-five feet or so," says Luke.

Lisa's estimate? "I say fifty feet in the air! Is this my imagination?? With a huge square hole in the centre to accommodate the fire pole that Ray got from heaven-knows-where."

Lisa tactfully suggested that it might not be a good idea for kids to sleep up there, doubtless with that "huge square hole" in mind.

"No, no, Frank," he assured her—he calls her Frank after Frank Nitti, Al Capone's gangland henchman, also known as "the Enforcer," because she was always telling on him when they were little—"you've got it wrong. It's actually safer way up there. You see, if it was only six feet off the ground, the boys wouldn't worry so much about falling out and they might get careless. This way, they will have proper respect for the danger, and no one will get hurt. Trust me."

In the summer of 2005 we were invited to nearby Keats Island for a family party. The water taxi scuttled back and forth from Gibsons Landing all afternoon, ferrying small batches of us to the government dock on Keats. Once there, Ray, Ian and I were crammed with a bunch of other people into a grubby old utility van that was making repeat trips to the dock to collect everyone. We bounced along a rutted dirt road through deep forest to the location of the party. At the edge of a large sunlit clearing, a sturdy old house sat on a rocky promontory overlooking the ocean and Bowen Island beyond. The place was a child's dream; there were games and activities and things to explore in every direction. A rope swing hanging from the impossibly high branch of an old maple tree had already attracted a lineup. Other kids chose Frisbee or croquet.

Never one for hanging about and hobnobbing, Ray decided to lead a little after-dinner expedition around the perimeter of the island, and he enlisted a band of young buccaneers who set off behind him, following a rough trail through dense brush. This trail emerges from the forest now and then to skirt the rocky cliffs, sometimes dipping to sections that can only be traversed at low tide by scrabbling over slippery granite boulders. A rising tide obliterates the way back. The sun had slipped below the tops of the trees when one couple noticed that their seven-year-old son, Ethan, was not with his friends. A pall fell over the merry scene as partygoers fanned out to look for him. One elderly guest pointed to a barely discernable path into the salal at the edge of the clearing. He had seen a group of people disappearing into the woods there, he said, but he couldn't say how many or who they were. "Surely they wouldn't take Ethan!" said the boy's mother, trying to suppress her growing fear. "He's too little!"

Panic had taken hold of us all when Ray and his companions emerged from the bush on the opposite side of the clearing, the little boy among them. Both the child's knees were scraped, and a thick line of congealed blood ran down his left shin. One of his running shoes was soaked with sea water. A giant smile covered his dirt-streaked face.

Ray didn't know what all the fuss was about. "I haven't lost one yet," he said, a little indignant at the notion that any harm would come to a child in his keeping.

The incident was a few years ago now. I don't remember how long Ethan was missing. Nobody called the Coast Guard, so it hadn't escalated into a full-scale emergency, but I do remember that later in the evening, the mother of the boy came up to me, locked her eyes on mine and said, calmly, enunciating each word, "I want to strangle your brother with my bare hands."

Ray will take on anyone in a game of chess. The reward for beating him has always been glory and bragging rights, but recently he upped the ante by making a magnificent chess crown, which is now coveted by all pretenders to the throne. He started by cutting steep zigzags along one edge of a flat piece of sheet metal, then bending it into a tall circle and bolting it closed at the back. The bolt goes through a horizontal slot so the crown can be loosened or tightened to accommodate a variety of heads, no matter how swelled. He spray-painted it gold. He's on the lookout for a nice piece of ermine to wrap around the bottom edge for that final, authentic touch. It's proving difficult to find—there seems to be an ermine shortage in Gibsons at the moment—but even "as is," the crown makes quite a statement. Beat Ray three times in a row and it's yours, but whatever you do, don't don it carelessly. It must be adjusted to ensure a snug fit, as the lower edge is sharp enough to shear your ears off if it's too loose, and the points can draw blood.

While Ray will graciously relinquish the chess crown to a victorious rival, he's always happy to win it back, too—and he doesn't mind wearing it around town. The sight of Ray driving down the road in his battered red pickup, wearing dirty overalls and a tall gold crown whose points catch in the ceiling upholstery, has turned more than a few heads.

When it's not being worn, the crown sits on the Royal Pillow, a tasselled job Ray found in a thrift shop. Right now the ensemble is being proudly displayed in the living room of the defending champion, our nephew Reid, who has taken to playing blindfolded and calling out his moves to an assistant. He's up to ten moves into the game before he has to look at the board.

"Kid's been kicking my ass," Ray mutters with satisfaction, using his best "old fogey" voice. "When I was a boy, we respected our elders. Wouldn't *dream* of kicking their asses!"

Nothing delights my brother more than introducing new players to the game, thus creating an endless supply of up-and-coming challengers. Besides, chess makes a great buffer. It is somehow socially acceptable, Ray has realized, to retreat to a corner with a partner and strike up a game no matter how many people are in the room. Miraculously, this does not seem to run afoul of the Goongbalong police.

As a way of safely and politely opting out of an engagement party he was attending at my house, Ray withdrew to a quiet spot to teach some basic moves to a bored little girl named Ireland, the child of friends of ours—she was perhaps seven or eight years old then—and by the time the party was winding down, he had declared her a future prodigy. A few days later he came to my house with a brand-new beginner's chess set. "Give this to Ireland," he said, tossing it on the couch beside me. "Tell her if she keeps it up, it won't be long before she's beating me."

I don't think anything would make Ray happier than being beaten by a little girl and ceding the chess crown to her.

Nothing but the Truth

We do earnestly repent, and are heartily sorry for these our misdoings.
— *The Book of Common Prayer*

Little children are notorious for their outspokenness, but as they grow up, they learn to censor themselves in the name of good manners. They become aware that other people have thoughts and feelings different from theirs, and their Goongbalong skills begin to flower. They come to understand that for the greater good—and their own—they must sometimes suppress their natural inclination to say whatever they think.

Ray possesses this understanding in theory only, in the same way that I understand $E=MC^2$. Which is to say, not very well. He tends to say what he thinks, whether it's "Wow, you're really pretty!" or "Wow, you're every bit as homely as Babs said you were!" I'm sure he would crawl under a rock if he realized that the latter comment, besides hurting my homely acquaintance's feelings, has the power to efficiently destroy my relationship with her. But he'll bravely try his luck with one comment or the other, knowing that he has a fifty-fifty chance of shooting himself in the foot.

If in doubt, the most prudent course is to say nothing at all—but pretending not to notice the obvious is not Ray's forte. He writes:

> As you know, one of my biggest objections to normal society is that you do *not* tell the lady that her dress is stuck in her bum and you do *not* tell me that I've made some foul—though of course the tally is always kept.

This tendency of his to make unedited comments has always confounded people—even slightly odd people like our own father.

"It seems that for Ray," Dad once said to me, "the truth trumps the pain it can cause the recipient. He told me he wouldn't hesitate to tell a woman she's fat. In fact, he would expect her to thank him for pointing it out!" Dad shook his head incredulously. "And yet his own feelings are easily hurt. Why can't an intelligent person understand that what offends him might offend someone else?"

That's a good question. For someone so thin-skinned, Ray can certainly seem insensitive. But I always knew my brother was not *trying* to hurt anyone. He was not weighing up the merits of pointing out the fat lady's flaws versus the amount of humiliation she would be spared if he didn't. The truth doesn't trump people's pain; the truth is all he has.

There are times, especially after he's had a nip of his favourite Scotch, when whatever barriers exist between him and the rest of humanity seem to all but evaporate. His shoulders come down from up around his ears and he loses that hunted look. At such times, tipped back in his old La-Z-Boy recliner, he is a philosopher—and a surprisingly keen observer of human nature. He seems able to reach deep into the workings of our Byzantine social machinery and put his finger on the troublesome parts.

With Ray, there is no soft-pedalling, no spin. He couldn't pander for social points even if he wanted to. Honesty is not the best policy for him; it is the *only* policy, and he is mistrustful of those who consider it to be just one of their options.

Though his honesty has gotten him into plenty of trouble, I can attest to the fact that it can be equally tough being on the receiving end of it. He has demolished me more than once with observations that are simply neutral statements of fact, meant neither to wound nor to flatter—which makes them all the more devastating. But that unswerving honesty is also the reason that commendation from Ray is so highly prized. His younger nieces and nephews in particular will go to almost any lengths to merit his approval.

Ray has always maintained that a little honest feedback would fix everything. "What I need—what I've begged for since I was a kid—is simple feedback. Just *tell* me when I commit a foul," he implores me. "I will be happy to offer a lengthy apology and gifts of atonement as needed." Problem solved. Lesson learned. Crisis averted.

He offers an example of what that might look like:

> Did I ever tell you about the time in Germany when I was saying goodbye to my friend Olav? We gave each other a hug and he later told me: "Zat vas zee koldest und stiffest hug I hef het zinz I hugged mein dead vahzer in his koffin." Now THAT'S feedback.

He succumbs to bitterness:

> But prompt and honest feedback would be nothing less than changing The Rules, and that's not going to happen, is it? I mean, why couldn't we have a code word? It could be as simple as saying 'Juju!' if I'm making a foul ... but of course that's not The Rules.

I have occasionally taken him at his word and approached him after he has made a particularly spectacular Goongbalong foul. I wait for a private time. I try to be calm and kind. But his back goes up no matter how gently I explain where things went wrong and what he might do differently next time. "Why didn't someone *tell* me?" he flails. "Correction delayed is worse than no correction at all!" Then he concedes defeat, but his words have a caustic edge. "Okay, you win. I'm a jerk. Consider yourself the victor." Ray thinks I'm not satisfied until I have subordinated him. And he still clings to the belief that only a few handy hints stand between him and perfect political correctness.

I had an opportunity to test the "simple feedback" theory when Ray was forty and my elder daughter Heather was fifteen. Ray had dropped by to borrow a ladder. He and I were standing in the driveway after loading it into his pickup when Heather wandered out to say hi to her uncle. I followed his gaze to her adolescent chest and realized that whatever he was about to say was not going to be good, but the words were out of his mouth before I could intervene.

"Whoa! Nice hooters, Heath!" he said brightly.

If only he had stopped there, the situation might have been salvaged. But he didn't.

"Pull your T-shirt tight so I can see how big they are."

Juju.

Heather, already an unfairly large bra size for her petite figure, had received plenty of unwanted attention at school and was excruciatingly aware of her disproportionately sized breasts. The shock waves emanating from her at Ray's remark nearly flattened me. Her face turned crimson. She took three slow steps backward and turned to flee the scene.

At that moment I realized a terrible truth: Ray was likely to lose his nieces one by one as they reached puberty if he continued making such ill-advised observations out loud. It would break his heart and that would break mine. I *had* to fix this. So I called him up later that evening. "Ray, I know you meant no harm, but you can't make comments about the size of a girl's breasts, okay? Heather was mortified! Couldn't you see her backing away from you this afternoon?"

Ray was instantly on the defensive. Flustered and hurt to the core at my suggestion that he had done something improper, he came out swinging: "Dirty minds assume dirty things," he said, "and I don't much care what you think. You disappoint me greatly with your pseudo-moral Victorian prudishness. I doubt that I will be able to cure you of it."

His vehemence took me by surprise, but I maintained my cool. I knew he had misread my motives.

"Look," I soothed, "I know you're not a dirty old man, but you can't expect a teenage girl to know that it's okay if her Uncle Ray asks to see how big her boobs are, but anyone else who wants a closer look is a pervert." I explained that commenting on bust size is not the same as commenting on hair length or height. But I was only making matters worse. He heard "dirty old man." He heard "pervert."

I tried a different tack. "What if one of our uncles had asked me to pull *my* T-shirt tight when I was a teenager," I asked, "so he could see how big *my* boobs were?"

There was a palpable silence on the other end of the phone, as though I had jammed a stick through the spinning cogs of Ray's brain. I waited while he grappled with this new scenario. When he finally spoke again, I could hear intense concentration in his voice. "Why is that different?" he asked himself in a strained whisper. "*Why is that different?*"

He knew something would have been very wrong if the girl had been me and it was my uncle commenting appreciatively on my budding breasts, but he couldn't figure out for the life of him why something that would definitely have been unacceptable for another man to say should not be acceptable for him.

The conversation frustrated both of us. My efforts to be helpful had backfired badly; whatever lesson Ray had learned, it was not the one I had intended to teach. I gave up trying to make him see things my way and simply asked him to make a mental note not to comment on a girl's bra size—ever. "Same goes for weight and acne," I said. "Never tell a kid they're fat or point out that they have a face full of pimples. Believe me, they already know, and it will just humiliate them. Okay?"

These things were stupefyingly apparent to me. I didn't realize at the time that pimples, weight and bra size are random dots that can never be connected in my brother's mind.

I reassured Heather that Uncle Ray had not meant to embarrass her. I reassured him that his niece loved him and that nobody thought he was a pedophile. My only motive in bringing up the issue, I explained, was to prevent him from inadvertently causing other nieces to shy away from their "funny uncle" as they grew up. God knows I had the best of intentions. But the damage had already been done; Heather's relationship with Ray never recovered. She was gun-shy of him from that day on.

And as for Ray, he remembers this whole incident differently. He retreated from me, believing himself a victim of a vicious power play by a sister who took pleasure in humiliating him.

So much for "simple feedback."

Over the years, accounts of some of Ray's more notorious fouls would reach me through the grapevine. I felt bad—always more for him than for anyone else. Despite having been badly misunderstood by him many times before, I'd still occasionally offer a little post-game analysis, but my efforts invariably elicited a predictable salvo of self-defensive arguments. Teach him *Goongbalong*? Was this a bad joke? How could I ask him to participate in this barbaric blood sport, he wanted to know, much less learn to like it!

Things improved with the advent of email in the '90s. We seemed to do better when we hammered out the big issues in writing, so I decided to once again approach the subject of his social impropriety—but this time, instead of waiting for something bad to happen and attempting damage control after the fact, I'd do it in a way that was less likely to sound like a direct attack on his morals.

In the following email, circa 1996, I make an exploratory foray into delicate territory, expressing puzzlement at his lack of progress in mastering the basic skills necessary to survive in a neurotypical world:

> I don't get it, Ray. You've been running around on the Goongbalong field for decades, and yet you still can't figure out the rules of the game. Think of all the fouls you could have avoided! The goals you could have scored! You should be a star player by now, a regular Goongbalong god! But you're still running offsides and taking penalties.

Ray didn't deny it. In his reply he gave me a glimpse into the painful conundrums that were his daily lot:

> That's true, but the first rule of G [by now we had shortened Goongbalong to "G" in our emails], is that penalties, though they are tallied against you, are not brought to your attention, so you can make a foul without even knowing it.

It's clearly not a matter of "practice makes perfect." Practice had not improved Ray's game.

> "It's true," he acknowledged ruefully. "I have made some bloopers, haven't I?"

But the topic was on the table, and because we were communicating in writing, the threat level was low. Ray was incredibly ready to engage. In the following email, rather than fighting me, he invited me to put myself in his place:

> Imagine that you are being forced to play Goongbalong for the first time. You are not told The Rules either before or during the game, and if you commit a foul no one tells you—not even the ref. You cannot possibly win, and yet you are expected to keep playing. At the end of the match your penalties are tallied up and you are killed—if you live long enough to make it to your own execution, because the playing field is studded with landmines whose locations are known to everyone but you.

Ray might well have been referring to a cocktail party, but he made it sound like some sort of brutish gladiatorial game where he is thrown naked and unarmed to wild beasts for the entertainment of bloodthirsty spectators.

He is more afraid of cocktail parties than he is of team sports—but he has problems there, too:

> It's funny, but in games like hockey, I have to stop and think for a couple of seconds before passing the puck because I can't remember who's on my team. It doesn't really matter to me who I pass to; I just want to make a nice pass.

He can opt out of hockey and football—and he usually does—but there's no opting out of the social arena.

Ray's teammates on the field assume he knows The Rules as well as they do, so when he verbally tackles one of them to the ground or hands the conversational ball off to the opposing team, they assume he's doing it on purpose. *What is this joker up to? Is he deliberately trying to throw the game?*

Ray knows when he has put someone ill at ease—he can practically hear the ref's whistle—but he doesn't know how he's done it or how not to do it again. And the problem isn't just on the Goongbalong field; it spills over into the "locker room"—the good-natured, ribald teasing that men use to telegraph their acceptance of one another:

> Let's take "light banter," for example. At work the guys are constantly joking around with each other. It's mostly a stream of "insults" that are not serious. It's fun and it bonds them. I enjoy listening to it, and I don't even mind being the target: if it's funny, I am amused. But I absolutely can't *do* it! I know perfectly well when we are in the "kicking a field goal" phase of G, which should narrow things down immensely, but it doesn't help. I have all the "data" I need to make a nice pass, but what comes out of my mouth is taken as a real insult. I have not the slightest idea why.

He resorts to sarcasm, but it barely covers his despair.

> It might be that on your planet one must face west when making a jibe, but east if the insult is serious. Here we have a situation where I commit a G foul, I *know* I have committed a foul—I have committed thousands of them—but I still cannot figure out what the foul IS. How is it possible to understand the rules for receiving the ball but not the rules for throwing it??? It's like some part of my mind is playing Goong-balong with ME, for God's sake!!!

It's a rare day when Ray uses all-caps and multiple exclamation marks in a row. I can almost feel his exasperation.

Determined to make me understand what "my" world looks like through his eyes, Ray now abandons the sports metaphors and tries another way. This time he uses his thorny relationship with that old arch-villain from his school days, spelling.

> I often know when I've made a spelling error, but that doesn't give me any help in fixing it. Why, just today I had to spell hig ... hygee ... hyj ... hije ... hygene ... hygiene! At every stop, I was aware of the mistake, yet unaware of what the mistake was. When I eventually got it, I knew it was right, too.

He has made the point brilliantly: knowing something's wrong doesn't necessarily help you get it right.

He finishes with a third analogy, this one from the computer world, to neatly sum up his quandary:

> It's very much a feeling of disconnect. My "Detect Error" engine can't seem to work it out with my "Fix Error" engine.

I once read of an experiment in which lab rats were fitted with shock collars and subjected to random zaps, purportedly to study the effects of chronic inescapable stress on their nervous systems. At first the rats literally climbed the walls in a desperate attempt to escape the torment, but in time, unable to figure out what triggered the shocks and how to avoid them, they broke down, becoming neurotic and withdrawn. That experiment might just as well have been done to demonstrate the painful reality of life on our planet for Ray—it's a chronic, inescapable stress. He knows just how those lab rats feel.

But while the poor rats hadn't done anything wrong, Ray does—all the time. He crosses unseen boundaries, *zap!* Violates invisible taboos, *zap!* Sends the wrong signals, *zap!* And as he twitches and grimaces with each new jolt, he sees that we are *all* carrying buzzers. It could be any one of us surreptitiously pushing the button, yet we all walk on by looking nonchalant, pretending not to see his pain.

We had been over Goongbalong Rule Number One many times by now—*No commenting on breast size, weight or acne!*—and yet Ray still had trouble remembering these things. But no one had ever told him not to notice a girl's moustache, so how could he be faulted when he did so?

The girl was a friend of my daughter's, petite, dark haired, and maybe sixteen years old at the time. In a room full of people, Ray, innocent of malice as always, squinted close to her face and said, "Hey, I see you've got a wee bit of a moustache there!" The girl's fingers went slowly to her upper lip, covering the shameful thing, and she disappeared into a bathroom, where I imagine she went straight to the mirror and saw for the first time those dark shadows at the corners of her mouth.

She secretly bought some sort of depilatory that involves slathering a sticky substance on the skin, pressing a cloth strip into it and then pulling it off with a quick jerk. As it happens, she was at the time taking a powerful prescription drug to clear up her teenage acne. One side effect of this drug is delamination of the skin; it loosens the bond between the dermis and epidermis. When she yanked the cloth strip, the outer layer of skin on her upper lip and partway up her nose was torn off.

When I learned of this, I agonized over whether to tell Ray. It would kill him. But what had he always said? *Feedback without delay is all I need.* How many times had I heard this refrain? He could simply not afford to make this sort of mistake again. So in the end I did tell him, hoping that a dreadful lesson would sink in at last.

As I gently told him what had happened to the girl, his eyes got a faraway stare. He put his hands over his ears and rocked back and forth. "*I can't have done that,*" he intoned, "*I can't have done that.*"

All these years later it still makes me feel sick to write about this incident—just as much for my brother as for that poor little girl—who grew up to be a model, by the way, her picture on billboards and in glossy magazines on three continents. But she continues to do battle with that shadow. My informing Ray of the damage that resulted from his innocent comment wounded him at least as deeply as his comment had hurt the girl. And it did no good. He might very well make the same mistake again with another self-conscious child.

He sometimes says he wishes Speaking Man would drop dead. And on this occasion, he probably wished I would do the same.

Two summers had passed after Ray's comment about my elder daughter's breasts had horrified her to the bottom of her teenybopper soul. And damned if he didn't do the same thing again, but this time the object of his innocent observation was my younger daughter, Lesley, now a shy fifteen-year-old. My heart sank.

This was a subject we had covered. We had thrashed it to death after the incident that had cost him Heather, and I had strongly advised him to commit the rule to memory: *No commenting on breasts!* It doesn't matter, I had said, if they resemble fried eggs or watermelons, sagging udders or surgically enhanced rockets. It doesn't matter if they are attached to young girls or old ladies, friends or strangers. Got it? Never, *ever*, I had warned him, make comments out loud about boobs. He should have had it down cold.

"*Why, Ray?*" I cried, as his cherished niece fled the room. "How could you make this mistake again?"

The price he had paid two years earlier had been so high that I had thought he would steer clear of the topic forever after—the way one might steer clear of a dark alley in which one had been mugged. But that's not what happened.

This time, I waited a day or two, then emailed him to ask if he might have any theories as to how he could have fallen into the booby trap again. "That's a Level One Goongbalong foul, remember?"

He wrote back:

Indeed. I know I committed a G foul.

But it seems to me that shapely girls are usually very proud of their figures and tend even to flaunt them, so why not compliment them on that point? I guess male relatives are supposed to pretend they don't notice. Anyway, I do have a vague understanding that one does not say such things. You can say that a girl looks lovely in many ways, but not in *that* way. But it is interesting that something as prominently displayed as a girl's breasts are not to be commented on.

There was a certain indisputable logic to that. But the thought of Ray losing a second niece compelled me to belabour the point. "I just don't understand how this happened," I pressed. "Not on this topic."

This time, with some distance between us, Ray was not offended. He responded in his characteristically forthright style:

My processing speed is part of the problem. I don't process language quickly—but it might be more accurate

> to say I don't access my memory quickly. I was playing
> some "answer the question quick" game a few weeks
> back, and the only time I ever got an answer out first
> was when I was the only one who knew the answer.
> Same as when I tried out for *Reach for the Top*.

When we were in high school, Ray had auditioned for *Reach for the Top*, a game show that pitted elite teams of brainiac high school students against each other in nationally televised trivia tournaments. He was hyped as West Van High's secret weapon and encouraged to try out. Why, Ray Andrews knew something about everything! Everyone was surprised when he didn't make the team—except him.

> I knew lots of stuff no one else knew, but if anyone
> else did know it, they always got the answer out faster.

This mystified me. Ray is usually in hot water for speaking too quickly, not too slowly. He is not a man who ever finds himself lost for words—even when he wishes he was.

The next time we were together, he explained it to me. "Okay," he said, "imagine someone is drilling you on your times tables. You have to answer random multiplication questions, one every five seconds, every waking hour for the rest of your life." He started clapping his hands in a slow, hard rhythm, while intoning: "7 x 8! 6 x 9! 12 x 5! Quick! You have no time to think. You're just supposed to spit the correct answers out perfectly without skipping a beat. You're not allowed to slip up or stumble or ask for more time. You can't opt out. If you get even one answer wrong, you're going to be punished, so you're scared the whole time."

I'm a little rusty on my times tables. The thought of this exercise made me feel anxious.

"But now," he continued, "let's say a few of those questions are booby-trapped. You know they're coming, but you have no idea when. If you answer *those* questions—say, 5 x 7 and 9 x 4—you won't even know you've committed a Goongbalong foul, but everyone else will know. Your penalty will be quietly noted and counted against you for the rest of your life. Oh, and by the way, you *have* to answer 7 x 5 and

4 x 9 or you'll be penalized, but *never* 5 x 7 and 9 x 4. Those two are certain death."

Ray's harrowing illustration was very effective. "Your hair's getting so long" is 4 x 9. "Your breasts are getting so big" is 9 x 4, just one random comment among many—but *that* one springs the booby trap. All the feedback in the world will not save him from stepping into it. Again, and again ...

I recently had occasion to try a variation on Ray's times tables test. Someone (who claims to be a friend) sent me a link to a little game that was making the rounds on the Internet. It had the fear-inspiring title "See How Smart You Are!" I decided to try this "answer the question quick" test for myself. I waited until I was alone before I opened the link.

Ready? asked my computer screen. I sat up straighter. I felt a prickle of adrenaline. My heart beat a little faster as my right hand clenched reflexively around the mouse. *Begin!*

The first challenge appeared: numbers from one to ten bounced around on the screen. I was supposed to chase them with my cursor and click on them in ascending order, the object being to see how many I could nail before the question timed out. They were moving pretty fast, darn it. I flailed away but only managed to catch a few before my time was up.

No problem. I'd ace the next one.

Two pictures appeared, one after the other. I had five seconds to study the first picture and five seconds to click on the areas that were different in the second picture before it faded away to be replaced by a word to unscramble, a numerical sequence to be completed and so on, for an agonizing five hours—or maybe it was only five minutes. I don't know, but it felt like an eternity.

I had started out with no small measure of confidence. I was going for the high score. But by the halfway point of the test, my breathing was shallow, my palms were slick, and I was randomly firing away with my mouse, desperate to catch anything. I couldn't imagine trying to complete one of these diabolical tests with anyone watching over my shoulder, never mind gauging my worthiness as a human being based on my performance. What if I never found out how badly I had done or which answers I'd gotten wrong, but my score was posted publicly for everyone else to gawk at?

It occurred to me that the test I had just done should have been called "See How Fast You React!"—not "See How Smart You Are!" Given enough time, I can count to ten, unscramble words, identify patterns and spot the differences between two pictures. I just needed the damn thing to slow down. My problem was not a lack of intelligence but a lack of processing time.

That computer game was humiliating but harmless. With practice I'd get faster because the correct answers never change. But that is not the case in real time. When we are interacting with other people, there is far more at stake—and no opportunity to keep trying until we get it right or do it over if we get it wrong. Conversations are fluid, shape-shifting things: the "right" answer changes depending on who we're talking to and what we're talking about—even where we're standing and who else might be listening. Does my experience with the computer game illustrate how Ray could make an egregious mistake like commenting on a girl's breasts more than once?

> Yes, it's that simple. I didn't have time to process it. You had told me that noticing a girl's breasts is a G foul—like 9 x 4—but when you're running down the field and people are yelling at you to kick the ball even though you don't know who's on your team or which goal you're supposed to kick it into, eventually you just take the shot.

Men notice breasts. The rules of G stipulate that they must pretend they don't. But in the heat of the moment, there's no time for Ray to root around for that crucial bit of information stored somewhere on his internal hard drive—in this case, "*Warning: pretend you do not notice your niece's breasts.*"

But as Lesley walks into the room, he thinks, *I'll be darned, will you look at that! My little Lolly is growing up. Now wait ... there's something important about her breasts that I'm supposed to remember ... I'm supposed to do something—or, oh God, is it* not *do something?*

Time's up—and standing right here in front of him is a sweet little girl in a training bra. With breasts.

Speaking Man winds up and takes his best shot.

MY SOUL WOULD SPEAK

In 2001 our cousin Don was hospitalized with a bone-crushing depression. Ray reached out to him by email as soon as he heard. Don responded, ever so politely at first, but as his exchanges with Ray continued, he began confessing some of his private agony, his feelings of worthlessness and his fears that he would never be himself again. I had been trying to keep in touch with Don by snail mail, but eventually he and Ray looped me into their email conversation, and I read back through their exchanges with a burgeoning sense of wonder. Don had been careful to end his letters on a brave, upbeat note lest he burden Ray with his pain. That sort of concern for others was typical of the man and did not surprise me. But Ray did. His messages were kind, insightful, encouraging, even funny in just the right places. And ladened with empathy. Here's an excerpt from one email:

> It's the strangest thing, Don. When I read your letters, I get the most incredibly powerful feeling of connection with you. I've been working on this email for a couple of weeks now. I'm no sentimental weakling, but I keep having to stop because I start crying. Feeling something of your pain has been a privilege for me, not a burden. And yet, it has been a burden—but one that I wouldn't put down for anything. There are pains that are to be embraced, not avoided, and this, for me, is one of those.

It was difficult to reconcile the writer of these words with the Ray who so often seemed to need help extracting his foot from his mouth. I filed paper copies of those emails in a box that eventually found its way to the back of a cobwebby closet under the stairs, but I never forgot about them.

Ray came shining through again in July 2007 when a beloved uncle on our mother's side passed away. I watched him drop a folded piece of loose-leaf paper on the coffee table of the home where our extended family had gathered to grieve and then make himself scarce before he could say the wrong thing. I picked it up, unfolded it, and instantly recognized his appalling handwriting.

Thankfully, one of my cousins kept that letter. I have corrected Ray's spelling and grammar here (and throughout this book), but the words are all his:

> I cannot say I have ever met a man I quietly admired more than my Uncle Dave. To a casual observer he may have seemed to have been "just" an ordinary man who led an honorable though unremarkable life.
>
> But Uncle Dave was not an ordinary man; he was a giant. A giant of gentleness, of kindness, of courtesy. He was the most pleasant person I have ever met. He seemed to have no ego at all, no trace of selfishness in his soul. He never spoke about himself, always about the other person, and his concern for others was so unaffected, so real. I saw him angry exactly once.
>
> He was the near-perfect model of what it is to be both a gentleman and a gentle man. I only wish I had known him better. I will cherish his example and my memory of him for as long as I live.
>
> — a nephew

Gentleness? Kindness? Courtesy? Here was Ray extolling the very qualities he himself had so often been accused of disdaining. How could this be? He was not opportunistic enough to use such a sad occasion to try to augment his standing in the family with insincere words of condolence. It occurred to me that I didn't know my brother very well at all.

Uncle Dave had been a modest man, living and dying without

fanfare. He was certainly not remarkable in any way that is rewarded with fame or glory by this world. And yet, the way my brother wrote of him, he *was* remarkable. Ray had gathered up the man's unshowy attributes one by one and made a literary bouquet of them. And while he had been stiff and uneasy at the gathering—no hugs, no tears—what comfort his words must have brought to our cousins.

How was this level of empathy and eloquence possible coming from someone who didn't even like looking people in the eye and who was usually guilty of insulting them in person? And yet, just as in the letter he had written to Don years earlier, his words thrummed with love and fellow feeling. The incongruity of it bothered me. The insolence, the awkwardness, the unintended slights—these problems that bedeviled Ray in real time never seemed to happen in his writing. Given time and space to formulate a reply, he could "hear" perfectly, and his responses were pitch-perfect. In writing, Ray could speak in the language of his heart with no risk of tripping over his own tongue.

I couldn't stop thinking about the implications of my belated discovery. After a few days I emailed to say how much I had appreciated his elegy to Uncle Dave.

"It was beautiful, Ray. Simple, yet profound."

He replied:

> Well, thanks. I strive for clarity and hit "Send" only when I have achieved it. The problem only arises when I speak. It most often seems like it's someone else speaking. The inner man, the silent man, does not like most of what he hears. The speaking man is often rude, sardonic and has an irritating voice and manner, and I'm always disappointed with what he says. No, I don't like him at all.

"Well, you truly are an enigma, Ray," I wrote back. "You seem to be an entirely different person when you write."

That, as it turns out, was an invitation. Ray's cue.

> It's true. My mind lives in the nonverbal half of my head. Words for me are hollow and inadequate,

phantoms of the living reality of thought and emotion—except for poetry, of course, which transcends the limits of normal language. Writing is just a shadow. But the only way I can communicate is in the one-dimensional world of text. Sad, isn't it? It's so limited, so puny, but it's the only thing I've mastered. My soul would speak with better tools if it knew how.

Ray had dared to be vulnerable. I couldn't risk scaring him away with a volley of intrusive questions about this "speaking man." But from that moment on, I knew that if I wanted access to my brother's heart and soul, I would have to bypass the speaking man altogether. I would communicate directly with Writing Man.

FINDING RAY'S PLANET

My desire to find Ray's home planet simmered on the back burner as the years passed. Then the first clue flitted by so quickly and quietly that I almost missed it. That clue was an unfamiliar term embedded in one sentence in the 1997 book *Glenn Gould: The Ecstasy and Tragedy of Genius*, written by Peter Ostwald, a practising psychiatrist who was also an accomplished violinist. I remember being drawn to the book; perhaps it was Gould's uncanny physical resemblance to Ray and a vague sense that the two had something in common.

Gould was catapulted to stardom at the age of twenty-three as a result of his sensational piano recordings of Bach's *Goldberg Variations*. But he was a star with some peculiar mannerisms. Most notably, he hummed as he played—a nightmare for recording engineers. And he always sat on a preposterously short-legged chair that his father had made for him, the seat precisely fourteen inches from the floor. Though padded piano benches were urged upon him at every concert venue by embarrassed promoters, he would sit on nothing but that chair, and he carted it around the world as his fame grew. The seat pad disintegrated over the years, but he refused to have it replaced, so he ended up straddling the bare wooden crossbeam, shreds of the original leather hanging from the frame. It seems Gould was as famous for his peculiarities as he was for his virtuosity.

It was in chapter three that I encountered the unfamiliar term. "Some of the behaviour [Gould] manifested ..." Ostwald wrote, "seemed to indicate a condition called Asperger Disease, which is a variant of autism."

I had never heard of Asperger Disease, but I made a note to look it up. (Asperger's is not a disease, but that's what it was called in the early days.)

Reading on, I marvelled at the words Ostwald had chosen to describe Gould's conversational style—they could have been written about Ray: "Speech flowed out ceaselessly and seamlessly, under great inner pressure. His vocal exuberance seemed like some kind of primal experience, a joyous discharge of emotion and intellect, mockery and fantasy, all designed to fascinate if not dominate the listener."[1]

That's my brother when he's on a roll. Ray is certainly no musical prodigy, as his playing on that poor, mutilated cello of his amply illustrates, so it was not musicianship these two had in common, and it was not *what* Gould said but the *way* he said it that seemed so deeply familiar to me. He often made the sort of deliberately provocative statements my brother likes to make.

Gould insisted that he was "not at all the gregarious type" and that he craved solitude, but Ostwald saw a man "demonstrating far more of a craving for companionship than for solitude." Just like Ray.

Peter Ostwald had a young family, a busy psychiatry practice, and a second job moonlighting as a musician. Often dead tired after evening rehearsals, he found himself unable to break free from Gould's orbit, sometimes playing music with him or listening to his soliloquies all night. As the hours ticked by, he would yawn ostentatiously and look at his watch in an escalating series of ever-more-obvious distress signals, but Gould was oblivious to these pitiful Goongbalong ploys—or perhaps he saw them for what they were and talked faster and played more furiously, so as to leave no opportunity for escape. Only when Gould was finally ready to call it a night would Ostwald be dismissed to stagger home to his wife and baby.

Glenn Gould "had a fantastic sense of humour"[2] and was fond of doing impersonations, particularly of German accents. This is one of Ray's parlour tricks too, and it's guaranteed to elicit laughs. (He also does a very credible Middle Eastern terrorist—but he usually saves that one for passport offices and airport security screenings.)

The more people in the room, the more Gould's anxiety escalated. He would seize control of the situation by going to the piano and playing something from his repertoire. This would force everyone into polite silence while still allowing their admiration for him to penetrate the sonic shield.

No such luck for Ray. All he has is his ability to speak well on a variety of topics and tell a compelling story. And what a charming raconteur he is! There's no one like him when he has a handful of enthralled disciples gathered around listening to him expound on any of his favourite subjects. You could light his hair on fire and he wouldn't notice. No unspoken signals will deter him—and at my house, that might include my husband, Ian, turning off the lights and going to bed. This is scandalously rude conduct for a neurotypical, as it contravenes the delicate series of Goongbalong procedures normally implemented when guests overstay—but Ian knows that Ray's probably so engrossed in what he's doing that he won't catch those hints anyway. So I'll interrupt: "Ray, it's a school night; we have to call it quits now." He will look startled, perhaps a little crestfallen, then he'll quickly decamp.

Glenn Gould's recordings of the *Goldberg Variations* were released in 1956, the year my brother was born. It seemed clear to me now that Ray Andrews and Glenn Gould, though separated by a generation, had both landed on Earth with a thud and been left to fend for themselves. Whatever this "Asperger Disease" was, my brother had it. I was certain of that.

Ostwald observed in Gould "a chameleon-like quality of eccentric behaviour, very appealing and entertaining, to be sure, but masking deep feelings of anxiety and fragility."[3] He wrote of Gould's "demands on the one hand to 'stay with me, listen, let me fill you with thoughts and ideas about myself,' and on the other hand to 'keep your distance, don't get too close.'"[4]

Glenn Gould was a notorious show-off, and yet—another paradox, this—he developed a revulsion toward his audiences: "It's dreadful," he said, "There's a kind of gladiatorial instinct that comes upon the case-hardened concert-goer, which is why I suppose I don't like him as a breed and don't trust him, and I wouldn't want one as a friend."[5]

In this I hear the echo of my brother's own mistrust of mankind "as a breed," with all those neurotypicals just itching to press their buzzers. Was Glenn Gould "mostly always terrified," just as Ray has so often described himself?

As Gould's celebrity grew, so did his neuroses. By the time he was thirty-one, performing in concert caused him such distress that he retreated to a studio and never appeared before a live audience again. Though safe now from the fawning hordes, his shattered nerves did not recover. His pockets bulged with pills of every description. He went through a succession of doctors and shrinks in a futile quest for relief from vague aches and pains—and always the debilitating anxiety that stalked him.

Gould lived his final year stooped, pallid and trembling, though he continued to play and record in his studio to the end of his life. On October 4, 1982, he died of a stroke. He was fifty. His funeral overflowed with admirers. As the eulogist said, "Everything about him was different ... Glenn Gould was a man apart."

By the time I closed Ostwald's book, I felt both a new foreboding and a new resolve. Ray was forty-five. I had to find his planet, and now I knew where to start looking.

I emailed Ray, using the "A" word for the first time:

> Did you know that Glenn Gould might have had a mild form of autism called Asperger Disease? At least that's what they're diagnosing him with after the fact.

Ray didn't miss a trick.

> That's right. It hadn't been invented in his lifetime—or rather, it was not yet fashionable. Certainly not the "diagnosis du jour," at any rate. I don't know if there's any such thing, but whatever Gould *had,* I *have.* Definitely. We're two dimes in a barrelful of nickels.

This bowled me over. Though Ray's reply was drenched in sarcasm, it did not slam the door on a diagnosis of Asperger Disease. I lent him Ostwald's book and waited for his take on it.

Reading Gould's story for himself did nothing but increase Ray's sense of rapport with the musician. He just wasn't sure about the "autistic" bit.

I don't think the Asperger's envelope is particularly well demarcated, and indeed I feel I have nothing in common with many supposedly autistic people. Nevertheless, there is this profoundly powerful sense of identification with GG. Brother! Fellow traveller! Yes, same language, same planet, no doubt about it.

There it was, in his own words. Twenty-three years after making my high-school promise, I had found Ray's planet. Only it wasn't Vulcan. It was a "disease."

Ray wasn't about to let me start congratulating myself on pegging him. How, he asked me, would this label change anything?

My point is simply that who has a syndrome and who does not is defined by the majority in the same way that who is a war criminal and who is a hero is defined by the victor. I am not impaired in an absolute way but only in a relative way. Okay, I do have SOME absolute impairments, like my handwriting and spelling, but "normal" people seem to me to have impairments that I lack. On balance, I don't consider myself to be a cripple—though I am definitely a "misfit" in the proper use of the term.

He then cited our niece Emily, a girl with significant learning impairments, as an example of someone who has been diagnosed half to death—and what good had it done her? By the age of ten she had been identified as having an alphabet soup of deficits and disorders, but Ray was unimpressed. According to him, these labels were a lot of useless jargon that did nothing to help her. Now he added some good-natured mocking to make a point about the new "disease" I was trying to pin on him.

Hey, I think we need some fresh diseases, and why not? We're coining new ones daily. Sheesh, Em has at least half a dozen of them, and you can make a good living diagnosing them. C'mon! Add a few yourself!

What I'd like is a new syndrome that puts me and GG in the same box but leaves out the zombies and head-bangers. The whole field needs a rework.

Fair enough; I had as many questions as Ray did. But for the first time, I believed there were answers out there.

Lost in Translation

Now that I was actively looking, it seemed that pieces of the puzzle were falling right into my outstretched hands. In 2007 I discovered on my own bookshelf a book I had been meaning to read for ages, called *Thinking in Pictures*. It had been written eleven years earlier by an autistic woman named Temple Grandin, a Ph.D. professor of animal science at Colorado State University. Thanks to a tour de force portrayal of her by the actress Claire Danes in the 2010 biopic *Temple Grandin*, she has become the most famous autistic person of her generation. Dr. Grandin uses her celebrity to advocate for autistics and to enlighten neurotypicals about the autistic experience, planting herself resolutely in the middle of that vast wilderness between the extremes of "us" and "them" so she can be heard by both sides.

The first three sentences of her book get straight to the point: "I think in pictures. Words are like a second language to me. I translate both spoken and written words into full-colour movies, complete with sound."

Grandin has cobbled together a vast library of "videotapes" of things she has seen and done. When stumped, she "plays" these scenarios over and over, trying to extrapolate how people in her current situation might be expected to behave. She admits the process is cumbersome: "Pulling facts up quickly is sometimes difficult because I have to play bits of different videos until I find the right tape. This takes time."[6]

Certain sentences that Ray had written, embedded in his hundreds of emails, seemed suddenly to jostle free from their places, rise above the top edge of my computer monitor and hover in the air:

My mind lives in the nonverbal half of my head.

I didn't have time to process it.

I don't access my memory quickly.

His description of his difficulties processing language had led me to conclude that his wheels turn more slowly than mine. But after reading about Grandin's process, I found myself wondering if his brain is actually attempting to do a *lot* of things in a very short time. I have come to believe this is closer to the truth. Speaking Man just ends up blurting out *something* while Thinking Man's search engine is still running.

> Speaking Man is trying to translate what he thinks Thinking Man is thinking, but he doesn't do a good job. Errors are made.

Temple Grandin has since expanded her pioneering work on visual thinking. Her 2013 book, *The Autistic Brain*,[7] explores other primary languages of thought. There are garden-variety "word thinkers"—I'd be one of those—but she now believes there are "pattern thinkers," too—among them, many noted artists, mathematicians and musicians, whose ideas come to them in ways that do not involve language.

Unlike Grandin, whose database is compiled from literal images and experiences, Albert Einstein created his "movies" by applying real-life scenarios in ways never before imagined, like riding light beams and bending space. These thought experiments were his springboards for understanding concepts that could never be demonstrated in a lab. Incredibly to me—but I doubt to Ray and certainly not to Grandin—Einstein called the translation of these concepts into words and mathematical symbols *a secondary step*, which he performed *after* he had already solved the problems using pure imagery. "I very rarely think in words at all," he once said. "A thought comes, and I may try to express it in words afterwards."[8]

Are Ray's words also a translation? A "secondary step"? When I put this question to him, he saw it as a fishing expedition:

> You'd be looking for something that highlights a difference between myself and "normal" people, but I

suspect that without actually getting inside each other's heads, we really can't know. I expect that most people think in pictures to some extent, and in words too, as the situation requires.

But my question had got him thinking about thinking:

People often think in emotions. They have a goal—make myself look smarter than Mildred—and they manoeuvre themselves in conversation to attain that. There is, I expect, no "picture" of a diminished Mildred, but there sure is the goal of a diminished Mildred.

I often think in "attractors." I *feel* the way an item will attract some things and repel other things, and I'll move it where it "wants" to go.

Years after, it occurred to me that Ray might be describing a form of synesthesia—literally, a "union of the senses," in which he experiences a melding of the "attractor" (the stimulus) and the sensation it triggers in a normally unrelated neural pathway. The next paragraph in his email seems to confirm this:

Mathematical thinking: Now there's something hard to put into words. The numbers have a sort of pressure or weight, and an equation is a balancing of those weights. I expect we have several other ways of thinking besides these, and that everyone uses all of them to one degree or another.

It's not words *per se* that cause the trouble for him. He speaks with lucidity and grace when he knows the topic back to front. It's the speed and unpredictability of conversation—the switching between a thought language and a spoken one in real time.

Einstein's theory of relativity revolutionized physics and astronomy, and nobody gives a damn about his processing speed now. Grandin designs and builds livestock-handling equipment in her head. She views it from every angle and runs cerebral test simulations. Glitches are found and fixed and modifications made until everything runs smoothly. The drawings are done later.

I remembered Ray telling me how he flew over and around a formless pile of sand and saw the castle he had already built in his mind.

Einstein was more interested in the relationships between objects than he was in the relationships between humans. This is true for Grandin too. Emotionally laden dramas like Shakespeare's *Romeo and Juliet* leave her bewildered. She chalks it up to her "sequencing difficulties"—too much back and forth, too many hidden motives. "I never knew what they were up to."

It comes as no surprise to me that Grandin is a *Star Trek* fan and identifies powerfully with Ray's alter ego, Mr. Spock, and with Data, the sentient android in a later incarnation of the franchise. Data's high-speed computerized brain lacks an emotion chip, so his efforts to imitate human idiosyncrasies and humour fall flat. No doubt, legions of autistic people can relate to his awkward attempts to fit in.

Grandin once said, "Autistics have problems learning things that cannot be thought about in pictures," and that is true of her. Not Ray. One of his favourite subjects is philosophy. He loves the Big Questions about truth and the nature and meaning of life. It's just more proof that autistic people are individuals with their own tastes and talents.

Ray reminds me, "We're *all* somewhere on the spectrum."

I figured I now understood Ray's problem perfectly: translating from thoughts to words takes time and energy. But there was more. Ray explained:

> When I say something on the spur of the moment,
> I'm hearing it for the first time just like you are.

Every word out of Speaking Man's mouth is a surprise to Ray! Can you imagine the performance anxiety? The inherent risk in each unrehearsed conversation?

Fear is a huge issue. I often find large social situations overwhelming, and I end up saying God knows
what. As you know, it can be disastrous.

For Ray, then, speaking extemporaneously is a sort of verbal Russian
roulette. He screws up his nerve, points the gun at his temple, squeezes
his eyes shut and pulls the trigger, hoping for the best but anticipating
the worst—and there's almost always a bullet in the chamber. But it is
not just the recipients of his spontaneous comments who will be upset. He will be too.

Ray isn't sure how much of his difficulty is unique to him (and/or
other Aspergians, he graciously allows) and how much is common to
humanity. "Lots of people have trouble *thinking* about speaking and
speaking at the same time," he says. "Maybe I'm just one of them."

There's a highly complex sequence of events involved in generat-
ing even the simplest sentence—and it requires the collaboration of
distinct neural pathways connecting different areas of the brain in a
seamless, lightning-quick relay. There are any number of opportunities
for that process to go awry—and Ray knows them all. "Writing," he says,
"is like playing chess; speaking is like playing tennis with a live grenade."

"Autistic people can't read body language." That's one of those blanket statements Ray doesn't like. He can read the big stuff—a wave, a
wink, a shrug—just fine. What he has trouble with is what he likes to
call, with a shudder of revulsion, "the language of evasion and hidden
meaning." Embedded in every interchange between neurotypicals are
coded messages that subtly shift and shape—and sometimes flat-out
contradict—the meaning of their words. Unfortunately for autists, the
unspoken part of the conversation is often the loudest part. Even the
"silent treatment" is not an absence of communication but a pungent
message in itself.

According to *The Definitive Book of Body Language*,[9] researchers have recorded almost a million nonverbal cues used by humans,
including 250,000 facial expressions. If that's true, very little of what
we communicate is delivered in the form of raw verbal data. Over a

third of the weight of a spoken message is delivered via tone of voice, inflection, rate, rhythm and stress, which together can infuse words with radically different meanings. Another 55 percent of the content is silent: the tilt of a head, crossed arms, a raised eyebrow, even the way we blink. The authors say that only 7 percent of the information in a spoken message is communicated by the words.

This is grim news for Ray, who is not fluent in body language. "Seven percent?" he sputters when I read him the statistic. "You're kidding! I'd have guessed 75 percent even amongst yourselves. Good God, if it's really 7 percent, then I'm blinder than I thought."

The way one person shakes another's hand conveys a universe of meaning to the shakee. *The Definitive Book of Body Language* devotes a whole chapter to this important ritual. It lists eight of the worst handshakes, each of which indicates levels of aggression and submission, confidence and control, interest and apathy. Among them are the Pump Handle, the Double-Hander, the Cold and Clammy and the infamous Upper Hand, in which the shaker rotates the other person's hand so that their own is on top, indicating dominance.

Would Ray be able to glean a few useful tips from the handshake chapter, or would he want to throw himself off a bridge in despair at the fiendish complexity of it all? I sat down beside him one night. "Did you know," I asked him, "that there are so many different hand-shaking techniques that this book devotes a whole chapter to explaining what they all mean?"

I expected him to shrink in horror but, much to my surprise, his face lit up. "I speak handshake!" he said, excitement in his voice.

I decided to test him with a classic Upper Hand. "But what if I do *this*?" I asked, as I reached for his hand and shook it, twisting it into a submissive palm-up position. "Do you know what this means?"

"Oh, I know what it means, and I correct it," he said, firmly rotating my hand back to a neutral position to indicate symbolic equality. "Not only do I understand the meaning of a good handshake," he told me, "I *teach* it. There was this one guy I met," he recalled, "a carpet cleaner, I think. Nice guy by the looks of him, but his handshake! Gawd, it was awful!" He shuddered at the young man's lack of proficiency in this most basic of greeting rituals. "I spent ten minutes with him, and I made him shake over and over. I wouldn't let him leave until he finally got it right. No, I speak *that* one native," he said with assurance. "I just don't look at people while I'm doing it."

Perhaps he can literally *feel* the other person's intentions—while at the same time exerting a measure of control over the interaction. Regardless, that particular bit of body language is one of the ones he considers "upfront and honest."

The handshake may be the only nonverbal ceremonial ritual in which Ray holds a black belt, but there are other subtext messages he understands passably well, and they do not involve physical touching:

> It's true that I have an inability to decipher the hidden, subliminal rules. Most of those escape me entirely. But some of the rules I understand perfectly— like when a person rolls their eyes, for instance. That one's easy for me. I know it the same way anyone else knows it.

To illustrate, he proffers the example of Lenny—a notorious gasbag who hangs around at the local marina. Lenny has a limited collection of anecdotes that he will unspool endlessly for anyone who will listen. Ray has become adept at sidestepping him, but one day he watched his friend Brandon get caught in the dragnet. Brandon shot Ray a googly-eyed glance over his shoulder as Lenny began reeling off a story that he had already heard countless times. Brandon made not a sound, but his message was loud and clear.

"That boy was in pain!" Ray tells me enthusiastically. "I felt it too!"

That evening I'm still smiling at the memory of his impersonation of Brandon's pleading eyes and slumped posture, and I see a chance to make my point to Ray via email:

> I read a whole lot of body language just as easily as you read Brandon that day. You can see that when you do "get it," it's not malevolent at all. It's just a way of transmitting valuable information quickly and without words—a kind of shorthand, I guess.

He acknowledges:

> Sure. It's just that on my planet there would be no
> need. Consider this correspondence, wherein we
> speak the same language (almost) due to the lack of
> a subtext. I'd suggest that we have not been hindered
> in any way.

The lack of emotional context in our text messages, I tell him, is precisely why we resort to emojis—those little faces with various expressions that help clarify the meaning of our words.

Ray doesn't use emojis, but he ends his email with a playful dig using a keyboard equivalent:

> Indeed, I'd venture that this sort of clarity would be
> best even between typicals. You should try it some-
> time!
>
> ;-)

Ray often gives up watching TV dramas because he can't keep track of the faces. This is a minor annoyance, but he has the same problem with faces in real life—and that can be terrifying. What is he to do when someone he's obviously supposed to know materializes out of a crowd and claps him on the back with a grin and a "Ray! How ya doin, buddy?"

Faces are constantly changing, each shift of expression indicating a shift in meaning. Smiles warp into teeth-baring grimaces that contort into frowns that explode into laughter—or is it grief? Ray tries to keep up as faces all around him telegraph information about their owners' emotional states. Not only must he try to decode it all on the spot, he is expected to reciprocate with matching expressions of his own. He can't do it; his face-recognition software doesn't work that way.

Mine does. People's facial expressions provide context to the information from my other senses. Hidden, masked or covered faces leave me feeling apprehensive. An article in the *Vancouver Sun*, entitled

"We are not a threat," quotes a woman, born and raised in Canada, who chooses to wear a niqab, the head-to-toe body covering that leaves only a narrow horizontal opening at eye level. She is not hiding from anyone, she says. Wearing the niqab simply makes her feel closer to her Creator.

"When confronted with a woman in a niqab," says a university professor quoted in the article, "there's a certain level of discomfort because we don't know how to behave. Without being able to see her body language, how can we know her intentions? ... Banning certain types of dress has never been the answer. We must, instead, learn to see the person behind the veil."

But how can we do that when we can't actually see the person behind the veil? One Muslim woman insisted on wearing her niqab while testifying in court and refused to remove it when ordered to do so.[10] A Supreme Court judge finally ruled that the woman must remove her niqab as it "masks her demeanour and blocks ... assessment of her credibility."[11]

If Ray had his way, would he want us all to keep our faces covered when we're speaking? He isn't quick to dismiss the notion. "That's a really interesting question," he muses. "I wish we could just listen to the words and forget about the mind reading. Don't get me wrong; I don't generally mind faces, but when things start to overload, then yes, I'd like it very much if they were covered. What matters is the idea itself, not the baggage. If I were a judge listening to arguments, I'd prefer to have the audio piped into my chambers. I wouldn't want to be distracted by the theatre of court." Here again, Ray's problem seems to stem not from a lack of information but from too much of it.

Freeze the action and it's an entirely different story. He has no trouble with *pictures* of faces. The first thing he does when he moves to a new home is put up his extensive gallery of family photos—all his important people in still life. Could it be that his pictures are easier on his eyes than the people they represent?

Despite his often-testy relationship with Aunt Nell during the years he lived with her, Ray sometimes did things just to be nice. On one occasion he presented her with a large framed canvas print of a painting he knew she admired—a portrait by Spanish painter Diego

Velázquez of his mixed-race Moorish slave, Juan de Pareja. His body is angled slightly away from the viewer, but his face is turned so that he looks directly out from the canvas. I stepped into Aunt Nell's house one day shortly after Juan was installed to find him surveying me from his place on the living room wall.

"Look at that level gaze!" Ray said as we stood together admiring him. "Neither subservient nor defiant. Just *confident*. He knows he's as good a man as his master. Velázquez knows it too, and he paints that mutual understanding onto the canvas. Juan was a slave, you know. Velázquez dressed him up in those clothes because he had been commissioned to paint a minor nobleman and he needed to practise. See how the hands aren't even finished? This painting was just a warm-up for the real one."

Years later I became aware of the face-processing problems of autists. I remembered Ray confidently interpreting every shade of meaning in Juan's expression. Why, I asked him in an email, did he feel such rapture for the portrait? His admiration had never waned:

> Anything less than rapture wouldn't do him justice. Juan speaks to the indestructibility of the human spirit. Did you know that he became a painter in his own right? In one of his works he paints himself into the picture and portrays himself as a nobleman, quite entitled to be there with the others of that rank. Pretty uppity for the son of a mulatto slave, eh? But as we see so clearly in the portrait, Juan considered himself to be nobody's property.

Ray *gets* this man's face. Adores it. This is what happens when he has the time he needs and no other sensory input competing for his attention. Juan de Pareja has simply obliged him by holding still there on the living room wall.

But Ray says there is much more to savouring Juan than simply having enough time to do so:

> It certainly doesn't hurt that he's static—but that's not the crux of it. I don't just "read" his expression; I

am nourished by it. Juan was a slave, but he is tougher and steadier than me, and he sees things exactly as they are. There *is* a world in his expression.

Ray then quotes from "Ozymandias," one of the poems on his top-ten list, which is about the great graven image of a mighty pharaoh, once feared and worshipped, now "a colossal wreck," face down in the desert sand. He weaves together the imagery of that crumbling statue and the portrait of the slave in a nobleman's garb to come to his own conclusions about human nature:

> Juan, his "master," the times, slavery, race ... the painting comments on all of it with a finality that reminds me of Ozymandias, only Juan is the opposite of him. Once you understand Ozymandias, there is simply nothing left to say about human vanity. Once you understand Juan, there is nothing left to say about slavery or racism. And it is all said without a single word.

Just the way Ray likes it.

It's one of those things "everybody knows" about autistic people—they avoid looking you in the eye.

But why is that? I email my question to Ray:

> If you're having a conversation with someone and you don't look at them, it makes you appear evasive, like you have something to hide. You're not hiding anything, so why do you prefer to look away? And eyes say so much. Why would you deprive yourself of crucial information by choosing not to see?

He writes back:

> Oh, I see quite a bit. Indeed, in my own way I think I see many things that are invisible to neurotypicals.

> But looking at people is scary. I don't like what I see
> most of the time. If I look away when I'm speaking,
> it's just words, but if I look at them, I see into their
> souls and am overwhelmed.

Ray knows he is expected to look at people he's conversing with, so he forces himself to do it. But making eye contact with another person activates a powerful energy current, like electricity. Eyes water and glint, stare and squint—electrocuting him with painful jolts of energy that bore deep into the recesses of his soul. The eyes are used judiciously even among neurotypicals—too much eye contact is seen as aggressive, defiant, prying or overtly sexual. Unfortunately, not *enough* eye contact sends a message too, and it's not a good one. We generally assume that the kid who stares at the ground when being questioned by a parent or teacher is guilty, ashamed and/or hiding something. And sometimes that's true. But there are other reasons too.

Ray writes:

> Sometimes I just don't want to meld with a person.
> I can't look into the eyes of someone who is lying to
> me or attacking me. But in any case, my "seeing" is
> often through a dark veil—I'm not always sure I have
> it right, or maybe I just don't want to believe what I
> see. And there are layers: the "seeing" is a kind of
> digging. I sometimes see right to the bottom almost
> instantly, but other times there is a brick wall. It sorta
> hurts to bang into it.

Ray's answer leaves me wondering if he's really *good* at seeing or really *bad*. Whatever the case, the idea that he avoids eye contact because he doesn't care about anyone but himself is misguided. Perhaps he cares too much.

For him, sustained eye-to-eye contact is distracting, uncomfortable, intrusive, even overwhelming—a tidal wave of uninvited intimacy. Seeing, then, must be harnessed, carefully controlled, rationed, or it can wash him away in a sensory deluge—in rather the same way the Vulcan mind meld threatened to flood Spock's carburetor.

Limiting eye contact is also an effective way of regulating sensory input. Ray must choose between what he sees, what he hears and what he says. I've often seen him close his eyes when he needs to concentrate.

It is impolite on his planet to invade someone else's privacy with brazen stares, and it rattles him when his privacy is so invaded. Most of us have had the experience of squirming under someone's penetrating gaze and wishing we could disappear. And we have all felt the need to look away in certain situations out of a sense of decorum. I think that Ray, with his exposed wires, just crosses that threshold earlier. Looking away might be not so much a choice as a necessity.

"What is it that scares you when you look at people?" I ask.

I see their fear and their pain. Better not to look.

Interesting. Because that's exactly what I see in my brother's eyes much of the time: fear and pain.

IF THE SHOE FITS

Sometimes Ray believes in Asperger's; sometimes he doesn't. He generally takes a dim view of my attempts to group him with anyone based on a set of symptoms, but he has always recognized other people who are wired the way he is. These are his "fellow travellers." I first heard him use that term when we were teenagers, and even then, I thought it sounded exotic and mysterious. Who *were* these people?

I figured I'd located one the day I met Dennis. Much to his wife's chagrin, he had spent thousands of hours building a massive steam engine that took up their entire two-car garage, floor to ceiling. I knew Ray would swoon over it, so I asked if I could bring him by. We were treated on a Saturday morning to a private viewing, complete with an enthusiastic and exhaustive commentary by its creator. After we left, Ray unabashedly pronounced Dennis "a man after my own heart, a fellow traveller."

And thus the steam engine man joined Glenn Gould in Ray's band of brothers.

Who qualifies as a kindred spirit, a man after Ray's own heart? I risked the question, even though I knew he was likely to see it as a naked attempt at stereotyping:

> Long before we had even heard of Asperger's, you instantly knew that certain people were like you. Looking back, do you think they were all Aspies? Do you feel more comfortable with them? Is it common interests that draw you together? What if their interests are different from yours? Might you still identify them as fellow travellers?

Sure enough, Ray was irked at this attempt to classify him as "Exhibit Ray."

> I have no idea if they are Aspies or even if there are
> any such things as Aspies and I wouldn't care one
> whit even if there is and they are. I'd give the subject
> as much attention as I would give to their shoes—
> none whatsoever.

It's a sore point for Ray, this neurotypical fixation with shoes. He wouldn't dream of judging another man by what he's got on his feet— and he's horrified that anyone else does. "You can tell a man by his shoes" goes the old saw, and this truism is still alive today. An article in *Medical Daily*, under the ominous heading *You Can Judge 90 Percent of a Stranger's Personal Characteristics Just by Looking at Their Shoes,*[12] states that shoes "serve as nonverbal cues with symbolic messages." Evidently a total stranger's age, income, social status and suitability as a mate can all be discerned by his choice of footwear. For Ray, who opts for comfort over style, these findings beggar belief. A world in which the calibre of another human being can be summed up by symbolic messages in his shoes is not a world he wants to live in.

Having made clear what does *not* constitute a basis for friendship, he continues:

> I feel comfortable with any intelligent, interesting
> people who aren't playing Goongbalong with me. If
> their interests differ from mine, that can be very much
> a plus—I'm open to new ideas and perspectives.

In his very next sentence he suddenly acknowledges the existence of Asperger syndrome and his own membership in the club:

> At least when I meet another Aspie, I know it isn't go-
> ing to be a contest, an endless jockeying for position.

Fellow travellers usually have something intelligent to say, and no ritual baring of teeth is required before they say it. They won't ask you how you are doing because they already know the only logical answer to that question is, "Doing *what*?" They have no idea how much higher or lower than you they are on the social ladder, so they're not sure if they're supposed to kowtow to you or you to them. Your shoes will never send them covert messages.

Now and again Ray will get lucky and cross paths with a fellow traveller. These chance meetings are exhilarating for both parties. But more often than not, people like him are solitary animals, lying low, taking no chances, avoiding the crowded Goongbalong thoroughfares. The Internet has done an admirable job of creating a *virtual* community, but there's something to be said for real live humans together in the same room. But for things to go smoothly they have to be the "right" humans, and I've developed an eye for those.

My friend Kathryn, a paralegal in Vancouver, enjoys attending the odd poetry or music night with Ray and me and our mutual friends here on the Sunshine Coast. After she remarried, she brought her new husband along to meet everyone. I introduced him to Ray.

"David's a lawyer, Ray," I said, priming the conversation. "He and Kathryn work together."

"Oh, interesting." Ray shook David's hand warmly. "What kind of law do you practise?"

"Personal injury, mostly."

A look of recognition dawned on Ray's face. "Ah! An ambulance chaser!"

David did not take the remark personally. He gave Ray a chance to redeem himself, and he did. A friendship was born. David is a deliberate sort of person, the kind of man who doesn't open his mouth until his thoughts are perfectly organized. He's also not very good at Goongbalong—a real selling feature in Ray's book. Maybe it's David's measured way of speaking or maybe it's his utter lack of interest in shoes—his own or Ray's—but whatever the reason, Ray is completely at ease around him. In fact, David now seeks Ray out for the occasional game of chess when he's visiting the Coast, and he doesn't mind getting clobbered.

For most people, a remark like the one Ray made when he met David would have put a quick end to any prospects of friendship. But I know that no matter how many penalties he has racked up, it's not because he doesn't care about other people's feelings. In fact, he says:

> I rather think that I am if anything too sensitive, but
> I'm somehow tuned to the wrong frequency. There is
> no faculty missing; rather, there is an incorrect tuning.

Had *I* used those words, "wrong frequency" and "incorrect tuning," to describe his social navigation system, I'd have been asking for a fight. But I take the opportunity to further the discussion while his shields are down:

> You know, Ray, you might be on to something with
> this "wrong frequency" idea. It may be small com-
> fort, but at least the computer eliminates this mis-
> tuning by standardizing the equipment we use to
> communicate. Nuance is lost—which is sad, at least
> for me, because it adds such a richness to spoken
> language—but it also does away with the problems.

Ray agrees:

> Quite right. I wonder if "nuance" (and that's a very
> good word for it) is something of value—I mean apart
> from being a needed skill in dealing with the natives,
> rather like knowing exactly how to bow to whom is
> a vital part of life in Japan. I wonder if "nuance" has
> any real content. I suppose it's an art form. If used
> gracefully, it could be beautiful. Alas! It's always used
> to hide, distort, evade, gift-wrap, anesthetize ... but I
> would view it that way, wouldn't I?

Most neurotypicals, if asked to express an opinion where they know that a truthful answer might hurt someone's feelings, will take pains to minimize the sting, swaddling it in softer sentiments. Ray does not do this, *will* not do this, except under extreme duress. In his eyes, a lie is a lie even if it is wearing dainty white gloves. If he thinks your new haircut is outlandish, he'll tell you so. If your makeup makes you look like a prostitute, he might feel duty bound to point it out. If he hopes never to see you again, he won't say, "We really *must* get together." But this doesn't mean he is without standards.

"I have a code of conduct just as strict as yours," he explains one evening, sprawled on our sister Trish's couch with his muddy runners on her coffee table. "It's just based on different things. It's not based on superficialities; it's not about keeping face or saving face. On my planet, honesty with oneself is the first virtue. When it is mastered, the truth cannot hurt you. Condescension, being ignored, deliberate assaults on your character—these hurt, but mere facts don't hurt, so they can be mentioned without wrapping."

Trish brings Ray a cup of coffee, which he takes from her almost unconsciously, never breaking his train of thought. Trish's eleven-year-old daughter is sitting beside her Uncle Ray on the couch, playing with her iPhone, oblivious to his discourse on manners. He suddenly notices her and realizes he has found the perfect way to illustrate his point.

"If I tell Tessa she looks like a bone rack,"—and here Ray grabs the startled girl's skinny thigh and joggles it from side to side—"if I say she looks like she's just been released from a concentration camp, apparently she will take it as a *compliment!*" Tessa smiles slyly, a testament to the truth of Ray's statement. "And yet," he continues, "to notice that a girl is fat is wrong. I'm confused! Both observations are true, but one is a G insult, and one is not. I can't even begin to imagine why that is."

Ray is on a roll. He puts down his coffee mug and leans forward. "On *my* planet, such things have no depth; they are not important. On *my* planet, an insult would be to question a person's motives, to accuse him of disloyalty, of cowardice, of dishonour. To point out a flaw is no more an insult than to point out that a door is ajar! Sure, I sometimes forget your rules and tell a woman she's fat or something. I know it's wrong—on *your* planet."

Ray might not mind his manners, but he sure minds ours.

TEMPLE

In 1995 the renowned neurologist Oliver Sacks wrote *An Anthropologist on Mars*, a book that was to change my life—and by extension, Ray's. The title story is a portrait of none other than Temple Grandin. Sacks flew halfway across the continent to interview her. After his plane landed at the Denver airport, he rented a car and drove the hour and a half to her office at Colorado State University, getting lost on the way. When he finally arrived, hungry, thirsty and frazzled, at her office door, Grandin plunged straight into a brisk monologue about her work. In a perfectly executed Goongbalong move, Sacks sent out silent distress signals, hoping she would notice them and offer him some refreshments. She did not. "After an hour," he writes, "almost fainting under the barrage of her over-explicit and relentless sentences, I finally asked for some coffee. There was no 'I'm sorry, I should have offered you some,' no intermediacy, no social junction."[13]

How many times had Ray walked through a door and let it swing closed in my face? How many times had I staggered up the stairs of my house with a child on one hip, a purse over my shoulder and a heavy bag of groceries in hand while Ray talked his way up behind me? He will take a seat at the kitchen table, only briefly interrupting his stream of consciousness—"Make me a sandwich, would you, Babs?"—before continuing to talk, heedless of my juggling of hungry kids, ringing phones and boiling pots. Of course he doesn't mean to be rude; had I asked for help, I would have received it. But boy, can I relate to Sacks, squirming in his chair, constrained by The Rules to suffer in silence—until his caffeine headache gets the better of him.

As a girl, Grandin would sit on the fence for hours at her aunt's farm, watching the cows. She had no trouble understanding their "simple, strong, universal" emotions, and she noticed how the steady pressure of the squeeze chute (sometimes called a cattle crush or standing stock) calmed them to the extent that they would tolerate inoculations and other indignities with little fuss. She craved the comfort of being squeezed like that—but whenever anyone tried to hug her, she experienced an unbearable sense of engulfment. She would stiffen, flinch and pull away. In her mind she began designing a machine that could squeeze her powerfully but gently, just like a hug—but one that she could predict and control.

In boarding school she built the first prototype. After many modifications to her original design, she was satisfied with her squeeze machine.[14] She could crawl into it and, by means of a hand control hooked up to a compressor, move the padded side walls in or out to exert a firm but soothing pressure on her body from shoulders to knees.

The contraption created a scandal. Faculty demanded that she remove it from her dorm, but one teacher, Mr. Carlock, defended it. He told her that if she wanted to find out why it relaxed her, she'd have to learn science. Grandin still publicly thanks Mr. Carlock for setting her on a path that led to her doctorate in animal science and a decorated career in humane livestock handling—not to mention better understanding of the needs of autistic people. I thought back with a rush of gratitude to Mr. Verhoff, the young teacher in the Caribbean who had let an adolescent Ray take the controls and "fly through knowledge" under his guidance.

Grandin's squeeze machine gave her the solace and pleasure she could never get from another person. After spending time in it, her ever-present feeling of "stage fright" abated. The weird autistic woman's device doesn't look so weird anymore. Today, deep-pressure therapy is recognized for its calming effects.

By professional standards Grandin is extraordinarily successful. Yet Sacks sensed an underlying sadness in her. "My work is my life," she told him several times. "There is not much else."

Sacks writes: "There seemed to me pain, renunciation, resolution and acceptance all mixed together in her voice ... Normality has been revealed more and more ... as a sort of front, or façade, for her, albeit a brave and often brilliant front, behind which she remained, in some ways, as 'far outside,' as unconnected as ever."[15]

Here it was again, this *aloneness* that has nothing to do with being alone. Is that why so many autists have worked themselves into solitary superstardom as Gould did? As Grandin has? Is work the only place where innovation and dogged dedication count for more than fashionable footwear and social diplomacy?

Sacks watched as Grandin demonstrated the use of her machine, visibly relaxing with the pressure. Her voice lost its strident edge. The process, Sacks noted, seemed to open a door "into an otherwise closed emotional world and allows her, almost teaches her, to feel empathy for others."

Invited to try it for himself, Sacks gamely crawled in and lay down on his stomach, experimenting timidly with the controls: "It was indeed a sweet, calming feeling—one that reminded me of my deep-diving days long ago, when I felt the pressure of the water on my diving suit as a whole-body embrace."

The pressure of the water ... a whole-body embrace ...

When I linked Temple Grandin's squeeze machine to the hugging sensation a scuba diver feels in deep water, I felt an instant paradigm shift in my mind. Suddenly Ray's free diving was not just a hazardous hobby. It was survival. Renewal. The opening of a door into a place where he was free and unafraid.

Ray was always trying to coax his family and friends to try free diving. I had long wondered why this seemed so important to him. Weren't there easier and far less perilous ways to have fun? Now it made sense. It's his way of showing love. Enveloped in water, he enters a state of grace that he finds unattainable on land. He wants everyone he cares about to join him so they can feel it too.

When I learned that Temple Grandin would be lecturing in Vancouver, I persuaded Ray to come with me and hear her speak. He seemed even more garrulous than usual on our ferry ride to the mainland, and I wondered if he was nervous, perhaps worried that merely being in the same room as this famous autistic woman would "out" him as another of her kind.

He was still talking as we took our places in the auditorium. I felt self-conscious when he posed his favourite rhetorical question at a volume easily heard by everyone around us: "Why do we need a syndrome to describe people who say what they mean?"

People were still milling about, looking for their seats, when I saw someone stomp purposefully onto the stage. I assumed it was a roadie coming out to do a last-minute sound check. *It's a man*, I thought. *Must be. No, wait, it's a woman ... and she's heading for the podium.*

The woman leaned a little too close to the microphone and said, "First slide, please."

It was *her*.

She was wearing a western-style shirt tucked into jeans, belted high at the waist with a big silver buckle. Her attire was an homage to her love of cattle and her vocation as a professor of animal science, but she had wasted no time on makeup or jewellery. Her wavy, greying hair was combed straight back in a manner designed to get it out of her face with the fewest possible pulls of the comb. There was no big smile and wave, no "It's great to be here in your wonderful city."

Ray leaned over to me and whispered loudly, "*I like her.*"

Of course he did. Temple Grandin couldn't throw the Goongbalong ball to save her life. She had spoken precisely three words so far, Ray had responded with three of his own, and I had already made up my mind: these two were from the same planet.

I was captivated by Grandin and so busy studying her mannerisms and watching Ray watching her that I don't remember much of her lecture. But I do remember the drive home.

"You liked her right off the bat!" I said with conviction. "She's *got* to be from the same planet as you."

But I received only a sharp retort from Ray. "How is my liking someone an indication that they share some sort of pathology with me?"

His challenge ignited another rousing discussion that raged all the way back to Horseshoe Bay and continued as we drove onto the ferry. We sat in the car for the forty-minute ride back to the Sunshine Coast, while Ray railed against the evils of Goongbalong. He attacked, I defended; I attacked, he defended. So much hot air was exchanged between us that the windows steamed up. Our conversation carried us right to my driveway, where Ray dropped me off before heading home. Then we carried on by email, always our preferred way of hashing things out.

Safely behind his computer, Ray was less combative:

> She seems to be looking into the distance all the
> time. Is anything like that true of me? I wouldn't be
> surprised, but of course I am the only person in the
> world who *can't* comment. Her gestures are both
> wild and illiterate. I consider that to be true of my-
> self as well. I've often wanted to learn sign language
> so that my hands would be able to say something,
> even if no one understood it. I think I'd much prefer
> speaking with my hands.

"I'm not saying you're a clone of Temple Grandin, Ray," I replied—
although I do find that his eyes are often fixed in the middle distance
when he speaks, just like hers. But knowing how touchy he can be
about my tendency to draw eager parallels between him and people
who acknowledge their place on the spectrum, I tried not to dwell on
the similarities:

> You're right: her gestures are kind of illiterate—they
> don't seem to have anything to do with her words. I
> don't find your gestures to be out of synch like that.
> Still, she clearly belongs with you and Glenn Gould.
> Same planet, I say!

My attempt to insert Grandin as a third member of some cohort of
oddballs that includes him and Gould was met with resistance:

> Maybe TG and GG and I do, in *fact* have some bio-
> logical condition in common, but I find the grouping
> too much of a stretch in purely useful terms. I laugh,
> TG does not. I like jokes, TG does not. TG seems
> emotionless, whereas my emotions are intense.
> OTOH [on the other hand], there are huge simi-
> larities. I suspect that the brain, the mind and the
> soul are so complex and so multi-faceted that it may
> prove impossible to make "hard" categories that do

more good than harm. Can we now claim that we can unscramble the egg of ourselves?

Maybe not. But that was not going to stop me from trying to unscramble the egg of Ray.

JUST RAYMOND

In his 1943 paper "Autistic Disturbances of Affective Contact," Leo Kanner, an Austrian psychiatrist on the faculty of the Johns Hopkins School of Medicine in Baltimore, noted two common themes in the parents of eleven strange young patients:

The first he saw fit to put in italics: "They all come of highly intelligent families."

I like that one. I think Dad would have liked it too.

The second: "In the whole group, there are very few really warm-hearted fathers and mothers."[16]

Uh-oh. The stage was now set for some serious parent-bashing that would continue on and off for decades. (Not until 1969 would Kanner "exonerate" parents of responsibility for their children's conditions.)

Another Austrian, pediatrician Hans Asperger, after whom the "high functioning" subset of the spectrum is named, had observed that the behaviours and characteristics of his young autistic patients were often evident to some degree in at least one parent.

Dad might have been inclined to argue that point, but there's a good case to be made for it.

In 1967, the year my brother turned eleven, Austrian child psychiatrist Bruno Bettelheim—those Austrians!—published a bestselling book called *The Empty Fortress: Infantile Autism and the Birth of the Self*. He pointed an accusing finger at parents: "The precipitating factor in infantile autism is the parent's wish that his child should not exist ... To this the child responds with massive withdrawal."[17]

Well, that just wasn't the case in my family. My parents were proud and happy to welcome their first-born son in July 1956, and they were pleased as punch with me, too, even though I arrived hard on his heels in November 1957. There's a studio picture of Ray and me when we were toddlers, and I must say, we were pretty cute. Mum tells me that she purchased new shoes for both of us to wear for the portrait and promptly took them back afterwards. She was already pregnant again when that photo was taken. I can only suppose that her enthusiasm—along with her disposable income—dwindled further as Anita, Lisa, Ian and Trish arrived in quick succession because there are no studio pictures of them. I'll go so far as to say that Mum and Dad almost certainly found themselves with more children than they wished ... but none of *them* are autistic.

☙

Our mum and dad were not the only ones wantonly contributing to the overpopulation of the planet in the '50s and '60s. A whole lot of children born into this world have been unplanned ... even unwanted. Most parents try to make the best of it, as ours did. Bettelheim did not spare "absent or weak fathers," but he aimed his most damning criticisms at "refrigerator mothers," cold-blooded reptilian creatures who spawned live young, then crawled back into the icebox again. Their babies responded to this icy detachment by withdrawing from the human race.

Fortunately for my mother, she was too busy cranking out babies to be doing much reading on the subject of child psychology. With five other children right behind Ray, she might not have noticed if he wasn't inclined to sit on her lap and cuddle. She is now in her eighties. I recently asked her if Ray was ever a normal little boy and if there was a point at which he "became" autistic.

"No," she said. "He was always just Raymond."

I asked her to cast her mind back to 1956 and tell me about her first pregnancy. She was, she reports, "young, strong and healthy" (although she smoked her way unrepentantly through that and all five subsequent pregnancies). No, everything was perfectly fine; she was sure of it.

"Dr. McDaniel did have me X-rayed while I was pregnant," she recalled. "I can't remember now which month, but at that time X-rays were not considered dangerous. I don't think I was ever sick and did not need medicine of any sort. They did try to push vitamins on me, but I refused."

The birth was uncomplicated, but a few months later, Mum tells me, little Raymond developed a high fever after a routine immunization—although at this late date she can't remember which one it was or exactly how old he was. He was just a baby, though, "a carrying baby," as Mum described him, maybe two or three months old. The memory of this event causes her to shudder even now, more than half a century later.

"He was very, very sick for several days. Dr. McDaniel said it must have been a real live batch of vaccine. He came to the house and stayed for several hours monitoring him. Gram came too. She walked him during the day, and I did night duty. It was pretty scary for a young mother. I thought he was going to die. Oh, God, he was such a hot, red, fevered little boy."

Few expectant mothers smoke anymore, most take their prenatal vitamins, and pregnant women are no longer routinely X-rayed—yet more kids are being diagnosed with autism than ever before. Any link between vaccines and autism has been repudiated. I do wonder about that high fever somehow altering Ray's brain circuitry, but we'll never know. There are plenty of other smoking guns.

It may not be fair that women have historically gotten the blame for things that go wrong with their offspring, but in the case of autism we just might be able to point the finger at the mother after all. Her immune system will respond to viral or bacterial invaders with a rise in inflammatory proteins, and the greater this rise, the greater the risk of central nervous system damage in her fetus.[18] Another theory has it that autism is an extreme version of the male brain,[19] perhaps triggered by high prenatal levels of testosterone in the mother.

And there's another way to implicate mothers. Babies are inoculated with bacterial flora during birth and while nursing. Even *one* course of antibiotics during pregnancy—something Mum might not have thought to mention—could have changed everything. It might be that what actually links the generations is not an "autism gene" at all but an inherited or shared set of gastrointestinal microorganisms.

Ray and I often discuss the latest "causes" of autism, and for a while we were swapping links to a spate of new studies suggesting a relationship between autism and gut bacteria. "Hey, wouldn't it be a hoot," I wrote to him recently, "if the whole thing came down to a lousy bunch of bugs?"

"Right," came his answer. "And the joke, as they say, is on me."

I've heard that older fathers are more likely to have autistic children. Dad was a grizzled thirty-three when Ray came along, but he went on to have five more children, none of whom are autistic. However, I often find myself wondering if some sort of weirdness gene has been making its way down through our paternal family line to splice itself into my brother's DNA, because there have been some very odd ducks on our father's side of the family.

None of us kids ever met Dad's father. Reginald Andrews was a British citizen who met and married a French woman in Baku, South Russia (now Azerbaijan), where she was employed as a governess to the children of a wealthy family, and he was working for a British oil interest. The couple did stints in Vladivostok, St. Petersburg, South Africa, Japan and Trinidad on oil company business, and in between they bounced back and forth between England and France. Each of their five children was born in a different country than the one before. Dad's youngest brother was born in Paris, by which time, Dad says, his father was more of a visitor than a parent. The kids all spoke French at home.

In 1935, when Dad was twelve, the family moved to Haifa, Palestine, where Reginald had taken a position with the Iraq Petroleum Company. It was his responsibility to calculate and direct the flow of crude oil through pipelines from Kirkuk, Iraq, into storage tanks on the coast, and from there onto giant oil tankers waiting in Haifa Bay. When one of those tankers was overfilled on his watch, he was summoned by the general manager to explain the resultant mess. He blamed a staff shortage. He alleged possible sabotage. He was promptly dismissed.

Disgraced, Reginald returned to England. Our grandmother, having just moved from Paris to Palestine with five kids, refused to budge. Neither she nor her children would ever hear from him again—and, of course, the opportunity for a yet-future me to know my grandfather and speculate as to whether he was on the spectrum took ship with him that day.

So Dad, not yet thirteen, quit school and went to work, pooling his earnings with those of his mother and older siblings. Though he was more comfortable speaking French, he did his best to pass himself off as British. At sixteen he was hired by a British company that was building a new oil refinery in Haifa. He rose through the ranks to the position of acting stores superintendent ("thirty thousand engineering items," he once told me proudly).

On May 13, 1948, when he was twenty-four, Dad moved to Canada with the money he had saved from his years at the refinery. The day after he left Haifa, Israel declared statehood. This was to be a pivotal event in his life.

Dad was driven to live down his lack of education. As a real estate developer, he never had a steady paycheque, but he was ambitious and worked with feverish intensity. Most of our countless moves were to display homes he built—grandiose things for their time, often with white carpets and swimming pools. Highly impractical for a horde of little ruffians to be let loose in, to say the least. These houses were invariably sold out from under us before we could trash them. Anyway, it didn't matter to us kids which house we lived in. As long as Dad's next project was in West Van, our familiar woods and beaches were never far away.

Our friends all had fathers who went to work in the morning and came home at the same time each evening, but it was never that way for us. Ray remembers standing at the window in his pyjamas when he was a little boy, counting headlights coming up the darkened street, watching and waiting for that one car to turn up our driveway. But most nights he had to give up, as Dad wasn't home until long after we were in bed.

"All my life I have had to live by my wits," Dad often told us. He was canny but strangely naïve, too. More than once he was wiped out financially, so he was left with a permanent fear of being "taken to the cleaners" and a tendency to write out contracts in reams of legalese—a habit he says he picked up during his many court battles. "I'm writing for the judge," he would say when anyone found his prose boggling. He was still "writing for the judge" to the day of his death, though it had been fifty years since he'd seen the inside of a courtroom.

I wouldn't say Dad was autistic, but he had an astounding ability to hyper-focus. He tended to tune out mundane details such as how many children he had and their names, but if he could swing the conversation to his special interest—the conflict between the Jews and the Arabs—his monologues were legendary. He was happy to share with anyone how the Balfour Declaration of 1917, which laid the foundation for the creation of the State of Israel, caused almost all the troubles in the world today. His grandchildren would dare each other to say the words "Balfour Declaration" within his earshot and time how long it took the victim to escape. As Ray said in an email when Dad was well along in years:

> Anyone foolish/brave enough to broach the subject with him should be forewarned that he will be in for a lecture that would make the Book of Job look terse and to-the-point.

When Dad answered a question, he had to start from the beginning—and no matter what the question was, the beginning was the Balfour Declaration. There was no "cutting to the chase," no *Reader's Digest* version. People tell me I have inherited this trait: I have to tell the *whole* story, even when they are beseeching me to get to the punchline. And writing is in my DNA. My great-grandfather was a newspaper editor; my French grandmother wrote her memoirs in longhand; Dad was working on his manuscript until he died—three guesses what the subject was!—and now I am writing a book. There has to be something genetic going on—but Mum gets a pass on this one; the blowhards are all on Dad's side.

Dad could deliver a world-class soliloquy, but when he had something really important to say, he much preferred the written word. He could write a "brief" so long, formal and pedantic that readers would soon find themselves sinking in a quicksand of commas, run-on sentences and subordinate clauses. It is fate's little joke that Ray—the one wearing the label—writes crisply and concisely and was as aggravated as everyone else by Dad's ponderous prose.

Mum rues the day I taught Dad how to use email. Though already in his eighties, he took to it with a passion. I braced myself whenever I saw his name in my inbox. Every sentence was brimming with *whereases* and *heretofores*, often with a little Latin thrown in for good measure. But despite his prodigious email output, Dad never did trust the

Internet, so after he'd sent his emails, he printed them out and drove around delivering them. An eighteen-page "memorandum" about a proposed joint real estate venture caused my brother Ian to consider moving to another country under an assumed identity.

Despite Dad's own strong proto-Aspergian tendencies, no one was more perplexed by Ray than he was. He was never asked to describe his son's difficulties in a "brief," but had he written one, it would doubtless have been a substantial document. Back in 1938, a man named Beamon Triplett wrote just such a letter to Leo Kanner about his five-year-old son, Donald, who was mesmerized by spinning objects, musical notes and number patterns and had a knack for memorization, counting and measuring, but did not respond emotionally to his parents at all. In fact, he acted as if they weren't there. Donald was about to become Kanner's Case One, the first person ever diagnosed with autism.

Much has been written about "autism's first child," but it is autism's first father, Beamon Triplett, who fascinates me. In advance of Donald's first appointment, he sent a thirty-three-page letter—single-spaced—describing his son's symptoms. After reading it, Kanner noted with a touch of understatement, "This much is certain, that there is a great deal of obsessiveness in the family background."

Our dad could have given Beamon Triplett a run for his money— and the similarities don't end with verbosity. Mr. Triplett was an attorney. Kanner described him as "meticulous and hard-working" and noted that "when he walks down the street, he is so absorbed in thinking that he sees nothing and nobody and cannot remember anything about the walk."[20] I laughed out loud reading this. Dad loved to tell people that he couldn't "walk and chew gum at the same time."

I don't know if Mr. Triplett had a car, but Dad did, and the harder he thought, the slower he drove.

I was once in the passenger seat while he expounded on the evils unleashed on the world by the Balfour Declaration, oblivious to the maddening *click-click* of his left-turn indicator. I squirmed politely for miles. Eventually I cut in. "Uh, Dad, your blinker is on."

He drove slower.

"Dad? Your turn signal?"

He became dimly aware that he was being hailed and performed an action designed to eliminate the distraction, the way one might wave absent-mindedly at a fruit fly buzzing around one's wineglass. He reached for his wipers and turned them on. Now we were driving at fifteen miles per hour down the street with the turn signal blinking and the wipers grinding dusty parabolas into the windshield. I slid lower in my seat, avoiding the eyes of pedestrians speeding by on the sidewalks. Stop signs, yield signs, flashing arrows and red lights were mere peripheral disturbances that my father blithely disregarded, as were the waved fists, upturned middle fingers and honking horns of other drivers who formed an irate conga line behind him when they couldn't pass.

Dad was never in a major accident, but I bet he caused a few.

SACKED

Ray was fired from Canada Post on July 22, 2008, his fifty-second birthday. This was ostensibly for a series of "minor infractions"—that's what he called them—like leaving mail in his truck overnight. The official charge was "Delay of Mail," which, according to Canada Post Corporation, is not a minor matter at all but a serious dereliction of duty with clearly stipulated penalties. Ray believes the charge was just a pretext for getting rid of him. He had developed a painful inflammatory condition in both feet, and after more than thirty-three years of making his appointed rounds as a postman in sun, rain, snow and gloom of early dawn, he had started missing work because it simply hurt too much to walk. Later he told me, "A lame letter carrier isn't good for much."

But it wasn't just his crippled feet. Ray believes his employer had a second ulterior motive for sacking him:

> I had a year's worth of accumulated sick time, and by firing me, the PO managed to in effect steal it. They would have had every reason to expect me to book off for an entire year, but I preferred to do my duty. However, the agony by the end of the day was such that I couldn't think straight, thus the mistake. As to being sorry, of course I was sorry. Does the question need to be asked? I wouldn't even have been caught if I hadn't reported it myself.

The truth was, he told me, that they had been looking for a way to get rid of him for years. The fact that my brother was trouble is probably the only thing the union and management ever agreed upon, and when they finally saw their chance to fire him, they took it.

Ray grieved his termination, but the arbitration that followed was a "hatchet job." The arbitrator's decision was received on June 3, 2009, but my brother's fate, he maintains to this day, had been decided before the trial even began. He swears he was never given a chance to speak in his own defence

 But Ray *did* speak. He requested a copy of the transcript, which I read with a sinking heart. According to that thirty-four-page document, he spoke plenty. During cross-examination, he was asked whether he was aware of the corporation's policy with respect to delay of mail. Instead of offering an apology or an explanation, Ray "entered into a rather lengthy debating contest with the counsel for Canada Post." It then goes on to read: "The Grievor, Ray Andrews, never indicated any regret or stated that this type of event would not happen again. His testimony was not marked by modesty and candour."

It was clear from the transcript that Ray had been given every opportunity to explain himself. Had he said, "Yes, I'm sorry I left mail in my truck, but my feet were so sore I didn't know what else to do," all would have been forgiven. But at no time did he mention his feet. Instead, he immolated himself in front of them all by suggesting, bizarrely, that a saboteur must have planted the mail in his truck. His allegations of "monkey business" were quickly shot down, and he was asked by the arbitrator—his judge and jury—what he had learned from this matter. All he had to say was, "It won't happen again," and he'd have had his job back. But according to the transcript, his response was: "I would be more like the other carriers and keep my back covered."

The transcript continues, "Mr. Andrews appeared to be offended that he had to defend himself because everyone should have been aware that he had always performed his job in the past and would do so in the future."

As I look back on this incident, I can almost hear Speaking Man lashing out in all directions as a frightened, cornered Ray tried to figure out what they wanted from him. But whether he missed their leading questions or his pride got in the way, in the end he refused to apologize, turning a salvageable situation into a career-ending catastrophe, just as our grandfather had done some seventy-three years earlier. Ray was found to be not sorry enough for his sins and dismissed. His letter of termination states: "Mr. Andrews, you have delayed the mail and failed to be responsible for your actions. This is considered a major misconduct for which the appropriate penalty is the termination of your employment from the Corporation."

Ray sees now that his actions were tantamount to self-sabotage. But in unrelenting pain from his feet, he had seen no other way out.

> I've since realized that I was committing "suicide," but I could no longer do my job.

None of this will ever make sense to me. Why on earth did he not just tell the truth? Even with his years of experience as a union rep advocating for other workers, and with a perfectly plausible, work-related explanation for his own predicament, he was unable to save himself. So at the age of fifty-two, after an entire working life delivering mail and only three years short of retirement, he found himself unemployed. Alone. Barely able to walk and staggering under the weight of a crushing depression. I didn't know about his state of mind at the time, as his demeanour remained the same as it had always been. As far as I could see, he had taken the whole thing in stride.

But it had come as a shock to his family. Everyone knows it's all but impossible to get fired from the post office. The institution has famously been mocked as a hotbed of kooks and conspiracy theorists— even *aliens*, for crying out loud!—and yet Ray, a loyal and long-standing employee whose quirks looked tame by comparison, had lost the job he had held since he was nineteen.

Thirty years earlier he had argued his way into that Seattle jail cell. Now he had argued himself out of a job. In both instances, he doesn't remember being allowed to say a word in his own defence. Yet an eyewitness in the first and a formal transcript in the second say otherwise. I now know that in each of these highly stressful situations Speaking Man was trying his best to save the day. But Thinking Man was, as usual, nowhere to be found in Ray's hour of need.

"Well," I told him in a desperate stab at cheeriness, "at least it took you thirty-three years to get fired!"

☺

After losing his appeal, Ray went into his room, closed the door and sat down in front of his computer. With no job to go to and Aunt Nell catering to his basic needs, he didn't have to venture out of the house at all. He knew he couldn't spend the rest of his life cloistered in his bedroom, but at least there, Speaking Man could do no mischief.

Although he has reproved me more than once for being too eager to ascribe everything he does to his "condition," I think it's safe to say that his affinity for computers has little to do with a fascination for technology. His computer acts as a security gate. It holds back even the most dangerous crush of Goongbalong players and funnels them toward him in an orderly queue, frisked of their weapons. Words—formatted, spell-checked and dressed in the sender's preferred font—assemble themselves in orderly rows like well-behaved little soldiers and march forth only on his command. Squadrons of incoming sentences—even those bearing disturbing news—marshal themselves in his inbox until he is ready to analyze them. They don't care what shoes he's wearing when he reads them.

Ray turned to his cyber-friends. "I have contacts around the world that I consider to be true friends," he assured me, "and our conversations, though typed, not spoken, are no less meaningful. It may not be a replacement for face-to-face socializing, but it does have its merits."

Indeed, it does. But no matter how many "virtual" friends and acquaintances Ray may have had, he was alone in that room. His days and nights began to blur.

For Ray and me, email has always been a portal through which our unadulterated thoughts can be delivered to each other without interference. And it was through this portal that he would eventually send a distress signal out to me.

THE CONFERENCE

In September 2008, two months after Ray was fired, I signed up for a day-long conference in Vancouver called "A Clinical Approach to Helping Adults with Asperger's Disorder." This series of seminars was clearly aimed at health care professionals, as I found out when I had to state my credentials in order to complete the online registration process. I gave myself a bachelor's degree in social work. My registration fee was accepted, and my badge (*Claire Finlayson, BSW*) was waiting for me at the front desk. I wore a pantsuit, carried a clipboard and tried to look officious in an effort to reduce my chances of being identified as a fraud and booted out the door.

There in the lobby was a display of books, all about Asperger's and the autism spectrum. I marvelled at the wealth of practical information before my eyes: advice for coping with school, job interviews, relationships. Advice for parents and teachers of Aspie kids, resources available in the community, support groups—so much help that Ray could have used, had we only known. I picked up a book called *The Complete Guide to Asperger's Syndrome*, written by Tony Attwood, one of the world's leading experts on the subject. It had been in print little more than a year. In the preface I read of the author's hope that the book "will enable someone with Asperger's syndrome to understand why he or she is different to other people, and not to feel dejected or rejected. It is also important for others to remember that there is always a logical explanation for the apparently eccentric behaviour of people with Asperger's syndrome."[21]

This was too good to be true. Here in these pages was "a logical explanation" for things that had defied understanding for fifty years! I purchased the book, sure that help would soon be on the way for my "dejected and rejected" brother. I walked into the first lecture with my nose in that book and didn't look up until the keynote speaker, Dr. Paul Dagg, a clinical professor of psychiatry, began his presentation.

In a day that turned out to be filled with unfamiliar jargon—everybody was quoting from something called the DSM-4, which I had never heard of—Dr. Dagg's lecture was in mercifully plain English. "They take a beating out there," he said of his Asperger's patients. "A lot of them are down in their parents' basements—and they ain't comin' out." He painted a grim picture of the social rejection often faced by people with Asperger's. People just like my brother. As he spoke with intelligence and compassion about the special problems of undiagnosed adults, I knew I was in the right place, but my elation was tempered with sadness—grief, almost—that for Ray, now a middle-aged man, there had been no choice but to square his shoulders and go for it with only a pointy-eared TV show alien for cover. No choice but to try his hand at love as a young man only to find out that his wife longed for something that was not in his power to give. He had walked around with a mail bag slung over his shoulder until his feet gave out, never channelled toward mathematics or astronomy or engineering because no one knew of his vast potential or how to tap it.

As Dr. Dagg's lecture was coming to an end, I gathered my purse, books and papers, ready to rush the podium and throw myself at his feet, hoping he would consent to see Ray and finally give him an official diagnosis. The instant the intermission was called, I made a beeline for the front of the auditorium, jockeying my way through crowds of milling doctors, psychiatrists and social workers. It became apparent that I was not the only layperson in the room, as other people were also bearing down on Dr. Dagg. I saw in their eyes the same hunted expression they no doubt saw in mine.

One woman who looked about my age got to him before I did and began pouring out the story of her brother-in-law, who was indeed hunkered down in her basement staring at a computer all day. He had been fired from a series of jobs well beneath his capabilities, he didn't have medical insurance, and he *really* needed a shower and a change of clothes. She and her husband were beside themselves trying to figure out what to do with him. Could he perhaps have Asperger's? Where could she turn for help? Dr. Dagg nodded sympathetically as she told her tale.

Then it was my turn. I presented my case and left the conference, clutching his business card. I didn't know it yet, but there was never any hope that he would be able to see my brother. With a busy psychiatry practice in Kamloops, he already had more work than he could handle—and there were plenty of autistic people in his own city who required as much time and support as he could offer. Without professional intervention, he knew they would likely end up moldering in basements too.

After the conference I devoured everything I could get my hands on about Asperger's. In the foreword of Tony Attwood's *Complete Guide*, autistic people had written of their huge relief at finally having a logical explanation for their troubles. Naturally I thought Ray would feel the same way—but he didn't. He read the book—festooned with my sticky notes, highlighted passages and comments scribbled in the margins—and handed it back to me a week later with the briefest of comments. "Some things I relate to," he said evenly. "Other things are not like me at all." End of discussion.

Far from experiencing the epiphany of recognition and relief that I had anticipated, he continued to resist me at every turn. *Thanks but no thanks.*

The more I learned about autism, the more irrefutable the evidence became that Ray was somewhere on the spectrum. We still had no official confirmation of the diagnosis, but I couldn't afford to wait around. Since he'd lost his job, he had become a virtual recluse. If other people knew what I now knew, they might make an extra effort to reach out to him. I shared the Gospel According to Tony Attwood with anyone who would listen, but Ray was not the only one to resist. I visited family and friends, thumping my new Bible and explaining that, to my utter amazement, I'd discovered within its pages a set of traits that described Ray to a tee—a scientific explanation for things that had baffled us for years!

I ran into thick walls of apathy. No one asked to borrow the book. Instead they fixed me with skeptical looks that told me they believed I was making excuses for my boorish brother. "Hey, Claire," said one friend at a backyard barbeque, holding aloft a hamburger patty in tongs, "maybe we should invite Ray over for an *ass burger!*" This prompted gales of laughter.

Undaunted, I went to see the biggest skeptic of them all: Aunt Nell.

Ray calls her Sarge. He had always found the sound of her hollering down the hall, "RAYMOND, YOUR LUNCH IS ON THE TABLE!" to be positively grating on his nerves.

He was in his room with the door shut when I arrived with my books and notes from the seminar. Aunt Nell made me tea, lit a cigarette and sat back in her favourite chair while I breathlessly related what I had learned. Ray has a "condition," I explained—no, *really!*— that sheds light on some of the very difficulties she was experiencing coexisting with him. Disbelief was written across her face. Though she maintains a grudging fondness for Ray, she will go to her grave thinking he is a tyrant who insists on doing things his way. "Raymond does whatever he wants, and to hell with anyone else, dear!"

My four neurotypical siblings seemed only mildly interested in the fact that they had an autistic brother. As for Mum, her first-born son had always been "just Raymond." There was no changing him and nothing to be gained from reading a book. She went back to her knitting.

And Dad? From the time Ray entered adolescence, he had been challenging our father's authority, and Dad found it exhausting. He once expressed his exasperation to me in an email:

> Raymond contradicts just about everything I try to teach him. I have given up trying to communicate with him politely because I get replies such as "you wouldn't understand," meaning he thinks I am too dense. We would all like to help him, but that will not be possible unless he sets about earnestly seeking to help himself.

Although Dad believed that Ray's conduct was deliberately uncouth and could have been easily remediated with a little earnest effort, he worried about his own culpability too. "I think I let him debate with me too much when we were in the Caribbean. I shouldn't have indulged him the way I did. I thought it was good for his intellect, you see."

Poor Dad. If only Attwood's *Complete Guide* had been available when his young son was wearing him thin. It was right there on page 26: "There is a great danger of getting involved in endless arguments with these children, be it in order to prove that they are wrong or to bring them toward some insight. This is especially true for parents, who frequently find themselves trapped in endless discussion."[22]

Surely Dad, of all people, would be elated to hear that he had not been responsible for his son's contrariness. He had not created Ray by engaging in verbal sparring matches with him. But Dad—yes, the one in our family who was himself a little *different*—figured it was not necessary to read *The Complete Guide*. Now that we knew what was *wrong* with Ray, couldn't he finally be repaired?

Maybe this new information wasn't going to instantly change the family dynamics, but surely the fact that he had a genuine neurological disorder would help Ray out there in the larger world that had been so unkind to him. Foot problems had to be an occupational hazard for letter carriers. Maybe there was some sort of compensation for a crippled mailman or an inside sorting job he could do. And while autism would make for a predictably poor outcome in court (or at least it does for Ray), maybe we could prove that he had blown his chances for reinstatement because of it. Perhaps his long-time employer could be induced toward leniency. I asked my brother if I could intervene on his behalf.

"Why not?" he answered. "I'm in the mood for revenge. They insulted me."

Then an idea began to blossom in his mind:

> Hey, wouldn't it be fun if I got a formal diagnosis and threw that before the arbitrator? I'd be a *victim* instead of just a regular white hetero male. Delicious! Nasty Canada Post Corp picking on the retarded! I'd get a million! Nuts, too bad I'm not black as well.
>
> Go for it. I'll give you a cut.

I contacted the union's grievance officer to plead his case, hoping that his Asperger's—if we could prove he had it, even after the fact—might be seen as a mitigating factor. When I asked if there was any chance that he might be reinstated if we were able to get a retroactive diagnosis, I was told in essence: "Nice try, but you're thirty years too late to be working that angle."

So Ray applied for unemployment insurance. To be eligible for benefits, he was required to prove that he was actively looking for work. A job interview, as I had learned at the "Helping Adults with Asperger's" conference, is torture for a person with Asperger's—no matter how proficient he is at The Handshake. Dr. Dagg had suggested in his lecture that the only way to get through it is to put his cards face up on the table and say, "Now look, I have Asperger's syndrome. I will suck at these things (list deficiencies). Nevertheless, this is what I can do for you (list proficiencies)."

Ray, of course, had no such strategy, and not even an official diagnosis to brandish about. He is not afraid of work; indeed, he believes that a man is only as good as what he accomplishes and that to be idle is to almost lose the right to exist. He applied for several jobs, all the while dreading being called for an interview, knowing he was doomed to fail. And that's exactly what happened.

"I went for one interview," he told me, "and it went so badly that it was truly comical. There is nothing on this planet I would less rather do than go for a job interview."

My heart ached for him. "Oh, Ray, it hurts me that you even *went* for a job interview. The process will do inestimable damage to your sense of self. Hell, it probably already has."

As usual, when trying to predict what my brother will do, say or think, I got it wrong. Ray assured me there was no damage done:

> It just gives me the chuckles. Situations like that I find quite funny—damaging though they can of course be to my career prospects. It seems to me that the most profound difference between myself and most people is that the ego is either missing in me or works totally differently. A failed interview has no impact on my "sense of self" at all. Believe it.

I wasn't sure I did. But Ray was not ready to be put out to pasture. He was only fifty-two. He had a fine mind and strong aptitudes in math, engineering and mechanics. Surely there was gainful employment out there for him somewhere. But several more botched job interviews later, he wasn't chuckling. Even though he maintained a stoical exterior, his dismissal from Canada Post had been a near-fatal blow.

I Am What I Do

"He never comes out of there, dear!" said Aunt Nell, waving her cigarette in the direction of Ray's closed bedroom door. "He barely eats! He just sits in his room looking at that goddamned *thing* all day!"

That "thing," of course, was his computer. Ray was always working on some project or other, often using computer-assisted design (CAD) programs he had taught himself, and he tended to be obsessive, so I thought little of it when he declined to come out to the kitchen for coffee despite Aunt Nell's hollering down the hallway, "RAYMOND! YOUR SISTER IS HERE!"

Nevertheless, with Aunt Nell insisting that Ray was decomposing in his room, I decided to check on him before I left. It was an unprecedented step. Although he had lived at Aunt Nell's for over a decade, I had never felt comfortable entering his inner sanctum.

I knocked softly.

"Yeah," came the brusque response from within. Opening the door, I saw my brother at his desk, bathed in the blue glow of his three computer monitors. He didn't turn his head. His curtains were drawn against the brilliance of the late afternoon sunshine. In the dimness of the room I could see plywood shelves resting on utility brackets he had screwed into the walls. They were groaning with files, books and artifacts of our childhood, many of which I had not seen for decades. The room was like a time capsule. Ancient computers, stripped of their housings, whirred and blinked. The walls were covered with photographs. There were framed pictures I had given him of my kids when they were little. Pictures of our parents, our brothers and sisters. Faded colour photocopies of various school photos, stapled or tacked up. Crayon artwork. Every niece and nephew, every child who had ever befriended him—all were represented on those walls. There, to my surprise, was my eldest daughter, who had maintained only a cultivated politeness toward her uncle since his unseemly comment on her figure. And my heart skipped a beat when I saw a thirty-year-old enlargement of Ian and me on our wedding day in the middle of it all.

I turned my attention to Ray. His dress and grooming had never been high on his list of priorities, and the light wasn't great, so although he might have been looking a little haggard, it was nothing I hadn't seen before. He was busy rewriting code for a web browser called Arachne, he told me, with collaborators from all over the world. He could barely tear himself away. He made it sound exciting. There were no obvious outward signs of distress. I told myself he was fine and left feeling somewhat reassured. As I was soon to learn, that was a grave mistake.

The days and weeks wore on and Aunt Nell continued to sound the alarm. I became increasingly concerned about Ray's overweening devotion to his computer project. It wasn't healthy. I prodded him via email:

> Seeing you holed up in your room for thirteen hours at a time distresses me. Dr. Dagg said that in all too many cases, people with Asperger's burn out and end up rotting in basements, never to emerge again. With you not working, I fear that's exactly what's happening to you.

I was right. But things were far worse than I could have imagined:

> Quite correct. May as well come out of the closet: I'm suicidally depressed. Don't tell anyone, and please don't worry—I won't do anything. The computer distracts me, that's all. It occupies my mind.

I believed him when he assured me that he did not intend to "do anything"—Ray is not a liar—but he was obviously in a bad way. How is it that no one, including me, had picked up on the extent of his depression? I began to wonder if the web browser he was feverishly working on was his way of ensuring that he made some contribution to the world before he died.

My next email addressed the gravity of his situation:

> You are a middle-aged man and you've been doing the same job since you were a kid. Now you've been fired. This would be catastrophic for anybody.

I consulted *The Complete Guide to Asperger's Syndrome*, which contains a section about the psychological impact of unemployment. There is a risk of clinical depression for both "typical" people and Aspergians who lose their jobs—but for an autistic person, I learned, such an event can be life-threatening. Attwood says:

> Unemployment means there is a lack of purpose and structure to the day, a lack of self-worth and, especially for people with Asperger's syndrome, a lack of self-identity, along with a real reason to keep going. When I ask adults with Asperger's syndrome to describe themselves, the descriptions are usually what they do, their job, rather than their family or social network.[23]

I didn't wait for a response from Ray. With the *Complete Guide* open on the desk beside me, I wrote to him again:

> I suspected the depression, although you are very good at hiding it and I didn't appreciate the magnitude of it. People with Asperger's often suffer with co-morbid conditions such as social phobia, intense anxiety and depression, but apparently Aspies are supposed to be poor at assessing their own emotional state. You seem well aware of your condition, so either you're more self-aware than the average Aspie, or the depression has gotten so massive that even you cannot help but recognize it. Yikes, Ray.

Only now can I see that my quoting passages from a book on Asperger's and using jargon like "co-morbid conditions" was rubbing salt in his wounds. And as so often happens, the greater my sympathy, the firmer the rebuff. My expression of concern seemed only to irritate him:

> I rather think that I am far better than most people at assessing the facts of any situation, my own condition not excepted. In fact I quite pride myself on the clarity of my thoughts, and if that's a disease, then I hope to God no cure is ever found.

Well, he was feisty, anyway. Maybe that was a good sign. I continued to probe, and he continued to answer my questions despite his anguish.

> I have no idea where I will live or what I will do. I'm wasting away. I'm lonely. I have no future. And to think there was a time when I was sure I was destined to have an interesting life ...

Ray would never have spoken these words out loud. Still, what he had written was so unnervingly at odds with his business-as-usual demeanour whenever he did come out of his room that it frightened me. What would become of him if he couldn't pull out of this tailspin?

I urged him to forge a new future:

> You have intelligence and a good work ethic on your side. You have a lot to contribute. You can't simply give up and surrender yourself to your obsession with the computer.

Ray's answer was chilling:

> It's happening. Don't quite know what to do. I'm losing my resolve, even my self-control. Not too much time. I don't care about anything here anymore. Goin' down.

This was my big brother, the one who had always had an answer for everything my whole life. Given the hopelessness evident in his words, I couldn't honour his request to keep his condition a secret. Left to his own devices, I believe he might simply have died of neglect. Aunt Nell would have kept bellowing down the hall three times a day: "Ray, coffee's on!" "Ray! Your lunch is ready!" and "*Raymond!* Your dinner is getting cold, for God's sake!" She would have kept on cooking, serving and clearing away his uneaten meals and pacing up and down the hall outside that closed door, not daring to knock.

The news spread fast in the family, but no one knew what to do—including me. The last thing Ray wants is a hug or someone looking deep into his eyes and telling him things will be okay. The Golden Rule doesn't seem to work with him—he sure as heck doesn't want me doing unto him as I would have him do unto me. And he was not going to stagger out of his bedroom and ask for help—ever. But I did unto him anyway by seeking professional help for his depression.

First, I wrote to his family doctor, asking for an immediate referral to any psychiatrist in the Greater Vancouver area that specialized in Asperger's. The letter was returned unopened; she had closed her practice years ago. My earlier petition to Dr. Dagg had been unsuccessful—and I knew the man was swamped—but I emailed his office again, anyway, imploring him for an appointment. This time I got an immediate personal response, but not the one I wanted. His practice was full, he told me with regret, and he had an impossibly long waiting list. He gave me the names of several psychiatrists in Vancouver, but those I called were too busy to see my brother anytime soon.

Dad figured he knew what the problem was: selfish pride. He'd seen it before.

> Raymond is far too young to retire and too clever to give up using his talents. I think he is like my father was. I was told that when my father was fired, he could have kept his job if he had apologized. Instead, he lost both his job and his family. Really, that was quite selfish. Pride was his problem, a factor that may also be afflicting Ray.

Ray found his own way to carry on. In 2010 he moved in with our parents in the coastal town of Gibsons and started a new work venture on nearby Keats Island, a partnership with one of his now-grown nephews in a fledgling company that specialized in marine dock construction, repair and maintenance, as well as barging between Keats and Gibsons. The idea was that the nephew would handle the customers and the jobs, and Ray, who had bankrolled the company, was to maintain the shop and equipment. Initially this new endeavour galvanized him, but within two years their working relationship had soured. Ray seemed to have gone rogue. The final straw might have come the day he swam up naked to assist on a job where our nephew and his crew were frantically finishing a new boat ramp for wealthy clients who were due to round the corner of Keats in their sailboat that very afternoon. Ray was asked to resign his directorship before he took the company down with him.

Yes, there are two sides to this story: Ray had put his time, money and whole heart into the company, and now that it was becoming successful, he was being pushed out. The loss of the job was personal this time, the wound near-lethal. It hurt far more deeply than his feud with the faceless Canada Post Corporation. The nephew had been one of Ray's favourite playmates. Now he was a traitor. Ray said he could never forgive him.

Not yet fifty-five, embattled, bitter and dreadfully sad, he retreated once again to his room, where the computer was there to lovingly hoover up what was left of him.

Ray had not been living with our parents for long before the three of them were driving each other crazy. Mum would serve dinner and make brave conversation. Ray and Dad gave one-syllable answers when asked direct questions, but for long stretches in between there would be only the sounds of chewing and cutlery clanking. As soon as he could politely leave the table, Dad would go settle himself in the living room to watch the six o'clock news, as had been his custom for most of his eighty-eight years—although as he got older the TV volume increased a little more each year.

Ian and I found ourselves being invited for dinner more often after Ray moved in, probably because we helped keep the awful silences at bay, but there was always tension in the air. "Only room for one alpha male in this house," Mum told me quietly one evening as Dad excused himself from the table. That night CNN was blaring the lead story about escalating tensions between the Israelis and the Palestinians in the occupied Gaza Strip—a subject that always held Dad's rapt attention. Ray strode into the living room, sat down, picked up his cello and started sawing away at it. Dad had long since given up arguing with Ray. He turned the TV volume still higher. Mum winced and covered her ears. Ray kept on playing as Dad, gritting his teeth, got up and stalked off to bed, seething. It was ten past six.

The situation was untenable. Ray was unkempt, morose, and threatening legal action against our nephew. As for me, I was still brimming with pent-up evangelistic fervour from the "Helping Adults with Asperger's Disorder" conference I had attended almost two years before. There had to be something I could do to rally everyone to his aid. As far as I was concerned, Tony Attwood's book was the key to my brother's survival. Why weren't they all grabbing it out of my hands, especially Mum and Dad? We were losing Ray—surely they could see that. Approaching everybody one by one had not worked. Appealing to them as a group might create some positive momentum. That is why I stopped in at my parents' place just past noon on a blustery fall Tuesday, and with the very best of intentions made a bad situation worse.

Lunch was already in progress. Ray was at the table, as were a couple of our sisters and their kids. Having cooked for a big family for so many years, Mum had kept right on cooking as her grandchildren came along. The high school many of them now attended was within easy walking distance, and Gran's food beat the alternatives hands-down. She was always stirring a pot of soup or chili and pulling fresh bread or scones out of the oven, so at lunchtime she could usually count on a crowd around her table, which is just the way she likes it.

I came in armed to the teeth with notes and pamphlets I had picked up at the conference and, of course, *The Complete Guide to Asperger's Syndrome*. Mum got up, set me a place across the table from Ray and served me a bowl of her leek and potato soup.

My strategy had been carefully thought out. I knew Ray hated being gossiped about behind his back. *The truth cannot hurt me*, he had said to me more than once. So I had already decided that everything I had to say that day would be said right in front of him. I thought he'd appreciate my forthrightness.

"I want to tell you guys about some of the things I've learned," I said to my assembled family, "things that are extremely relevant to Ray's situation." The chatter subsided as I held up *The Complete Guide.* "People with Asperger's say this has been a game-changer for them. Listen to this."

I opened the book to the first page and began reading out loud the glowing reviews penned by well-known and accomplished autistic people, all of them singing Attwood's praises.

My favourite was by Liane Holliday Willey, author of *Pretending to be Normal.* She calls Attwood "Saint Tony" and explains the "stupendous" impact his book had on her life:

> It explained the whys behind who I was, and in doing so, it gave me the building blocks that would enable me to become who I am today.

> Everything about me was in jeopardy of evaporating into thin air—my marriage, my self-esteem, my identity, my ability to form relationships and keep a job ... [Attwood] gave me the strength to come out to the world and admit I was only pretending to be normal. That strength saved my life.[24]

Was this not *exactly* what we needed?

It was too late for Ray to save his job or his marriage, but it wasn't too late to reclaim his self-esteem. His identity. Maybe even his life.

I plunged into the book, reading passages I had marked as particularly relevant to Ray's situation. I interspersed them with my own helpful commentary. "Ray can't change the way he's wired," I explained, "but if everyone knows his handicaps are real, we can make allowances—learn how to work around them rather than being eternally perplexed at his resistance to doing things our way." No one made eye contact with me. The kettle boiled and Mum got up to make her usual "three-bagger." I waited while she brought the teapot over and sat down again. Didn't want her to miss a word.

Now we were on Chapter Two: The Diagnosis. I could hardly wait for this part—it was the pièce de résistance. If there were unbelievers in the room, they were about to be converted. I listed off the diagnostic criteria for Asperger's as my soup got cold:

- Socially inappropriate behaviour—*check.*
- Marked impairment in the use of nonverbal behaviours such as eye-to-eye gaze—*check.*
- Lack of social or emotional reciprocity—*check.*
- Formal pedantic language. "Haven't we all wondered at Ray's insistence on calling people he meets 'sir' or 'ma'am'?" *Check!*
- Clumsy body movements. Peculiar, stiff gaze. Difficulty interpreting social cues—*check, check and check again.*

"So Ray's never going to pick up on subtle hints," I said with conviction as he sat quietly across the table from me, eating his lunch. "For instance, you can't look at your watch and expect him to divine that you're telling him it's time to go. We have to say exactly what we mean and not hope that our body language will fill in the parts we're not saying. That's not going to work." I looked around the table to make sure everyone was with me. Ray's face gave nothing away, but I was sure Thinking Man was cheering for me in there.

He wasn't.

In retrospect I can see why Ray didn't care for my "Asperger's for Dummies" presentation, but what he said came as a nasty surprise. "You can't speak Aspie, so don't even try. I find your attempts highly condescending."

I tried to squelch my shock. After all, could I—the one trying to explain to the less educated that people with Asperger's are not trying to hurt their feelings—have my own feelings hurt right in front of them all? It was a classic blunder, and one I was determined not to make. *We have to say exactly what we mean.*

Heat rose in my cheeks. I tried to control my voice. "You say you welcome prompt and honest feedback, Ray, so I'm going to give you some: I'm trying to help here. What you just said was unkind."

Zap!

No one at the table moved or spoke. Ray knew he was in trouble. His response came in the form of a question delivered to the wall somewhere over my left shoulder. "Nice ... scarf?"

I meant well that day. I really did. But a little knowledge is a dangerous thing. It was, I know now, the height of arrogance on my part to believe that after attending one conference and reading a few books on Asperger's, I could explain my brother to his own family.

The rest of lunch was a sombre affair. I went home to lick my wounds.

When I spoke to Ray again close to a week later, it was from the safety of my computer:

> Tell me if you meant what you said at lunch the other day. Do you really not want me to try to understand you?

My question was whiny and emotional. I didn't care. From now on, I would speak "Babs." Ray could take it or leave it.

Maybe he was relieved to see me in his inbox again, but his answer showed how far I was from understanding how he felt about being outed in front of his family:

> Lunch is worth discussing. It illustrates something that quite worries me about all this "coming out" stuff. See, I'm afraid that if it ever becomes official, so to speak, I'll stop "trying." Once I have the "A" tattooed on my forehead, everyone is going to be immunized against me hurting them, so I can stop worrying about it and let myself be myself. Scary, no?

Yes, it *was* scary. And he wasn't finished. He saw the rubber stamp hidden behind my back:

> I prefer to think of myself as an individual rather than as a nice specimen of the disability. You may not be aware of it, but you never stop trying to explain every last little thing about me as a symptom of the "disease," and I wish you'd stop—it is belittling,

condescending and inaccurate. It is a caricature of almost the same sort as a blonde girl must endure but worse because everyone knows that the latter is a joke.

Next came a warning:

> I hate to admit it, but this label could throw a switch that is better left unthrown. In my current state, the burden of "trying" is crushing, but I need to frame myself—and have others frame me—in such a way that I am given no excuse to drop that burden. To illustrate: A Regular White Guy gets drunk and crashes his car. The judge socks it to him, tells him how disgracefully he has behaved. The guy serves his time and smartens up. Rewind the universe. Now take the same guy in the same situation but put a "status" card in his wallet. The judge tells him he's a victim of white oppression so it's no wonder he drinks, tells him that it's not his fault and lets him off—and he goes straight back to the bar just like he is expected to do.

Trying to ignore the many ways his analogy was offensive and distracting—*Oh, Lord, has he used this on anyone else?*—I read on.

> See what I mean? I'd rather just be a jerk because a jerk can be asked to—can be expected to—do better. I can't allow myself to just get weirder and weirder. What you are trying to do with this Asperger stuff could have unintended and even disastrous consequences.

I was still smarting from his rebuke at Mum's, and this new admonition quite unnerved me. He was telling me he had been in an emotional turmoil at lunch—"crushing" was the word he had used—but there had been not an inkling of it, not a clue that he was even slightly uncomfortable as I merrily dissected him right there on the dining room table. Now he was warning me about "disastrous consequences."

"But Ray," I wrote, "I've been trying so hard, and yet you dismiss my attempts to communicate candidly with you as unhelpful and condescending." I sounded peevish and petulant, even to myself, but I wanted him to know how hurt I was.

His answer, in contrast, was logical:

> For you it's an emotional equation: Comment on failure = rejection or attempt to hurt. For me it is understood—it need not even be mentioned—that *all* efforts to help are appreciated and that failures in mastering a very difficult task are to be expected and have no emotional content at all. On my planet we are not only NOT insulted when people point out our flaws, we are complimented. Your efforts are not unappreciated, but they have been so far unsuccessful.

Looking back, I have to admit that in this case it was me who had fumbled the ball; I was so focused on the goal that I had trampled my own teammate. Saint Tony had shown me the way, and I had visions of a new world for beleaguered Aspies and their families everywhere, with Ray in the vanguard and me trotting proudly beside him. Instead, he'd kicked me in the teeth.

Had I blown it for good?

No. I have not lost the Writing Man as I had feared; he's got too much to say. Just as a barnacle extends its feathery appendages into the water when it's safe and abruptly withdraws them into its armour-plated carapace when it's not, Ray is willing to eloquently—almost joyfully—answer my questions when they are posed from a safe distance. But he is not going to let me pry him open and poke around at the gooey contents of his shell.

I was surprised at the conciliatory tone of his next email:

> I have been trying to understand your language my whole life. I am surrounded by it and am almost constantly trying to speak it, but I still fail quite often. Yet you are put out by the idea that you—who have only been trying to speak Aspie for a few years and

who have only me to practise with—should not have
mastered it yet.

So far, you've been trying to teach yourself by yourself
and, sorry, it hasn't gotten you very far. But if you
really do want to learn to speak my language, I'd be
more than happy to try to teach you.

Learn his language? *No thank you*, I thought bitterly. It's nothing
more than a licence to be rude. I spurned his offer of free tutoring.

Fine, he said. He wasn't sure I would have been up to it anyway:

My language is simpler than yours, as it lacks sub-
terfuge, innuendo, dominance and all that fun stuff.
But it won't be easy for you to actually converse in it
because you will have tremendous difficulty achiev-
ing the nakedness that is required—the directness,
simplicity, courage, clarity, trust and honesty.

I was in no mood to be shown the Path of Enlightenment According to Ray. I was an angry little neurotypical with bruised feelings, and
I let my fingers fly. I typed out and deleted several sizzling emails in
which I accused him of hiding behind lofty notions of moral supe-
riority while blowing poison darts at people who were trying to help
him. But I erased my tirades one after another, in the end settling on a
neutral statement of fact:

Most of us appreciate honesty and directness, Ray.

To my brother this was neither neutral nor a statement of fact. His
rebuttal came swiftly:

You most surely do *not* appreciate honesty. You
consider it rude. The more complex the evasive
dance, the more one shows concern for the other.
It's a sort of verbal ballet and the best performances
get the highest praise. On my planet, such evasion is
considered an insult.

But we're not *on* your bloody planet, I wanted to scream. Instead, I typed:

> So our language is indirect, sly, dishonest, convolut-
> ed, cowardly and unclear. Have I got it about right?

That seems to have summed up his position perfectly:

> Yes, sorry, but that's exactly how I feel.

Ray's next words made clear that he was anything but sorry:

> It seems to me that "normal" folks never say any-
> thing without some intent to stab or stroke. I speak
> without any intention to do either most of the time.
> I just say what strikes me as interesting. There's no
> emotion attached to it. For types like me, things are
> *just* what they seem. "We" don't spend any time
> trying to look into each other's minds. "We" simply
> listen to what is said.

"We"? Ray still regularly challenges the existence of any syndrome describing a group of people that includes himself, but he certainly seemed to acknowledge his membership in that email. He continued:

> I react emotionally to your language the way I react
> to maraschino cherries. Phoney, artificial mocker-
> ies—no! Blasphemies of real cherries! Full of hidden,
> dangerous chemicals. Poisonous monstrosities. Lies
> within lies.

He was obviously getting worked up. I tried to interject a little humour into the debate:

> Gee, Ray! Here I was trying to convince you that you
> could be happy eating a diet consisting solely of em-
> balmed fruit. Hmm, this *is* a tall order! How will I *ever*
> succeed?

To my dismay, he took me literally:

> You mean you've been thinking that I could come to
> LIKE it? Jesus! Never will that happen! Never!

That was that. It was time to throw in the towel. I typed out my resignation:

> Well, that pretty much puts an end to our correspon-
> dence then, doesn't it?

> —

> Why? You yourself agreed that our written conversa-
> tion has been a great success, no?

> —

> A success? We've gotten nowhere. I don't want to
> continue this just for your amusement. It seems
> there's no chance you can learn anything from it.

It's a pattern I have come to recognize: every time I am about to limp off the field, Ray throws a Hail Mary pass to keep me in the game. And that's exactly what he did here:

> I would rather say we should *both* learn something
> from it. Nevertheless, I *am* on your planet. I am
> obliged by simple decency to learn the lingo. Not to
> try would make me a brute and a moron in my own
> eyes, which would be even more distasteful.

I had been hammering away at him for so long that my acknowledgement of his "incurableness" must have been interpreted as a sort of surrender. But he was clearly not ready to be carried off the field:

> Hey, I'm not that crippled. With a bit of coaching, I
> could probably learn to play G well enough to at least
> survive. I get the *principle* and I'm certain I could
> do better. It's possible I'm blind to some social clues,

but maybe I can come to understand those things too in a normal, empathic way.

I was still reeling from his adroit switch of position.

But how will you accomplish that, Ray, when you can't see the yield signs, the warning signs, the stop signs? No one knows you're blind to social cues. A proper diagnosis would convince people to cut you some slack, damn it.

I threw in a challenge for good measure:

But this is all contingent on you not being too scared or too proud to present yourself to a shrink and be labelled with a "disability."

I braced myself for the anticipated backlash, but once again he surprised me:

Quite the contrary, I'm already trying to pass myself off as autistic to anyone who'll buy it, even if I don't. Labels can be useful in dealing with "normal" folks.

I felt as though I'd rammed my shoulder against a heavy door that I had never been able to budge, and this time it had unexpectedly flown open. Ray had been bucking like a bronco at even the *idea* of being labelled. Now he was trying to capitalize on it? This was a switch! I guess he could see the rationale: a diagnosis might come in handy in a pinch, and besides, he probably didn't have the energy to argue with me anymore. But on some level, he remained deeply conflicted. He still fought that label, still feared it, still worried that it would reduce him to some*thing* instead of some*one*. He made one last appeal to our common humanity:

Cripple that I am, we seem to communicate just fine, don't we? See, if you just let it happen, I'm easy to understand. I'm afraid that having to run everything I

say through the Ray-has-Asperger's interpretive filter
might do more harm than good. Understand?

I understood, but I did not agree. I was certain that a diagnosis
would open more doors than it would close, and given the state Ray
was in, he wasn't in a position to make much of a case to the contrary.
I phoned Dr. Dagg's office one last time. But his caseload was already
overwhelming, explained the harried receptionist. Some of his young
patients were suicidal. A middle-aged man who had gotten this far on
his own steam was never going to make it to the front of the line.

We were on our own. Still, Ray would not permit me to lower the
bar. There would be no pandering to his supposed disabilities. No ad-
aptations. No concessions. No excuses. Writing Man would prove to
me that he was not blind:

> Look, don't be too condescending here, Babs. I read
> a universe of unspoken communication:
>
> Beauty.
>
> Love.
>
> Em's smile.
>
> Kids having fun.
>
> Truth.
>
> Music.
>
> Poetry.
>
> Do you think these things don't communicate to me
> instantly and with power? They knock me over! But
> they are not the same as the machinations and lies
> and double-dealing of "polite society" where every-
> thing is a manoeuvre and a display and an act.

TRAILER TRASH

Ray had saved quite a bit of money working full-time and living modestly at Aunt Nell's for fifteen years, and his brief stint with our parents after that was rent-free. In April 2011, when he was fifty-four, he got a mortgage and bought his first home, a dowdy, down-market trailer in Poplars Mobile Home Park, less than five minutes from my house. "Can't miss it," he said to me with a hint of pride when I asked for directions. "Just look for the most depressing one in the place!"

His first order of business was to unscrew and remove all the kitchen cupboard doors so he could see everything at a glance. This elicited much hand-wringing on the part of myself and the other females who had shown up to help him get sorted out and pretty the place up a bit. But aesthetics were not on his agenda.

Over the years he had assembled a collection of mismatched wineglasses, cups, saucers, plates and glasses, which he put in the cupboards under the counter, where most people keep their pots. Once an object has accrued meaning, Ray will not throw it out. Unpacking one of his boxes, I was startled to see a pitted old pewter teapot stamped with the letters IPC—Iraq Petroleum Company. It must have been a gift to our grandfather from his employer during his days in Palestine in the 1930s, something he had left behind when he vanished out of his family's lives. I have no idea how or when Ray acquired it. It is not something he intends to use, unless a contingent of Iraqi petroleum executives comes to Gibsons for tea, but he put it in a prominent place on a shelf within easy reach just in case they do.

He insisted that his kitchen drawers be left empty. Cutlery was assigned to a Rubbermaid divider on the counter, along with all the other bits and pieces that "normal" people tuck away in drawers. He fashioned a pot rack out of a two-by-two and ran it the length of the counter above the sink. He swathed his ancient refrigerator in two-inch-thick Styrofoam to improve its efficiency and stacked canned food on top of it. He tacked up his poster—*Never question authority: they don't know either*—beside the kitchen door.

He hung his family pictures on the walls of his office. Then he carried in a dusty old fake potted fig tree that I recognized from one of our childhood homes.

"Ray," our sister Lisa said, making a face, "that's pretty dated. You don't need a plastic tree, do you?"

"Ma gave it to me," he said simply and set it by the living room window.

He placed his cello—the one with its elegantly scrolled head amputated and guitar string winders sticking ghoulishly out of its neck—on a stand beside his La-Z-Boy. Against an adjacent wall sits an out-of-tune piano. Ray doesn't play, but no one else wanted it, and it had been in the family for three generations, so he found room for it.

A few weeks after moving in, he saw an ad for an old wood-burning stove, going for cheap on Craigslist. He recruited a couple of our teenage nephews, and together they muscled it into his trailer—contrary to the clearly stipulated rules of the Poplars strata corporation.

"Don't you think you should ask first?" I queried as he was laying cinderblocks on the living room floor.

"If they catch me, they catch me," he said, and he cut a hole through the ceiling for the chimney.

After Ray had settled in a bit, we threw him a housewarming party. He was touched and opened every gift with solemn appreciation. None of those presents will ever be thrown out or given away. No matter how worn or ratty they become, they will be added to a growing collection of things that will be with him for the rest of his life, along with that old pewter teapot and the plastic fig tree. His past is all around him, on display in those open-faced cupboards and on his walls.

My housewarming gift was a shower curtain and some matching towels, but as a bit of fun, I had also had a navy-blue T-shirt printed with the words TRAILER TRASH in white block letters across the front. I knew Ray would see the humour in it—and he did. Everybody loved it. He gamely put the shirt on and posed for a picture to great mirth and applause.

It was not until I was home in bed that night that it struck me: my gentle joke had potentially placed him in real jeopardy. I could see him joining the strata council and wearing that thing to his first meeting, thereby insulting every single one of his new neighbours without even opening his mouth. And it would have been me who set him up.

With the weather improving, Ray began the annual tune-up of his old BMW motorcycle. When I stopped in on a fine May morning, he was on his knees in his carport tinkering with the bike, an array of tools spread out around him. "Just getting Reinhold ready for summer," he said briskly, without looking up.

It feels wrong, almost rude, to refer to Reinhold as an *it*. "How long have you had him now?" I asked.

"Bought him in October '82, so he's just turned thirty-eight." Ray rebuilds him about every five years. "It's almost that time again," he said, patting Reinhold's metallic green cowling.

"Sometimes," I said, "you get this *look* when you talk about him. It's almost bordering on, well, outright affection."

"*Bordering?*" Ray looked up at me, shocked. "He's my best friend. I can trust him. I have a deep respect for anything made with precision, care and craftsmanship. You get to know the machine intimately and it becomes a trusted companion, almost a person. Better than a person— in some ways, anyhow."

Our younger brother, Ian, is an auto mechanic, and now that Ray doesn't have a job, he sometimes drops by Ian's shop to help out. "It's really no trouble," he says. "I like salvaging hopeless situations and solving problems." On one of these occasions he reorganized the contents of Ian's toolbox to make things more efficient, sending Ian into a quiet, cherry-red apoplexy. After thirty-five years as a mechanic, Ian liked his toolbox precisely the way it was, but he couldn't bring himself to yell at someone who meant so well.

Ray's own workshop is a model of efficiency, but when he's working in Ian's shop, he tends to create a disaster zone around himself while his attention is fixed solely on the job at hand. Ian can't stand disarray, but he knows Ray will ultimately step out of the chaos with one immaculate and perfectly working engine part. And there are times, he admits, when Ray is a miracle worker. Those thorny electrical malfunctions, the ones Ian hates most, are the ones Ray likes best. He's used to being misunderstood, and I bet he knows just how those parts feel.

He also doesn't like to see perfectly good machinery go to waste—and that happens a lot with computers these days. So when people upgrade to new systems, Ray rescues their old ones. He has amassed an extraordinary collection of cast-off parts and artifacts spanning the computer age.

Recently I called him in a panic. The hard drive of my computer was failing. This little circuit board contained the twenty years of email archives upon which I was basing a book about him. If I lost it, we were sunk. Could he help?

"Well, I can't very well refuse, can I?" he said. It was not a question. He knows the importance of that correspondence to both of us.

I'm at his door in a flash. I hand him the failing hard drive and follow him into his dark, musty-smelling office. He sits down at his desk and cracks his knuckles. "Pull up a chair," he says, without noticing that the only chair available to me is heaped high with books, papers and files, and his dirty work coveralls are flung over the lot. I move the stuff onto the floor in batches and pull the chair up close beside him. Ray has already decanted ice cubes into Ziploc bags in anticipation of my ailing hard drive's arrival. "Heat is the enemy," he explains, as he wraps the hard drive in a towel, places it between the bags of ice and hooks it up to life support. "If we can keep it cool, we should be okay. If this doesn't work, there's one more thing I can try, but it's drastic and there will be no turning back. Failure *is* an option. You have to accept that."

While Ray works on my computer's brain transplant, I have time to take a good look around. His office is dingy and cluttered, but I begin to discern a certain kind of order—and I suspect he wouldn't take kindly to some do-gooder trying to tidy it up for him. Shelves groan with books and memorabilia. File folders, like the contents of his kitchen, are out where he can see them. They cover the top of his file cabinet and most every other available horizontal surface as well. Clustered on the fake wood panelled walls are his pictures. I can see he's hung them roughly the same way they were organized in his room at Aunt Nell's. There I am again with Ian on our wedding day, somewhere in the middle. Spreading out from the epicentre like the rings on a tree and spilling over onto an adjacent wall are pictures of suntanned kids at Ruby Lake. Kids with elementary school sports day ribbons pinned to their shirts. Our sisters. Mum and Dad. There is Yvette, the wife of his youth, who left him more than thirty years ago. Perhaps more surprising still, I see not one but two pictures of the nephew who asked him to resign from the business they had started together on Keats Island and who went on to make a solo success of it. The nephew Ray said he would never forgive.

The big L-shaped desk hums and blinks with resurrected computer relics. Ray sits with a semicircle of antique monitors all facing him. Three old computer towers are stacked precariously to his left, one on top of the other, the side panels of their housings removed. "We geeks like them this way," he says when he sees me looking. "Easier to see what's going on." Their exposed fans fill the room with a soft whirring.

Ray uses a DOS word-processing program that was written at the dawn of the computer era. He sees no reason to "upgrade" to a system that hides its glitches behind cutesy little icons. He has memorized all the codes for various DOS functions; they are second nature to him. He's sure I'd like DOS too, if I'd only give it a chance, though he's all but given up trying to convince me.

My email files start to flow through the intravenous line connecting my faltering motherboard to one of his computers. Strings of numbers and letters begin scrolling onto the centre screen. Never mind that my file names are gone, as Ray's computer has replaced them with indecipherable file tags—they're alive! He watches closely as the download proceeds, berating me for my haphazard file structure. "This is a total mess, Babs," he chides. "Windows hides all this stuff from you, but I can see the entire file tree at a glance. Look at this—you've got stuff everywhere. With Linux we never have this sort of chaos."

I remember when he set up our aged parents with their very first computer from his stock of obsolete parts and taught them how to do things his way. Dad worked on his book for hours every day, and we got used to seeing the old man squinting at the blocky white letters on his small blue screen, a long list of handwritten keystroke commands taped to his desk for reference. Since there is no one—save perhaps a few souls on the outer fringes of geekdom—who knows how to operate a system like this anymore, only Ray could help Dad when he ran into trouble. If Dad called when Ray was in the middle of something, like sprucing Reinhold up for the summer, he would just have to wait. Given Dad's own workaholic tendencies, the forced downtime drove him around the bend. Ray would eventually show up and fix whatever it was, of course, but this sometimes involved taking the computer apart and leaving components strewn about the living room or covering the kitchen table for days on end.

Ray sometimes made Dad feel stupid, though I'm sure he didn't mean to. One day, exasperated when Ray still hadn't shown up after repeated appeals for help, Dad finally called a computer tech. The man stood in the doorway of Dad's office, blinking in amazement, a look on his face such as one might have seen on the face of the first archaeologist to enter Tutankhamen's tomb. But the tech couldn't fix the thing. Dad drove to London Drugs and came home with a four-hundred-dollar computer that ran Windows. Ray tried to shrug it off, but he was hurt. No denying it. He felt that our parents had sold out.

Ray saved my email files, by the way. He and Reinhold came over and delivered my entire archive on a CD. No thanks required.

THE NEPHEW PROJECT

Ray committed a level-ten Goongbalong foul in February 2012 when he went to visit our then fifteen-year-old nephew Reid in the hospital. Reid's family had broken down—exploded is perhaps the more accurate term—and now, dangerously depressed, he had been taken by ambulance to CAPE: the Child and Adolescent Psychiatric Emergency ward of the BC Children's Hospital in Vancouver.

There's not a lot to do behind the locked doors where those kids at risk of harming themselves are kept. Reid was not allowed a pen or pencil in his spartan room, nor was his guitar permitted. There was a deck of cards, but in a supreme example of psych ward irony, several were missing. There is so little stimulation in the CAPE unit that if you're not crazy when you go in, you very well might be by the time you get out.

Ray thought the boy might enjoy a game of chess to occupy some of the endless hours, so he took a ferry and two buses to the hospital with his board tucked under his arm. That first visit transpired without incident. The second visit a few days later went horribly sideways. On that occasion one of Reid's aunties and a few of his cousins from Gibsons had travelled by car to the hospital to see him. Ray had gone along, again bringing his chessboard. The rule at CAPE is no more than two visitors at a time, so he waited in the foyer as various relatives took their turns pressing the buzzer and being admitted into the secure part of the ward. When his turn came, he rose and gave the door a few good yanks as though it was stuck, ignoring the call button. This is not the way he remembers it, but at least six people watched him do it.

What follows is Ray's written account of what happened next. It is a rare, insider's eye view of life on the Goongbalong playing field.

He opens with a comparison of his first uneventful visit and his second:

The first time I visited the Cuckoo's Nest, it wasn't a disagreeable experience at all. I beeped to request admission through the "risk of flight" door, and a pleasant, smiling nurse pushed it open from the inside with a "Come on in!" air about her. I did so and had a nice visit and a game of chess with Reid. I won. I won't say the place felt like home, but neither did it feel like a maximum-security prison under lockdown.

Last night was different. I pushed the buzzer as before and was sort of expecting the same thing as last time. Bad mistake. This time a nurse comes to the door and opens it just enough to wedge herself inside the gap. She looks like she's expecting me to storm the place and she's bracing herself to make sure I don't get past.

"Who are you?"

"My name's Ray."

"What do you want?"

"Um, I'm here with my family to see my nephew, Reid."

She backs up out of the gap and pulls the door shut. I watch through the window as she walks away. A couple of moments later, some goon ... er ... guard ... er ... orderly shows up, opens the door enough to stick his head out and glowers at me.

"It's okay," I say. "You can let me in. I'm here to see my nephew. I've already spoken to Nurse Ratched over there." I didn't mean to say that, honest; it just came out. Can't even think why.

Slam! The door closes and locks.

Nurse Ratched, for those unfamiliar with the character from the 1975 film *One Flew Over the Cuckoo's Nest*, has been named the fifth-greatest villain in film history by the American Film Institute. Even Louise Fletcher, who won an Oscar for her portrayal of Nurse Ratched, says she can't bear to watch the film.[25]

We pick up the story as Ray stands nervously in the waiting area, bouncing on the balls of his feet. He sees staff members conferring with one another inside, shooting glances at him through the gridded window of the heavy metal door. He continues:

> Time now becomes hard to measure. But eventually Nurse Ratched comes back. This time she comes right outside the door but still holds it open a crack. She is in enemy territory but is ready to retreat behind her battlements in a flash if necessary.
>
> "I understand you called me Nurse Ratched. That is very disrespectful."
>
> Her voice is almost mechanical. Everything about her tells me that she herself could use some of the goo-goo pills she's forcing down Reid's throat. I am dismayed that this person is in a position of power over my nephew. I know that I am in Deep Trouble.
>
> "I'm very sorry, ma'am, I was just kidding. It's just that the last time I was here, people didn't seem to be so uptight. I was just hoping to have a game of chess with Reid, that's all."

At this point, the other family members in the waiting area are pretending they don't know Ray. Most of them later recount that they heard him say "Nurse Ratched" at least a dozen times. One cousin, head in hands, muttered, "Somebody shoot me." But nobody came to Ray's rescue.

He brings his account to its grand finale:

Other words may have been spoken; I'm not really sure. My brain feels like it's in one of those movies where the hero and the girl are running for their lives, while all around them things are blowing up with showers of sparks everywhere. I might have said something to the effect that I'd be happy to be strip-searched if that was thought necessary.

She goes back inside and slams the door again.

I run.

Though Ray's account of his disastrous visit to the hospital was written to sound hilarious, the situation with our nephew was not. Reid was released after a week in the hospital, thoughts of suicide still plaguing him day and night.

Two powerful medications were not controlling his symptoms—the dose of one was doubled and he got worse. We couldn't tell if the drugs were keeping him alive or contributing to the problem.

Three months before his breakdown, Reid had begun taking long-term antibiotics for a mild case of acne. The gut microbiome and its relationship to mental health had recently become an area of fascination for me. Could it be that the antibiotic was somehow contributing to his crisis? I begged him to stop. But he resisted. His face was his only vanity. He wanted to look good at the end.

Nothing I said or did seemed to help. Then I had an idea. Who knows better than Ray what it feels like to be told that the way you see things is all wrong? To be the only one of your kind, answering a call that no one else hears, for reasons no one else understands? And Ray had done battle with his own feelings of despair and hopelessness. I phoned to ask for his help.

Whatever he was doing when I called, he shelved it. "Sure, bring him over."

The three of us sat down in his living room. It was the first and only time I have ever been served tea by my brother. Reid patiently explained why death was the only way out and why nothing was going to change that. Ray listened carefully without interrupting. Then, using the same tone he would use if talking about, say, what toppings to order from a pizza menu, he said to our nephew, "If you want to kill yourself, go ahead—but please do it with a sound mind. To be the captain of your own mind, you must first have control of it."

He used his beloved motorbike to illustrate the point.

"If I want to ride Reinhold off a cliff and die in a blaze of glory, so be it—but for God's sake don't let me die because my brakes are faulty! To say that one does not want to function properly is like saying that one does not want to be who one really is. Only a coward would say that, and I don't think you're a coward. Live or die, but don't half-live. And before choosing death, why not give life a try? If you haven't got yourself firing on all cylinders, you don't even *know* yourself. What could be more pathetic? Oh, and by the way," he added, "they say being dead is really boring."

Somehow Ray's dispassionate exploration of Reid's options worked where my efforts had not. The boy agreed to humour us with a six-month trial of a powerful micronutrient formula that has a track record for reducing or eliminating symptoms of mental illness. It wasn't going to work, he said, but he didn't want to leave us wondering if it would have. So, despite incessant thoughts of death, he acceded to our request.

He was as good as his word. He stopped the antibiotic, which we immediately replaced with probiotics. He faithfully swallowed a therapeutic daily dose of micronutrients, along with fish oil, extra vitamin D and amino acids. As his mood lifted, his doctor began cautiously titrating his medications downward. He turned a corner within days. So intent had he been on this mission to end his life that he experienced grief and a temporary loss of purpose with the change in his thinking, but he fought his way through it.

Now nineteen, Reid has a girlfriend and a job. He has a Ducati motorcycle that his Uncle Ray helps him maintain. He's taken to playing chess blindfolded, with only a mental map of the board for reference. His opponents move his men as he directs. He recently beat Ray four games straight.

"That's gratitude for ya," grumbled Ray in his best old-geezer voice as he handed over the chess crown. Reid wears it with regal pride when defending his title.

I felt the need to thank Ray. Knowing he would hate it if I made any sort of display of my gratitude, I chose a simple email:

> I've been leaning out over a great chasm, trying to grab Reid's hand, and I can only lean as far out as I do because you're holding my other hand and I know you won't let go.

His reply was gracious.

> Well, thanks, I'm touched. More than that, it gives me a very deep vindication. I long ago stopped trying to be someone else because (a) it was a huge and exhausting effort, (b) it wasn't working anyway, and (c) I always hoped that someone, somewhere, sometime might be able to benefit from who I really am.

How Does Your Garden Grow?

It was a cool March morning in 2012 when Ray showed up at my house.

"Got any white pillowcases?" he asked, dispensing with the small talk as always.

"White pillowcases? Well, I *do*," I admitted reluctantly, "but ..." He disregarded my pathetic little Goongbalong roadblock and waited for a proper answer.

I tried another tactic. "Uh ... what do you need them for?"

"Can't tell you."

Among the gifts he had received at his housewarming was a certificate from my then twenty-eight-year-old daughter Lesley for "one cooking lesson, time and date of your choice, menu of your choice, all ingredients supplied by me. Offer valid for one year." Time was almost up, and the coupon was about to expire. Today was the day, he said. I wasn't sure what pillowcases had to do with anything, but I handed them over and immediately wrote them off in my mind.

That evening around six o'clock I got a phone call from Ray: Did Ian and I want to come for dinner? I quickly shelved my own dinner preparations. We were at Ray's door in ten minutes flat.

He was stirring gravy with a whisk in his steamy little kitchen while Lesley scrubbed baby carrots at the sink. "Lol really knows a lot about this stuff!" he said with genuine admiration. Both he and Lesley were wearing homemade chef's hats, consisting of white poster board taped into cylinders, with my white pillowcases stapled to the tops so that they bloused out fetchingly over the sides. Ray's hat was comically tall, Lesley's shorter.

When she had arrived with the groceries, Ray had two finished chef's hats waiting, only he had miscalculated the diameter of hers—it slid right over her head and came to rest on her shoulders. Thus he had spent the first part of the cooking lesson adjusting it while she seared the roast and peeled the potatoes. Even after alterations it was still a little big, the bottom edge coming to rest at her ears.

"Why the different heights?" I asked, trying to sound blasé while feeling a rush of delight at Ray's unqualified enthusiasm for his cooking lesson. He walked over to Lesley and put his arm around her, yanking her close. His free hand still held the whisk, which dripped gravy as he used it to indicate his domain with a sweeping gesture.

"It's *my* kitchen so that makes me the head chef," he explained, as though that much should have been obvious. "My hat has to be taller to denote my position. Lol's just the sous-chef."

"It's true," said Lesley, her head tipped back so she could see out from under the brim of her hat. "Uncle Ray did most of this himself."

It was a big night. Ray had never cooked anything this ambitious in his life, yet here before us was a set table, lit candles and a complete roast beef dinner with all the trimmings. And although he'd had help, he had participated in every step of its preparation—once the hat problem had been resolved, of course.

Dinner was delicious. It seemed to me that Ray had settled into his new home in splendid fashion.

After Lesley had gone home, Ian and I lingered at the table with Ray, and that's when we learned that the transition into his own place had not been as smooth as we had thought. Perhaps the wine had softened him up, but for the second time in his life he told me that he was severely depressed. And just as had been the case after his dismissal from the Post Office some four years earlier, it completely blindsided me. Just one month earlier he had sallied to our nephew's aid and made a powerful case for living. Besides, given Lesley's loving gesture that very day, the spirit of fun he had shown in making those chef's hats, the food, the wine, the company ... I couldn't have been more shocked if he had dumped my dinner over my head.

Sympathetic noises would do no good. I took a quick glance around his kitchen.

For most of his life Ray has been able to inveigle various women into cooking for him. But since going it on his own, he had been living on some very dubious foods, all of which were on display: stale white bread, sugary cereals and pancake mix. Perhaps the vilest of Ray's kitchen staples was the flat of instant noodle soups that he kept on top of his fridge. All he had to do was peel the lid off the Styrofoam bowl, pour boiling water over a block of shrivelled white noodles, add a packet of "flavouring," and *voila*! Lunch was ready, with no dishes to wash afterwards.

In fairness to Ray, it must be noted that his diet was no worse than that of many single men. But hunger always seemed to sneak up on him from behind, and he tried to ignore it until it became an emergency. Whatever it took to fill the hole with as little fuss as possible, that's what my brother was doing.

I held up a giant bag of garish orange Cheezies. "You should know better than this, Ray! How is your brain supposed to run on this stuff? It's no wonder you're depressed."

He didn't even try to defend himself. "It's strange," he said. "I have no empathy for my body—it just carries me around. I wish I could ignore it. I know that's a shitty attitude, but there you go." He shrugged.

"It *is* a shitty attitude!" I replied. "You're probably halfway to scurvy."

He could try cooking decent meals, I suggested, but he didn't like that idea much. The notion of having to fuss over food or cater to his constitution was repugnant to him. And he had already heard my sermon on supplements. While they had been a terrific idea for our nephew, he himself just wasn't a pill-popping sort of a guy, he explained. We both knew that no vitamins could cure his boredom and loneliness, nor could they compensate for a diet of instant noodle soup, Kraft Dinner and Cheezies. But now, having just confessed to another debilitating depression, he had little room to weasel away.

He knew all about my interest in the microbiome and my evangelism for nutrition—including supplementation where necessary—and resorted to sarcasm. "I see," he said acidly. "You want me to join your little religion."

But he didn't put up much of a fight. Pain was crashing around in his body. He groped for the words to explain it. "I feel like ... like I've been poisoned." His brain, he said, seemed to be pressing against the inside of his skull, pushing at the back of his eyes. "It's pressure, like a headache that doesn't hurt. I can't really describe it." He rubbed his fingertips through his thinning hair. "You know, it's not the loss of my body that bothers me," he continued, betraying not a trace of the bleakness of spirit that lay behind that matter-of-fact tone. "It's the loss of my mind. My brain's all foggy. There's this dull, thick, stupid feeling. I can't concentrate. I can't *think* anymore. And without my mind, I'm not much good to anyone."

I had a stash of my vitamin/mineral formula at home, and a bottle of essential amino acids. I bought fish oil, vitamin D and probiotics and drove straight to Ray's the next morning with the whole works. "Take these every day," I said, "just like it says on the bottles. Oh, and you have to keep the probiotics in the fridge." I watched as he dumped the contents of all five bottles into a big bowl, jumbled together like candies. That way he might remember to take them, he said.

Sometimes when nutritionally deprived people take the right micronutrients in the right amounts, they begin to feel better. And in my experience, almost without exception they attribute this improvement to something *else*: the firing of that miserable colleague at last, or the fact that they have restarted their exercise program ... Anything but the supplements.

Ray suspected he was suffering from Seasonal Affective Disorder, and there might have been some truth to that. The Pacific Northwest was just starting to emerge from its winter darkness. Plus, living on his own for the first time in perhaps twenty years, without Mum or Aunt Nell there to make his meals—and without the family and friends those meals tended to attract—he had endured long stretches of unaccustomed solitude. But I was sure his depression had been compounded by the fact that he had deprived himself of what little daylight there was by covering all the windows in his mobile home with quarter-inch Styrofoam panels to conserve heat, so even during the day he existed in a sort of gloomy twilight. Nothing could convince him to take those damn panels down, including my offer to pay the difference in his heating bills.

He knew he was in rough shape, but he was still reliably rebellious when told what to do. I worried he'd be so resentful being bossed around that he might deny any good effect from the supplements even if he felt better. But he assured me he had no intention of being that petty. "Don't worry," he said. "I'm not afraid to give credit where it's due. If this stuff works, I'll make a fine testimonial."

"Okay, well, get your head around it and get started."

There was no fight left in him. "Whatever you think best," he replied meekly.

Keys in hand, I stepped out his door but turned back. "Soon you'll be throwing away your crutches and leaping about like a spring lamb."

He responded with brave humour. "Okay, Reverend, get me to the Promised Land."

I went home and made my official prediction: if he began to feel better, he would attribute his improved mood to the spring equinox, which, as it happened, was to occur the very next day: Tuesday, March 20, 2012.

Two days after I had dropped off the supplements, he emailed to say he thought the fog might be lifting:

> You know, I'd swear I feel less brain fuzz already ... but there's a problem with your little experiment, Babs. This afternoon when the sun came out, I started to feel better. You see, we've just passed the spring equinox, and ...

Ray has long talked of pooling family resources and starting a commune, growing all our own food and becoming entirely self-sufficient, a grand ambition for a man who had never so much as planted a single seed or kept a houseplant. (Plastic ones don't count.)

But in the spring of 2013, after a second winter on his own, Ray decided to start a vegetable garden. By that time he had stuck with his vitamin regimen—more or less—for a year. His depression had lifted intermittently, and his thoughts were clearer, but he wasn't exactly in robust health. He'd been sitting inside for months, pasty and puffy, his feet wracked with pain so intense that walking was practically impossible first thing in the morning. Though he had his wood stove and an endless supply of free firewood stacked outside his kitchen door, he had once again covered his windows in light-sucking Styrofoam to conserve heat, and it seemed to me the more we urged him to take those panels down, the longer he kept them up.

But now he was out surveying his yard, with a view to feeding himself off the land. Not being one for half measures, he started by building sturdy garden boxes and covering his front yard with order-ly rows of them, leaving just enough space to push a lawn mower be-tween them, should he be so inclined. He filled the boxes with dirt he dug from underneath his mobile home. The soil was poor, and rookie though he was, he knew it needed augmenting, so he added dead leaves and kitchen scraps, including the skeletal remains of his barbecued chicken dinners. Not content with these measures, he decided to add some cellulose by layering whole newspaper sections into the dirt. He found out from our sister Anita, an able gardener, which cool weather crops he could plant, and he sowed the seeds thickly into the big boxes.

Next he made a greenhouse to get an early start on his warm weather crops, nailing shelves to the sunny south side of his trailer and covering them with sheets of heavy opaque plastic. He also made his own custom seed trays out of corrugated plastic, fitting them with removable inserts so that when his seedlings were ready for transplant-ing into his garden beds, all he had to do was slit the duct tape at the four corners of the box to flatten it and lift out the inserts one by one with a pancake flipper. Each individual cube could be replanted in his garden without disturbing the growing roots.

When the newspaper in his garden beds didn't seem to be break-ing down fast enough, he repurposed a drill, fashioning a novel "bit" for it by shaping one end of a two-foot length of broom handle to fit into the chuck. Then he drove nails through the broom handle at various angles all the way to the bottom. It reminded me of a giant, vicious-looking, self-propelling curling brush. He demonstrated it for me. He immersed the nail-studded rod in a drywall bucket filled with newspaper and water, fired up the drill, and in no time he had whirled up a fine slurry. Each flat received a different ratio of papier mâché to dirt, so he could track the results and learn which worked best. He experimented with the proportions until he found a consistency that would hold its shape, not drying out and turning into bricks or crum-bling into a handful of rubble. A few seedlings rotted in wet mush and others were baked solid before he got that problem sorted out, but once the ratio was right, he had flats of happy summer veggies coming up in his greenhouse.

We were all thrilled with Ray's newfound initiative and did what we could to provide encouragement and practical help. I was delighted when he phoned me on a cold, clear April morning to announce that he was a father: his radishes had sprouted! He could barely believe it. I quickly dug up a bucket's worth of strawberry plants from my own garden and drove over to his place to congratulate him on the blessed event. I found him outside in his overalls, bent over one of his raised beds, watering the new babies with painstaking care. On closer inspection, I saw a dense line of tender new radish shoots, freshly dampened on both sides. "Whoa, these will need thinning, Ray," I said. To demonstrate, I crouched down and gently pulled out a few seedlings. I ran their threadlike taproots between my thumb and index finger to pull off any loose soil and popped them into my mouth, resolutely ignoring a chicken thigh bone and a piece of the *Vancouver Sun*'s classified section peeking out of the soil. The chlorophyll in these little plantlets would be so good for Ray; why get hung up about a little dirt?

"See?" I said as I plucked and nibbled the peppery sprouts, "These are delicious! You can tell what they're going to be even at this stage—the leaves taste just like the radishes will. You've planted them way too close, though. You've got to give the roots room to swell. But don't waste these little guys—they're full of nutrients. You can throw them in salad or scatter them on your scrambled eggs. Better yet, just nip off the taproot and eat the tops as you thin them, like this."

I was still chewing on radish seedlings when Ray informed me that he had been watering his garden with urine.

"Diluted, of course," he assured me, "five to one. With all the cellulose I've got breaking down in there from the newsprint and leaves, I figured I needed nitrogen, and pee is a good source of that. I checked. Besides, it's free."

As Ray's garden flourished, the deer began making dawn raids, hopping the low picket fence around his yard to feast on tender lettuce and beet greens and delicately nipping the blossoms off his scarlet runners. Determined they would not get another morsel, he went to work devising a system to frighten them out of his yard, involving a timer, a motion sensor and a noisy rotating sprinkler nozzle mounted on a pole. When he was ready to unveil it, he called me. "Hey, you should come by sometime and check out my new deer-soaker."

Next time I was passing Poplars, I remembered to stop at his place. Ray pulled his rubber boots on and led me around the side of his trailer into his yard. Right away I noticed the strawberry plants I had given him a few weeks earlier, neatly set out in one of his boxes. They seemed to have "taken." I wandered over to take a closer look while Ray fiddled with some gizmo mounted to a pole. Suddenly a jet of water hissed in a stuttering arc across his garden toward me. "What do you think?" he asked, his voice raised over the noise as I backed up, trying to get out of the line of fire. "Still needs some fine tuning." Indeed it did, I agreed, having been cornered against the fence and my midsection strafed with staccato bursts of cold water. "Oops, still need to adjust that," he conceded. "Come see what I've done inside."

In Ray's trailer there is a rectangular pass-through between his kitchen and living room, maybe four feet high and five feet wide. In this space he has rigged up a wide shelf that he can raise or lower by pulley. Anita has planted and labelled trays of seeds for him, and he places these on the shelf, lowering it to water the seedlings, then raising it back to almost ceiling height and securing it there, over his head and completely out of the way. A long, thick extension cord loops from his kitchen light fixture to a series of fluorescent tubes he has installed at the top of the cut-out, so that when the shelf is raised to maximum height, the seedlings sit bathed in broad-spectrum light. Here, his babies—cucumbers, tomatoes, squash—grow sturdy and strong, waiting to be transplanted outside when the weather is warmer and Anita says it's time. "She's the expert," Ray says. "I just do what I'm told." In keeping with Ray's genius for getting women to do his bidding, it seems that Anita was doing most of the grunt work—including purchasing the seeds, planting them, weeding, harvesting and sometimes even cooking his garden-fresh produce for him—while he thought up and built novel accessories for his farming enterprise.

He has come over a few times to look at my vegetable garden, and we compare notes. His radishes are enormous; mine never came up. My six different kinds of salad greens blow his pitiable attempts out of the water. His peas are tall and robust, but he can't seem to grow spinach worth a damn, and mine's a roaring success. His beets are a bust, but he has fat asparagus spears thrusting through the soil. As we stroll around my raised beds, he stops at the end of one box where I've stuck a few tulips. He touches a pink petal.

"I know, I know," I say, almost apologetically, sure of what he must be thinking. "Not exactly practical."

"Oh, I wouldn't say that," Ray replies. "What could be more practical than a flower?"

THE LANGUAGE OF GOD

Ray should have been a math teacher. He knows that now, but he's closing in on sixty-five and thinks it's too late. How he would have thrived, the classic absent-minded professor, holed up in his own classroom at some venerable university. When he talks about mathematics, he adopts a worshipful tone:

> Math is the language in which God describes the universe. You can't understand much of anything in science without it. Math can be elegant, even beautiful in much the same way that music can be. No one owns math, and no one rules it; not even God can make two plus two equal five. Before math, all men are created equal—no one has any authority, and anyone can discover as much of math for himself as he chooses. When you prove a theorem by yourself, you stand as an equal with the first person to have proven it. Pythagoras and I are brothers. The truths of math are absolutely true; they are not subject to dispute or interpretation or revision. In a world of noise and pointless going around in circles, math gives us clarity and certainty.

Mathematical principles make perfect sense. They never trick him, never change, and never ever let him down. There are no "exceptions to the rule."

He wasn't always a natural with numbers, however. I had forgotten that until I unearthed some of his early report cards from a box of memorabilia brought up from Mum's crawl space. His elementary school arithmetic marks were straight Ds. I was floored. I don't remember a Ray who flunked math.

I queried him about it by email. Yes, he said, it's true.

> It's the reason I sympathize with kids. I remember
> hating math. Trying to "do" it without knowing what
> I was doing or why or how it really worked.

It was in Grade 7, he explains, that the light of logic began to dawn.

> When I awoke, it was to science first, but then I re-
> alized that math was the language of science, and
> so math bloomed too. This not only makes sense, it
> is the whole key to my teaching method; had I been
> good at arithmetic, I'd never have come to love math,
> and I'd not be any use as a teacher. I'm a "convert"
> and thus have the love that only a convert can have.

Ray's been teaching math ever since to anyone who cares to learn. His method is a complete rethink of the standard curriculum. He has never met a math textbook that didn't deserve a good bashing, and that's always his starting routine—almost a pre-game warm-up: "Look at this! What do they think we are, *morons*?" It energizes him. He keeps threatening to write his own curriculum, but I think he'd miss the fun.

Don't even think about rushing him, either. There have been countless times over the last twenty-five years when a kid has appealed to Uncle Ray for help with a school math assignment. Questions 1 to 18 on page 139 might be due the next morning. But instead of getting straight to the homework, Ray embarks on a free-wheeling romp through the wonders of mathematics. Page 139, questions 1 to 18, will have to wait for another time. First the foundations must be laid firmly in the young mind. "Thou shalt not be in a hurry," Ray says. It's one of his Ten Commandments of Math.

"I will not focus on assignments, and I pay almost no attention to tests," he told my teenage daughter, Heather, many years ago as she sat grimly at the table, arms crossed, head craned away from an open Grade 10 math textbook still leering at her untouched after an hour and a half of her uncle's scintillating oratory.

"It doesn't matter if the book is even opened," Ray told me, flipping the text closed with his index finger after I gently entreated him to get to the homework, "so long as we explore some worthy aspect of the subject. It will all loop back eventually, trust me."

He left our house that night thoroughly invigorated. Heather went to bed in a cold sweat and bombed on her test the next day.

But sometimes Uncle Ray is the only game in town. Even now, when he is asked to help some poor child bogged down by math concepts, his patience is infinite. He quickly locates the place where the child's knowledge broke down, and he will set about repairing it. Then he will fly with that child as high as they are willing to go. Given time, he can coax the most resistant doubter toward faith in the unshakeable principles that order the universe. Just don't call him if you're on a deadline and looking for a shortcut.

Unfortunately, Reid's crisis was the final straw for his twin brother, Connor, who had what might be called a "nervous breakdown." With Reid in hospital and their family in pieces, both Connor and his younger brother, Seth, came to live with us.

As the weeks passed, Connor made a slow but steady recovery, and he and Seth adjusted to their new living situation. The time came to figure out what to do about school. Connor hadn't been going for a month, and Seth's attendance was sporadic at best, despite all the bribes and incentives I could think up. With only three months left in the year, neither boy was going to pass his grade, and both had backlogs of uncompleted work from the years before. Seth, at the age of fifteen, figured he'd dug himself into a hole he could never hope to climb out of. School staff warned me that both boys were "hanging by a thread."

I wanted to find out why they hated school so vehemently. Were we trying to force them to do things they were incapable of doing? I requested formal psycho-educational evaluations to identify their academic strengths and weaknesses. I braced myself for bad results but was shocked at just how bad they were. On a bell curve, Seth's math fluency tested in the first percentile—where you'd put the point of your pencil down on the paper to begin drawing the curve. Connor, sixteen, was in the same boat. And it wasn't just math dragging down their averages: for both boys, reading comprehension was practically nonexistent. They were labelled with multiple learning disabilities.

Ian and I were determined to help them salvage what they could of the school year. We started with Seth, as he seemed less fragile. Ian took a crack at the first set of questions in Seth's math textbook, but he turned out to be a little rustier than he thought, and I knew I couldn't possibly teach high school math, having last contended with it somewhat unsuccessfully forty years earlier.

Ray would help. I drove to his place with Seth's abysmal psycho-educational assessment in hand. I found him in his garden.

"Hey Ray, would you consider tutoring Seth? He's failing everything, and he's pretty much given up on himself. His math score is *one percent*! Look at this! It says he's profoundly learning disabled ..."

Ray was watering a line of beet seedlings with his special five-to-one blend. "Seth is not disabled in any way," he said flatly without bothering to look at the report.

Ray had often made dismal prognostications for the boy's future. *Nice kid*, he'd say, *but he'll probably fetch up on the end of a shovel if he doesn't become a drug dealer.*

"Would you at least read this?" I asked, following him as he moved to the other side of his garden box.

Still he would not deign to look at the sheath of papers in my hand, so I read an excerpt out loud: "Seth does not intuit mathematical relationships. His overall performance is in the *well-below-average* range. He meets the DSM diagnostic criteria for a 315.1 Mathematics Disorder."

I looked at my brother expectantly.

"*There is nothing wrong with Seth's brain.*" Ray enunciated the words very clearly, as though I had perhaps not heard him the first time. He set his watering can down, straightened up and brushed his palms together, as though to indicate that the subject was now closed.

"But this was done by a psychologist," I protested. "They know what they're doing."

That got his attention. "Please," he said, "don't condescend. They may know what they're doing, but I know what I'm doing too. Let the pundits read their tea leaves. I am well aware of what Seth knows and what he doesn't know, and I know better than they do what he's capable of."

"Well, will you come over and help him, then?"

"Certainly. Any time."

"How about this afternoon? Spend an hour with him and I'll make you supper."

"Deal," he said. "A bachelor never turns down free food."

I went home and broke the news to Seth. "Uncle Ray's coming over at four to work on your math homework with you."

Seth looked pained.

"At this point, kid," I said, "he's probably the only person on the planet who believes in you, so you'd best be grateful."

At precisely the arranged time, Ray wheeled into my driveway on his vintage ten-speed bicycle. Watching from the kitchen window, I felt an upwelling of affection. He looked like some sort of rare tropical bird. He was wearing a vivid turquoise V-neck pullover (I'm pretty sure it had once been Aunt Nell's) and his modified navy-blue sweatpants. He had cut off the elastic just above the ankles and normally wore them with the ragged bottom edges flapping around his calves, but now they were stuffed into white tube socks pulled high so as to prevent the baggy fabric from getting caught in the bike chain. He sported a fluorescent lime-green skateboarding helmet with a flashlight firmly affixed to the top with wide purple rubber bands, the kind that hold stalks of broccoli together. A red nylon backpack completed the look.

He dutifully removed his shoes at the front door and sat down at the kitchen table, so focused on the lesson ahead that he forgot he was still wearing his backpack and his helmet until I gently reminded him.

"Hi, Uncle Ray," said Seth, smiling sheepishly as he ambled into the kitchen.

"Hi, kid."

"Aunty Claire says you're the only person alive who believes in me."

Ray's head snapped up. "Believe in you? No, I don't *believe* in you," he said, lingering on the word. "You're a lazy teenager and you might very well end up as a drug dealer. Shit, you know what? Even a drug dealer has to know how to do basic math! Oh no, I don't *believe* in you. But I don't think there's anything wrong with you, either. I'll teach you anything you want to know, but I will not chase you." He jabbed at

Seth's math textbook. "We can knock all of this off in a month, tops, but we're going to have to start by backfilling the holes in your knowledge. Math is linear. You can't do Grade 9 math on a Grade 5 foundation, so we have to get you up to speed. The schools teach math all wrong—it's too slow! It's almost like they're *trying* to make you hate it!"

Seth nodded, relieved, no doubt, that his career prospects were no longer under scrutiny. This only served to spur Uncle Ray on.

"Kids these days are not taught how to learn!" I think this last bit was aimed in my direction. "They're taught how to perform like little monkeys."

Uh-oh, I thought. *Here we go ...*

Seth stood leaning against the counter while his uncle trashed the system that I was desperately trying to keep him in.

"I will not teach kids how to pass tests," Ray continued. "When I'm finished with a kid, he *will* pass a test. It's a given. But we gotta go fast. Gotta keep the iron hot."

He turned to his nephew. "By the end of the school year, I want you tutoring other kids." In response to the look of horror that blossomed on Seth's face, he said, "Nothing less."

Ray's diatribe continued. "Learning shouldn't be a 'top down' sort of thing, with the teacher as the boss and the student as a sort of employee." His face suddenly brightened. "It's like making love," he said. "The less you worry about who's supposed to be on top, the more fun you'll have!" His voice became more reflective. "I'm always thrilled the first time a student contradicts me and the first time he or she proves me wrong. I feel like I have given birth to a new person. All right, lad, let's begin."

Seth slid into the seat beside his uncle.

"The learning environment must be free of anything unrelated to math," Ray intoned. "Get rid of all this stuff." With both hands he corralled my African violet, the salt and pepper shakers and a few other bits and pieces and pushed them roughly away. "Our minds must be clear; the table must be clear."

Seth scrambled up and caught the salt shaker as it tipped and rolled toward the edge of the table, quickly removing it and the rest of the offending objects. Ray made him wipe the table and fetch the necessary supplies. He barked orders: "Ruler! Calculator! Compass!"

Seth retrieved these items from a cupboard, and I was dispatched for sharp pencils, paper and erasers. This became the opening ceremony for entering the sacred realm of mathematics.

Ray came every few days. He had agreed to tutor his nephews for no pay other than food, so I was usually in the kitchen while they worked. At the start of each session I made a point of setting the oven timer for an hour, so Seth would know that the lesson had an end point. He looked balefully at the timer as the minutes counted down. I would put veggies and dip or a bowl of almonds on the table to tide them over while I made dinner, and they devoured these snacks unthinkingly, Ray's mind on the task at hand and Seth's on how much longer he had to sit there.

Ray's patience was a marvel. When Seth gave a wrong answer, Ray stopped him. "What's the first commandment of math? *Thou shalt not guess.*" He went over the problem again and again until Seth got the concept. I found myself getting it too, being drawn in by Ray's exquisite teaching ability as I washed lettuce or stirred a pot of chili.

"It doesn't matter if the question has two digits or two hundred," Ray told Seth. "If you understand the principle, the method is the same. Don't get scared off by big numbers."

Seth had by now resigned himself to the fact that he would be attending school every morning followed by tutoring sessions with his Uncle Ray most afternoons. His favourite video game would have to wait. He stopped resisting. It wasn't long before he came home with the news that he had passed his math final. With 90 percent.

And on they flew, through science now, and the more I listened, the more I appreciated Ray's consummate skill as a teacher. He wove together chemistry, biology, astronomy and physics. He used his old fogey voice, his Mahatma Gandhi voice and his German führer voice. He badgered, wheedled and cajoled. But always the bedrock upon which everything stood was math. Sometimes the books were not opened, and assignments were not done.

"Math doesn't have to be dry and lifeless," Ray told the boy one day. "The master builders of the great cathedrals had only the simplest arithmetic written on paper, but they could *feel* the balance of their work in their minds. The thrust of the buttress must balance the thrust of the vault. It's an equation solved not on paper but in the consciousness of the builder—but it's no less a math problem for that."

I was standing in the kitchen the day Seth forgot when his hour was up, and he forgot that he was "learning disabled."

"Uncle Ray, you know those signs on bridges, the ones that say how much weight they can take? How do they figure that out?"

Seth had *asked a question*. Not because it was going to be on a test, but just because he was curious. I kept on peeling potatoes, but my heart leapt. As for Ray, he was charged with a joyous enthusiasm. "Math, of course!" came his answer. "*Math*! Bridges are engineered using applied physics, and all physics is just applied math. Have you ever heard of the Golden Gate Bridge? It's one of the most beautiful bridges in the world. It was built way back in the 1930s. The senior engineer was a man named Charles Ellis. He didn't have computers like we have today, not even a calculator like this one!" Ray held up Seth's little solar-powered scientific calculator. "He had a clunky old mechanical adding machine as big as a cash register, a table of logarithms and a slide rule. If he wanted to multiply by twelve, he had to crank this lever twelve times." Ray pantomimed the pulling of the lever as he spoke. "Can you imagine having to do that? But he had the very same principles you are learning right now. He filled books and books and books with handwritten calculations. And you know what? The Golden Gate Bridge is a masterpiece! It will last forever. Because of *math*."

I had stopped working and was leaning with my back against the counter, entranced. Ray became vaguely aware of me. "Babs," he said absent-mindedly, "I could sure use a cup of tea."

Once Seth was rolling along nicely, it was time to initiate sixteen-year-old Connor. He sat politely in the chair, eyes downcast. One leg bounced up and down. He looked defeated before he had begun. Ray probed gently for his weak spots.

"So, then, what's the formula for determining the surface area of a cylinder?"

"Um, two times base area plus lateral area?" Connor's answers were tentative, always given as questions.

Ray abandoned his lesson on calculating surface area. "Okay, let's go right back to the basics. Eight times eight?"

"Um, sixty-four? No, sixty-two? Is it sixty-four?"

Ray could sense the young man's lack of confidence. "My God," he said softly, closing the textbook, "this isn't even *about* math." He turned to Connor. "You know what's wrong with you, kid?"

Connor shrugged and looked at his hands drumming the edge of the table.

"Your problem isn't math at all! It's that you haven't yet realized that you are a free man. You're still dragging your chains around, thinking you're a slave. 'Yes, Bwana. Yes, Masa.'" Ray put his hands together and bowed obsequiously, as though to a whip-wielding plantation boss. Then he straightened up and looked at Connor. "But those chains no longer bind you. You just haven't realized yet that you can walk away any time! That's the difference between me and you, kid. I go where I want; I think what I want. You don't lack the brains, but you've got to lose the chains."

Ray wasn't about to let Seth lose his momentum, so he alternated between the two boys, always adapting his lessons to their individual levels. Soon Connor was picking up speed, and to Ray's surprise and satisfaction, was found to be "not so stupid after all."

It is impossible not to love math the way my brother teaches it. I didn't dare sit down at that table myself—how would I ever extricate myself?—but if I had, he'd have made me feel like I could do it, and he wouldn't have let me go until I did. I believe my African violet would have been calculating the surface area of cylinders and the volume of spheres had the Nephew Project not come to an end when Connor moved out in March 2014, followed six months later by Seth.

The boys have graduated to girls and cars. Both Uncle Ray and Aunty Claire are now receding figures in their rear-view mirrors. Ray shakes his head and mutters, hopes he has not wasted his time.

They are still too young to appreciate what he did for them. All they know right now is that they have escaped his clutches, but one day—when they amount to something—they will have their uncle to thank in no small measure.

Something happened to me as I watched Ray sitting there day after day teaching those reluctant teenagers. It ceased to matter to me that he is "a nice specimen of the disability." I often forgot about his autism—I know he'd be glad to hear that. He was just a man doing something important and altruistic, and I found myself genuinely admiring him. He never once told Seth or Connor that he loves them, but he certainly demonstrated that he does.

The New and Improved Ray

While Ray was coming over regularly to tutor our nephews, he became the guinea pig in a little experiment. It was "double blind"—though only in the sense that neither he nor I knew we were conducting it. Our laboratory was his digestive tract.

It all started with my daughter Lesley nagging me to try raw milk. She had found a source—a small organic dairy whose cows were fed grass rather than grain—and was using it regularly herself; in fact, she had become such a snob that she declined to use my "store milk" in her tea. I've heard that milk from commercial dairies can be laced with hormones and antibiotics, and I had two growing teenagers living in my house, so I agreed—in principle—to try the raw stuff.

Next thing I knew, there was a litre of cow juice sitting in my fridge, a thick layer of cream at the neck of the bottle. I couldn't quite get my head around the idea of drinking it. Adding to my squeamishness, there was no "best before" date anywhere, so I had no idea how old it was. The boys reacted to it as though it was a rattlesnake coiled in the fridge. Realizing no one was going to drink it, I decided to try making yogurt, and if there were no takers for that, I'd use it in baking. I bought a cooking thermometer and a packet of "friendly" bacteria from my local health food store and made my first batch.

Eight or so hours later, the contents of the jar were solid. I couldn't bring myself to taste it. After all, I had been suspicious of it when it was just milk, teeming with bacteria, and what had I done but inoculate it with even *more* bugs. Set free from their little foil prison, they had reanimated themselves, gobbled up the lactose and congealed the milk, and they were still in there, very much alive, wriggling, writhing, replicating ...

I held up the jar, imagining millions of lactobacilli with their little faces pressed against the glass, staring back at me. I knew this yogurt was probably good for me and gave myself a pep talk—*come on now, down the hatch!*—but ultimately, I was unable to put a colony of bacteria—however friendly—into my mouth. I tried sneaking a bit into Seth's store-bought strawberry yogurt, which he always ate as fast as I could buy it, but his eyes went slitty with the first spoonful. He was on to me.

The accidental experiment began—though neither Ray nor I knew it yet—one Saturday morning in June 2012. Ray was going over some math concepts with a dishevelled Seth, who had rolled out of bed just in time for his prearranged eleven o'clock tutoring session. I announced my intention to call a halt to the lesson at twelve thirty. This would give me a chance to get some decent food into Ray, as I had promised to do in exchange for the free tutoring.

Ray sometimes came to my house on an empty stomach despite the morning being well along. He'd start getting cranky, scrunching up his face, rubbing his forehead and making stupid math errors. At this point, recognizing the signs, I'd usually rustle up some scrambled eggs or homemade granola. But on that particular morning I remembered the jar of yogurt sitting untouched in my fridge. Ray usually shovels food into his mouth without paying any attention to what he's eating, especially if he's engrossed in something as enthralling as math, so who better to flog the stuff on?

I kept a surreptitious eye on him as I puttered around the kitchen. He downed the whole bowlful. Even said it was good, as I recall.

The next morning, a Sunday, I was surprised to see him at my door before nine. There was no tutoring session scheduled. But Ray wasn't there about math.

"Hey," he asked me, "do you have any more of that yogurt?"

"Sure, why?"

"Because last night I didn't have heartburn."

I had no idea that heartburn was a problem for Ray. He hadn't mentioned it in years, and I guess I had simply forgotten about it while he had quietly continued to cope as best he could.

"I take up to twenty Tums a day," he explained, as my eyes flew wide open in dismay, "and before bed I mix up a big batch of baking soda and water and swig it straight from the jug all night to control the burn. But last night ... *nothing*. It had to be the yogurt. There are no other variables. It's a miracle."

There were other small miracles afoot as well. In addition to his hit-and-miss vitamin regimen, Ray had started eating more produce from his garden—especially if he could recruit Anita to pick and prepare it for him—but he was still highly resistant to the suggestion that he further edit his diet to control his symptoms. "I just don't think of myself as one of those people who has to be careful of every little thing he puts in his mouth. A bachelor should be able to eat anything he wants," he said with a hint of petulance.

Ray's gut apparently doesn't know he's a bachelor. It consistently punishes him for his failure to discriminate between foods that cause discomfort and those that don't. He knows which rich and greasy foods ignite the blowtorch in his chest, but he indulges anyway, relying on his ever-present Tums to douse the fire. I've seen him bloated and belching, fingers spread wide over his distended stomach after a spaghetti dinner at Mum's, resigned to his fiery fate.

Besides creating an endless revenue stream for GlaxoSmithKline, Ray's reliance on Tums was neutralizing acid where it was needed, in his stomach, thus impeding digestion and assimilation of nutrients into his bloodstream. With his body's acid/alkaline balance thrown off, nasty little microbes could take up residence in his damaged gut, rather in the way that drug gangs and petty criminals will infest a rundown part of town. And while Tums quelled his pain, it was like paying protection money to the mob; bad things happened when he stopped.

Now here he was standing at my door asking if I had any more yogurt. I donated the rest to what looked like a good cause. He took it home and polished it off over the next few days. The relief from his heartburn was immediate and sustained.

I've been in the yogurt-making business ever since, and the more of it Ray eats, the better he feels. It has become his new fire fighter—and a surprisingly potent one at that. Instead of suppressing his symptoms, he is now continuously inoculating his gut with good bacteria. They are slowly but surely taking back their old neighbourhood.

Seeing such noticeable benefits in Ray, by the way, I am happy to report that I now enjoy my own yogurt tremendously. I've gotten used to the idea of whole civilizations of microscopic living creatures sliding

down my throat to meet their fates in my innards. They're delicious—
especially with a bit of my homemade raspberry jam stirred in.

As Ray's gastrointestinal symptoms abated, strange things started
happening. Things I could never have anticipated. He began making
eye contact. Thanking me for lunch. The first time he put his plate and
fork in the dishwasher, I stared dumbstruck. When he phoned one day
to arrange a math lesson for Connor, he opened with, "Hi, it's Ray. How
are you?" I nearly dropped the phone. How was I? *How was I?* Stunned,
actually. I had never heard that most common of Goongbalong pleasantries come out of Ray's mouth—ever.

In August 2013, with Ray and I now devoted yogurtees, we attended
a conference at the Vancouver Trade and Convention Centre called
"BrainSolutions." We were there to see the Yogurt Lady. A microbiol-
ogist, she claimed that her family has been making yogurt for the last
750 years. The lady knew her bugs. She told the audience that bacteria—the good, the bad and the ugly—are the true rulers of the world
and that the balance of these organisms in our guts affects us physically, emotionally and yes, mentally. The gut, she explained, engages in
a constant, incredibly complex chemical and electrical dialogue with
the brain. This was bad news for Ray, who preferred to think of his
stomach as a bubbling vat of acid and his intestinal tract as a simple
tube that propelled waste to its ignominious end. Bacteria, said the Yogurt Lady, are smart little critters, working in their own best interests,
just like their human hosts do. Disturbingly, to me at least, she claimed
that our bodies are made up of 90 percent bacterial cells and only 10
percent human cells.

After her lecture, we stayed in that big, air-conditioned conference room for the rest of the afternoon to hear other speakers on various aspects of brain health and neuroplasticity. During a talk on brain
imaging, Ray abruptly got up and disappeared. I experienced a frisson
of apprehension. He likes nosing around where he's not supposed to
go. Was I going to find him hanging from the ceiling, trying to improve
the acoustics? Being detained by security for attempting to re-enter the
auditorium without showing his ticket? Swimming across Burrard Inlet

naked? But no, he reappeared a few minutes later with a paper cup of cold water for me. Most people would not feel much beyond a cursory gratitude for this small kindness. To me, the moment was monumental.

Probiotics *is* rocket science. Not only must we know the genus, species and strain of bacteria we are using, we must make sure it is packaged with its "supernatant," or culturing medium, nourishment for the little guys as they while away the days in suspended animation in our fridges, waiting for the perfect conditions to spring to life. Good thing I didn't know any of this when I first walked into the health food store and picked up the only refrigerated probiotic they carried, or I might never have gotten started.

The beneficial bacteria in real live yogurt do far more than take the burn out of heartburn—they actively synthesise nutrients. *No bugs, no benefit.* So when we added the yogurt to Ray's supplement regimen, I think we stumbled onto a truly effective therapy for his malfunctioning microbiome. With the good guys regularly cruising his gut, more nutrients are being converted into usable forms and ferried to his cells. And there are spinoff benefits too. Most of the neurotransmitters thought to regulate mood and social functioning are produced by nerve cells that line the intestinal tract. As Ray's gut began to heal, it seems to have sent a memo to his brain, which then started quietly repairing its shredded synapses. He has a new self-awareness, and this has expanded to include more awareness of others. My heart jumps a little when Ray's eyes meet mine. I'm still not used to it, and I'm sure he isn't, either.

My husband, Ian, who has known Ray for forty-five years, says he is "a changed man." When I passed this comment on to Ray in an email, he was contemplative.

> Strange, I feel "better" but not "changed," although many people are using the latter term. Scary to think one can change and not even be aware of it. Am I different?

He is. Everyone can see it. Anita spends a lot of time with him, helping him eat better and haranguing him when he doesn't. She said in a recent email:

When Ray's had a good spell of doing things right, he's clear, handsome, funny, much "looser," more conversational, engaging, kind even. Ray's paradigm is shifting.

The yogurt easily handles his minor dietary indiscretions, but his indigestion returns with a vengeance after he's eaten greasy foods: a burger and fries at the pub is like swallowing a ball of fire. Worse still are the depression, brain fog, stiffness and bodily pain that follow like the four horsemen of the Apocalypse. But he continues to dine out whenever he's invited, with no regard for the consequences. The company's worth the price he pays for it, I guess, but the next day he knows he'll be "as stiff as the tin woodman in *The Wizard of Oz* before he gets his oil can."

"Restaurant food hits me hard for some reason," he says, shaking his head. "Last time I was at the pub I had a veggie plate and some pita with dip, and the next day I was set like concrete. Couldn't even tie my shoes. There does seem to be a definite 'death bun' effect."

Any way you slice it, he turns out to have a very delicate system indeed, and when he abuses it, he pays with an inferno in his esophagus and a big, fat, foggy head.

"Heck," I said once after he had experienced a run of good days, "maybe this whole time your brain's just been swollen."

"Well," he said cheerfully, switching sides the way he likes to do, "there's this college dropout who got his head kicked in outside a karaoke bar—remember that? He got really good at math and became a whole lot more like me, so maybe I really *do* have some sort of brain damage. Note the common gesture of hitting oneself on the side of the head when one wants to think more clearly. Go figure."

I'm not going to try whacking Ray in the head to see what happens, but I do dream of locking him up like a lab rat and feeding him through the bars of his cage. He's not entirely opposed to the idea. "Yeah, too bad I couldn't be put in a controlled environment," he says, "where some proper experiments could be run."

Friends and family are loath to believe that vitamins and yogurt could have anything to do with the changes they have seen in Ray. They like to point out that there are other more obvious factors at play in this "new and improved" incarnation, and these I happily acknowledge. First of all, while he was tutoring our nephews, he had a reason to get up in the morning: teaching engaged his mind and made him feel useful. Plus, it ensured plenty of nonthreatening human contact. In addition to the salutary effects of teaching, he was, between Anita and me, being fed nutritious meals on a semi-regular basis. He was definitely eating more vegetables. There were even days when his entire dinner was made from his own garden, as he told me with no little pride. These things are not lost on me; they have to be part of his transformation. But I don't believe they alone can account for the changes we are seeing.

Could it be Writing Man thanking me for lunch, bringing me water? It's a bold claim for a layman like me to make, but I'm going to come right out and say that my probiotic yogurt, along with high-quality vitamins and a better diet, seem to have initiated positive neurological changes in my brother. I'm not touting a "cure" for autism, and there might be—no, there *are*—other factors at play that I have missed, but I suspect that Writing Man and Speaking Man are converging, that Ray's brain, grateful for the reprieve from near-constant inflammation, is knitting those two disharmonious fellows into one more cohesive entity. Importantly, Ray reports an embryonic empathy for his own body. He once spoke to me of a mysterious room in his brain that he knows is there but cannot enter. Has the swelling gone down enough that he can at least get a peek inside?

I can't prove any of it, but my intuition tells me this all has something to do with bugs. Call it a gut feeling.

Was the "new Ray" just a flash in the frying pan? A temporary aberration? Or have the changes held? The acid test, if you will, came in June 2015.

Ray, Mum and I were on our way to Vancouver to celebrate a milestone: our niece Emily's high school graduation. This was a day many had doubted would ever come, given the academic challenges she faced. Ray was packing an expensive pendant he had commissioned for the occasion: an 18-karat gold scale model of the constellation Auriga, containing a glittering yellow gemstone to represent its brightest star, Capella. The necklace, he said, was a fitting tribute to someone who had surmounted so many obstacles. A girl who shone as brightly as Emily deserved no less.

At the ferry terminal we ran into my friend Kathryn, who was returning from a weekend at her Gibsons cottage. Kathryn—Ray calls her Kate—has the rare distinction of being the only person I know that Ray hugs of his own free will. (Kathryn and her daughters all have souls.)

The four of us were sitting at a picnic table in the shade, waiting for the 4:30 sailing, when up strolled twenty-seven-year-old Edith, who was returning to the city after a few days with friends on the Coast.

She and her siblings had grown up on the Sunshine Coast with my kids. As a teenager, she had quickly distinguished herself as one of Ray's brightest young acolytes: she was a night swimmer, a poetry lover and a stargazer. She has never been afraid of him, so he has never been afraid of her. She has an open-hearted curiosity about the world, an intelligence and a *teachability* that inspired him. She had seen a good bit of the world between stints at work and school and had just returned from six months volunteering in Central America.

Edith had changed her appearance radically in the ten years since Ray and I had last seen her. The sides of her head were shaved in urban neo-hippie style. A thick swath of long black hair ran down the middle and was piled on top of her head in a messy heap. One arm was tattooed from wrist to elbow with a cascading series of moons in different phases. I wondered in passing if Ray's influence had anything to do with that. She had various piercings, including one through the septum of her nose, in which she wore a thin silver ring about the diameter of a dime.

It was hard for me not to stare at this new incarnation of the girl I had once known, but of course, Goongbalong rules of engagement dictate that we must conceal any shock or consternation we feel at a person's appearance—at least until we have performed the customary greeting rituals. Mum and I were prevented by our adherence to the code from doing anything in that moment but offering an appropriate greeting, which is what we did.

Ray's opportunities to insult or alienate Edith were legion. *Oh no,*

I thought, as I waited for him to blurt out his first impressions, *here it comes.*

Mum's pleasant smile never wavered, but it was directed nowhere in particular. I could tell she was bracing for impact.

"This should be interesting," whispered Kathryn under her breath.

But Ray did not say, "My God, what have you done to your beautiful face?" He did not ask her if she had just been unhitched from a plow, or what tribe she belonged to.

What he said was, "Oh, hi, Edith, long time. Nice to see you. What have you been up to?"

Edith took a seat at our picnic table and chatted amiably with us about where she had been, what she was doing back on the Coast, her future plans and so on. It was small talk. Chit-chat. And Ray was shooting the breeze like a seasoned professional. I sat stunned. I had spent seven years chronicling his social ineptitude, its fallout, and his patient and profuse explanations as to why it could be no other way. My work was going up in smoke. Who would believe me now? *This* Ray was knocking the Goongbalong ball right out of the park.

When our ferry was finally called, Edith left us to find herself a quiet spot on the outer deck to read, but the rest of us—Ray, Kathryn, Mum and I—reconvened on the passenger deck for the forty-minute sailing to Vancouver. My brother's graceful social performance was ringing in my head.

"Ray," I said after a while—I couldn't resist—"you didn't comment on Edith's appearance."

"Well, of *course* not!" He pulled in his chin and wheeled to look at me on the bench seat beside him. "What did you expect me to do, embarrass the girl publicly?"

I chose my next words carefully. "But ... this is something new for you. Edith looks so different! Normally, you would have said the first thing that popped into your head. Kathryn, Mum and I—we were all waiting for you to comment on her appearance."

"Oh, I *knew* what you were all thinking!" he retorted. "And the truth is, sometimes I feel like saying something rude just because it's expected of me. It's a well-known thing in psychology—and I'm not talking only about Aspies, it applies to everyone—this tendency to rise to what is expected of us or to lower ourselves, as the case may be.

The class clown is funny, the bad kid is always getting into trouble, that sort of thing. I knew you were all waiting for me to say something scandalous—and I almost did. Fortunately, I have a little more self-control than that."

Ray isn't quick to embrace any dietary trends, especially the "gluten free" and "low carb" ones. "Whatever they say now, they'll change their minds in twenty years anyway," he grouses over his instant noodle soup. "Yesterday butter and eggs were from the devil; now it's wheat. What will it be tomorrow? Steamed kale, for God's sake?" And when held to account for his own foolish dietary choices, he trots out the old standby: "What can I do? I'm a bachelor. I eat what's put in front of me."

Despite his half-hearted protests and lame excuses, he has clearly demonstrated the correlation between how his body feels and functions and how his brain feels and functions. He's not even really trying to deny it anymore. Having seen his response to a few modest self-help measures, I suggest that maybe he's been right all along and there *is* nothing fundamentally wrong with him. Maybe he's just an exotic hothouse flower who requires exquisitely precise conditions to bloom.

True to form, Ray switches positions as soon as he's won me over to his side:

> Let's not be too hasty here. The cascade of genetics, natal environment, gut toxicity, various traumas and who-know-what-else will produce complex, layered outcomes. It might be very difficult to take it all apart. No!—it will be impossible to take it apart. The latest research suggests that everything before now is not only wrong, but absolutely *backwards.* No sooner do you get the "Autistic" label successfully pasted onto my forehead than we find out that most of what we thought that label meant is probably wrong.
>
> Sheesh! Hard to trust these people ...

Regardless, Ray functions better and feels happier—and seems less autistic to everyone else—when he's doing the right things. I can't help it: I get excited about his potential and frustrated with him when he fails to take responsibility for his own health.

I was at his house recently when he was burying his morning yogurt in brown sugar, and the look on my face only prompted him—I swear—to throw on an extra shovelful. So although the trend is positive—I actually heard him decline some reheated pizza at Mum's the other day—he still has setbacks where pain and depression get the better of him. But after his lifelong "lack of empathy" for his own body, he's finally learning that it pays to be nicer to it.

He worries sometimes about what I'm trying to turn him into. I tease him a bit about the dangers that lie ahead if the trend toward better health and improved social skills continues. "At this rate," I say, "I think you might have a future in politics."

"Who knows?" he says, and is that a trace of fondness I hear? "And maybe I'll finally start to notice people's shoes!"

Improving his diet will not make Ray any less Ray, will it? If he ends up less grouchy and more engaged, how is that a bad thing? "You can keep your love of philosophy, music and math," I wrote recently, "but anything 'cured' by vitamins and/or yogurt should be cured, right?"

His default position remains as follows: Argue with everything Babs says.

> Can we be so sure about that? The paradigm of "disease vs. wellness" would have us believe that if I was cured of my brain fog—and I'd love to be cured of my brain fog—it would leave the rest of my faculties untouched: the "bad" would go, the "good" would stay. Fine. However, when we talk about curing autistics, we are implicitly saying that all the traits that define autism are similarly "diseases" to be cured. The fact that Aspies probably all agree that we don't care very much about people's shoes makes that trait a marker of autism and thus a "disease," and one should strive for a cure. It follows from the paradigm, does it not?

However, if we broaden out our thinking a bit and move incrementally away from "sick/well" and "good/bad" into "assets vs. liabilities" or "gain this, lose that," then things become a bit less clear.

The dark skin of Africans is a "disease" when they live up north, because it impedes the formation of Vitamin D; on the other hand, the light skin of Caucasians is a "disease" when they live down south for the obvious reason. But we don't say that melanin is a disease; we say that pigmentation is beneficial or not, depending on the situation: as a person gains protection from sunburn, they lose the ability to make D. Gain one, lose the other. Perhaps that's the better paradigm at my end of "the spectrum."

Now, just as one could, in theory, develop some treatment for the "illness" of light-coloured skin for a whitey—some medicine that would facilitate the production of melanin—so one might indeed develop a treatment for the autistic symptom of, say, not caring about shoes. But just as "curing" my pigmentation deficit would help me in some ways, it would hinder me in others—I'd have to supplement with D if I was living up north. In the same vein it could well be the case (really, I'm being only half facetious here) that the "cure" for my not caring about shoes could have the side effect of diminishing my love of logic.

Which (to finally get to the point) is to say that had Ma taken more D when she was carrying me, my brain might very well have developed in such a way that I cared deeply about shoes but didn't give a damn about math! Scary thought, eh?

THE KINDEST CUT

My friend Lana and her seven-year-old son, Carson, were coming to the
Sunshine Coast to spend a weekend with us. I had met them through
mutual friends in Vancouver when Carson was four or five. Even back
then, the boy had made quite an impression on me. His vocabulary
was off the charts, and he had seemed more comfortable with adults
than with his peers. Lana, a single mother, told me that he had been
reading fluently since the age of three.

I thought right away of introducing him to Ray, who might be
able to offer him a little fatherly attention, or at least some intellectual
stimulation. Lana readily agreed. We arranged for Ray to come over
on Saturday afternoon. While we were waiting, I offered Carson some
paper and a jumbo pack of coloured felt pens—the kind that come in
tiers on a plastic riser. He had no interest in drawing, but he arranged
fifty-eight of the sixty felt pens in a perfect colour spectrum. Only the
metallic silver and gold pens stumped him.

Ray strolled into the kitchen and said, "So you're Carson. I hear
you're pretty smart."

"Yup," said the boy.

"What's your favourite subject?"

"I like them all, but if forced to choose, I'd have to say math."

"Hmm. Math, eh? Do you know your times tables?" Ray was starting low.

"Yup."

"Can you do fractions?"

"Yup."

"Can you find the area of a sphere?"

"Yup."

"How about quadratic equations?"

"Umm ..."

I have no memory of the actual questions Ray asked Carson (though I bet they both do), and I'm sorry if I've gotten them wrong. All I know is that each question reflected an escalating level of mathematical complexity, and Carson hung in there like a champ. He had finally flagged—at quadratic equations or calculus or rational root theorems or whatever it was. At that point his mother, who had been sitting at the table with a cup of coffee, listening to the exchange, interjected gently. "Ray, he's *seven*."

Three years later, Lana found a bright, centrally located apartment in Gibsons, a five-minute walk from her favourite coffee shop. Lana worked from home as a copy editor, starting at 3:30 a.m. so her work could be finished and posted on international websites by the start of business in other time zones, and often she had to work late into the night, catching sleep where she could. Her off-kilter schedule kept her somewhat socially isolated.

As for Carson, he had always been home-schooled, and he had no friends in this new town. His mother was battling to keep him from being consumed by his favourite interactive computer game. I asked whether a regular school might perhaps provide some socialization for him. Of course Lana had thought of that, but reading between the lines of her answer, I discerned that there was no elementary school on the Sunshine Coast that could accommodate the boy's challenging mix of emotional immaturity and oversized intellect. I wondered aloud about certain issues he seemed to share with Ray, but Carson's mother was well aware of Asperger's syndrome. She had concluded that her son did not have it. But after meeting him on that one occasion, Ray told me in an email:

> He "has" whatever it is that I "have." Call it what you will.

Ray didn't much care either way. He took a shine to the kid and invited him down to the beach to practise swimming and diving—which by now I had come to recognize as one of his grand gestures of friendship and goodwill. It was a fine evening, so Lana and I picked up a few snacks and a bottle of white wine and headed down to Franklin Beach, where Ray was waiting for us. We spread a blanket while he and Carson waded into the ocean and swam out perhaps forty feet. Lana kept a wary eye from shore as she sipped her wine.

Three quarters of an hour later, Ray emerged from the water, a hypothermic but beaming Carson at his side. "Kid's a natural," Ray proclaimed.

I knew right away that Carson and his mother would fit in well with our little poetry group and was pleased when they joined us at our beach fire one summer night. We were working on Shakespeare's Sonnet 116. One of Ray's favourites, it speaks of love as a guiding star to sailing ships in a storm.

Carson blazed through the poem, leaving the rest of us in his dust. He memorized the whole thing that night and will, I have no doubt, be able to recite it for the rest of his life, backwards and forwards.

Carson was a baby-faced eleven-year-old when his mother announced that they were moving to Scotland.

About a week before they left, Ray asked me to stop by his place. He had something to give to Carson. I knew it wouldn't be something shiny and new. Ray doesn't buy gifts for people; when he feels impelled, he gives away his treasures, pieces of himself. I pulled into his driveway and unrolled my window, and he handed me a rusty hunting knife with a seven-inch blade. I took it from him gingerly and laid it on the passenger-side floor. "Every boy needs a knife," he told me. "This one's carbon steel. Mind you, not all carbon steel is good, any more than all lasagna is good, but this blade must have some pretty decent alloy. Most knives nowadays are low-grade stainless, which is basically incapable of holding an edge, although my cleaver is very good—straight from China, where chefs still know that what matters in a knife is the edge. Don't worry about the rust; it doesn't affect anything."

I drove that wicked-looking thing around on the floor of my car for days before Ian finally brought it inside and wrapped it carefully with newspaper and masking tape. Meanwhile, Ray fretted that I had forgotten about it. He nagged me in an email:

> Do you still have my knife? I wanted Carson to have that. Nuts, a boy needs a hunting knife, now doesn't he?

I could think of no child who needed that rusty blade less than Carson did, but I assured Ray I'd see to it that his gift was delivered in time.

Ian and I caught up with Carson and his mum for a final good-bye breakfast at a Vancouver cafe before they headed to the airport. We handed over the package. The sonnet-quoting boy unwrapped the knife and held it up by the tip of the blade over his eggs Benedict, admiring it from all sides before his mother suggested he might not want to brandish it in the restaurant.

Weeks later Ray received an email from Carson, now living in Edinburgh:

> The hardest knife ill-used doth lose its edge ... I can
> no other answer make but thanks, and thanks."

Ray cried.

KISSING THE MERMAID

I have a picture of one of our nephews in his grandparents' pool. He is maybe four or five. He is triumphantly breaking the surface of the water while clutching a spoon that Uncle Ray had dropped into the deep end for him to retrieve. In the photo, the boy is holding the spoon high above his head as though it were an Olympic gold medal. A look of pure joy and exultation lights up his face. A whole crop of kids, including mine, learned to swim and dive under Uncle Ray's watchful eye.

As my kids and their cousins grew older, they spent time at the beach or made day trips to Ruby Lake with Uncle Ray and came back clamouring to tell of their triumphs—personal bests in depth and length of time underwater, always met with the benediction of Uncle Ray's approval. My sisters and I fretted quietly about sending our children on these excursions, but Ray assured us that there are inviolable safety protocols in place—"Hey, I've never lost one yet!"—and so we trusted him with our children. Besides, any time we went along and watched from shore, we saw nothing but enthusiastic kids having fun while learning to respect the authority of the water.

Then one summer day, long after my kids have grown up, Ray asks if I'd like to give free diving a try. My instinctive reaction is "*Me*? No thanks!" but I stifle it. Having my brother ask me to dive with him is an honour, one I've not been offered before. It is like being asked to take communion.

It's low tide at Hopkins Beach, and the water is full of silt from the muddy mouth of the Fraser River. Ray is waiting for me. We walk the length of the pier to his pile of dive gear, and he tosses me a mouldy old wetsuit, ripped and stained and smelling of seaweed and other people's sweat. I gingerly wriggle into it. He yanks the zipper up my back, squashing my chest flat. The shoulders are wide and empty and almost touching my earlobes. It is not a flattering look on a short, fifty-five-

year-old woman, but Ray is oblivious. He hands me a mask and snorkel. Clutching them, I leap off the end of the pier. It's a long way down,
and the cold water is a shock to my system, but I'm too self-conscious
to engage in any of my customary stalling.

He has already set up his diving rig thirty feet beyond the end of
the pier. I estimate it's thirty or forty feet deep out there—more than
I'll need. We both know I won't be setting any records today. A plastic
five-gallon jug bobs at the surface, with a yellow polypropylene rope
tied to its handle. I know it will be held taut by a brick or rock of appropriate weight at the other end. With some trepidation I swim with Ray
out to this makeshift buoy and put on my mask and snorkel. I hold onto
the jug with one hand, treading water. I keep my eyes on Ray's face as
he prepares for his descent. He seems to become unaware of me as he
directs his concentration inward, filling his lungs with long, slow, deep
breaths. Then he dips soundlessly below the surface. I tip my face into
the water. Right away my mask starts to fog up, but I keep watching as
he executes a graceful turn and begins pulling himself headfirst down
the rope. The creamy soles of his feet fade quickly into the olive-green
depths until I can see no trace of him. I hang there, aware of the quick
in-and-out of my own breathing through the snorkel.

It seems an unbearably long time before I see a ghostly shape ma-
terializing beneath me, and Ray comes slowly into focus as he ascends
from the gloom. He takes his time. When at last he breaks the surface,
he is serene.

"Now you try—oh, and be careful. There's a red jelly at about four
metres. They sting."

But I just can't do it, can't get past the anxiety of pulling myself
upside down into that murky water—never mind running face first
into the trailing tentacles of a passing lion's mane jellyfish. Ray is patient with me. Again and again he encourages me to try. I finally give
up, heart hammering, after having attained the pathetic depth of 2.5
metres. He is nothing but kind, leaving the door open for me to try
again another time.

Back on the pier, we peel off our wetsuits. Ray, unselfconscious,
pulls some shorts on over his soaking wet Fruit of the Looms and strug-
gles into a T-shirt, which rolls and sticks against his damp skin. He can't

stand clothes when he's swimming and only wears them when he absolutely has to as a concession to public decorum. As we walk back to our vehicles, each lugging a plastic crate of wet gear, I ask him if he ever free dives naked.

"Not if I'm diving to any depth," he says with a mildly reproachful tone. "It's ice cold down there! You wouldn't survive without a wetsuit." And then as an afterthought, he adds, "Except when I kissed the mermaid. I did *that* stark naked. No mask. No fins." He wrestles his T-shirt down. "But that was a stunt."

I stop walking. "You kissed a mermaid?"

"Sure, the mermaid at Saltery Bay."

I've never seen her myself, but I know instantly which mermaid he's talking about. She is a ten-foot-tall bronze sculpture, sunk offshore in a rocky cove for the pleasure of scuba divers.

"At low tide she's about eighteen metres down, but when I dove on her she was sitting at about twenty metres. It was dark and absolutely freezing down there. It took all of my physical ability and discipline. I tell you, *that's* mind control."

"Did you have someone with you?"

"Not that time. I was alone. I'd say that was probably the high point of my life."

The high point of his life. Way down there, alone in the suffocating dark ...

Later, in an email, I ask Ray to explain what exactly it is he loves so much about free diving—because I certainly hadn't attained to any rapture during my pitiful attempt. His answer invokes both music and poetry:

> Hard to explain, really. There are "reasons," although listing them is sort of like giving the "reasons" why one likes Brahms.
>
> I dive to explore the beauties and mysteries of the water world.
>
> To do so without the encumbrance of scuba gear.
>
> To explore my limits, physical and mental.

To slip the surly bonds of earth and "fly" through the
water.

He enters "the zone, a very, very Zen feeling of total calm and total
awareness at the same time."

Ray's longest breath hold is five minutes and thirty-seven seconds,
and his deepest dive is thirty-five metres. The world record, he informs
me with neither modesty nor immodesty, is well past one hundred
metres. That's about as far as a man can get from the human race on a
lungful of air. And that is where my brother finds his greatest peace.

THE CHESS GAME

In the spring of 2013 I met a slender, handsome young man named Eddie. Not quite sixteen, he had just been diagnosed with Asperger syndrome. (He squeaked in just before Asperger's was merged under Autism Spectrum Disorder in May of that year.) He was deeply embarrassed about his new label, but he consented to share his experience with me—although he wasn't sure he was quite what I was looking for. In his first email to me, he wrote:

> I do not mind sharing my diagnosis with you—however, I trust you will understand where dignity can and must be preserved. Furthermore, as per your request, I would be very happy to help you with your research, although I doubt I will be your most informative test subject. From my perspective, I am 99.2 percent normal, and sometimes I wonder if I even have Asperger's or if I am just a smart kid who didn't really learn the ropes of social interaction. (I am attempting to adapt now.)

Did I mention this kid was fifteen?

I asked him if he accepted his diagnosis. His answer showed the same unflinching candour I've come to expect from my brother—yet it also betrayed a deep ambivalence. The 0.8 percent of himself that was not "normal" was causing him a lot of angst:

> I do in fact see many Aspergian traits within myself. They particularly emerge whenever I am in a social setting, and it would be both foolish and ignorant of me to ignore the determinations of professionals in a field that I have barely dabbled in myself. Like it or not, they're probably right.

Perhaps my own doubts about my diagnosis come
from wishful thinking—like wishing I could abolish
the awkwardness I feel in large crowds. Unfortunately, the cold, hard facts are there, and there is no
changing them.

Eddie faces his situation with brave resignation:

Loneliness is something that underlines my life. But
instead of just living with it, I have been trying to embrace it. I am trying to learn to enjoy being alone, to
treasure the moments of introspection.

He is utterly bewildered by his difficulties. He sees guys who are
clearly less "normal" than he perceives himself to be, and yet they
are hanging out with friends and flirting with girls, while he tackles a
chemistry project alone in his room. He can construct a sentence that
vaults him into the super-nerd stratosphere, but somehow he finds the
simplest conversations with his peers excruciating:

I don't know what to say exactly, and the ensuing
awkward silence is rather disconcerting. Every time
a gap in the conversation opens up, my mind races furiously to come up with something better than
"Quite rainy, isn't it?"

He doesn't appreciate his mother's urgings to "get out there" and
make friends, and he dismisses her concerns about his spending so
much time alone:

She used to complain about how much time I put
into my interests, until I retorted that I was exhibit-
ing extreme focus—a useful skill. I haven't heard any
negative comments since.

When Eddie is locked onto a project, he works with fanatical attention to detail:

> I make sure every element of every project is as per-
> fect as I can make it, and I will nòt let up until I have
> completed it to my satisfaction. Some call it obses-
> sion, I call it focus. Others say I'm stubborn, but I call
> it persistence. These qualities allow me to produce
> high quality work—but at a very slow pace, which
> puts me constantly at odds with the contemporary
> systems of authority.

Ray has made a very similar argument:

> Why must "normal" people always see difference
> as a thing to be squished, not a resource to be har-
> nessed? Who is to say what the "correct" balance is
> between focus and flexibility? I often get tunnel vi-
> sion and can't let go of a problem until it is solved.
> But is that really dysfunctional? Sure, there are times
> when it's not the right thing, but there are other times
> when it is the *only* thing that will get the job done.

More and more, Eddie is forsaking his research projects and the arduous hours of "clerical work" that his teachers require in favour of an online multi-player video game. Through his avatar he interacts with creatures conjured and controlled by other unseen players. It has become more than a game for Eddie. It's hard to leave a world where he is strong, capable and confident, able to use his keen intelligence to form alliances, dodge traps set by his enemies and slay virtual monsters.

There was really nothing I could do to help him, but I knew someone who could: Ray.

I invited Eddie to come to my house to play chess with my brother, a seasoned Aspergian. Eddie responded with worries that his game wasn't up to snuff. Once I had allayed his fears as best I could, I emailed Ray. Would he consider playing chess with this boy?

He agreed immediately.

> Sure, absolutely. Any time.

"That's great, Ray," I wrote back, relieved that he hadn't accused me of trying to herd him into a room with another one of his kind to satisfy my own curiosity. "I'll arrange it. It will be good for Eddie to have something to occupy his clever little mind that doesn't involve a computer." Then, as an aside, I added, "He is drawn to the computer like a duck to water, of course." I pictured Ray nodding knowingly, but he was actually a little affronted by my glib assumption:

> There is no "of course-ness" about it, which is to say that I don't take it for granted that any and all persons with Asperger's will like computers—though most of "us" probably do. The addiction to interactive games is no special trait of Aspies. As always, you are too quick to stereotype.

After shooting down my stereotype, he breezily substituted one of his own:

> Interesting, though, how these games seem to attract males so much more than females ...

He was right, though: most hard-core gamers are males, and most Aspies are males. There's bound to be an overlap. (Incidentally—or not—an unusually high proportion of autistic people are left-handed, as Ray is).

According to the Extreme Male Brain theory of autism, women are usually better at verbal tasks and "empathizing," while men excel at spatial tasks and "systemizing" (defined as the drive to analyze or construct systems). I like this theory. If there is an empathizing-systemizing continuum, I'm hanging off one end and Ray is dangling off the other, and it looks like Eddie's right behind him—except that he has systemizing options that were unimaginable in Ray's day. As most video games are designed to appeal to boys, it follows that "extreme boys" like Eddie would be almost helpless to resist. And the more time he spent in the alternate world of his avatar, the more unwilling he was to come back to this one.

So every day, when Eddie's homework was done and there were

still hours to go before he would be allowed to slip into his other skin, he sat alone in his room, learning to treasure those moments of introspection.

I introduced Ray and Eddie by email and invited them to set a date and time to meet at my house for a game. Both expressed interest, but the logistics of arranging it seemed quite beyond them. When I told Ray to propose a time so I could check to see if it suited both Eddie and his mother, who would be driving him, he made me sound like some sort of micromanaging freak: "The sooner the better," he said. "Anywhere, any time. No need to worry about the 'delicate social implications.' No advance notice required. Nothing to plan." But it was never going to happen unless I managed the delicate social implications.

It all came together. Eddie's very pregnant mother arrived at my door with her stiff-as-a-board son bringing up the rear. Ray had come early, thank goodness, and was waiting in the kitchen, his chessboard already set up on the table. As Eddie entered the room, Ray rose, extended his right hand and assessed the boy's handshake. "Ah, there's a decent grip!" he said warmly. "Not too hard, not too limp, just the way I like it. Full marks." Eddie had passed Handshake 101. There was no mention of the weather, but as I recall, there was some discussion about bowing to one's opponent before a contest and how much better the Samurai Code was than the crap that passes for manners today. Then the two of them sat down to play.

I joined Eddie's mother in the living room, and we chatted, mostly about the impending birth of her baby. I caught snippets of Ray's encouraging commentary: "Great, you've got me on the run." Then, switching into Old Fogey: "Watch out for my knight, sonny. Old age and treachery will get you every time!" He seemed to strike a perfect balance, parrying back and forth between challenger and cheerleader. As is his custom with first-timers, Ray let Eddie win.

The second Eddie and his mother left, Ray leaned back in his chair. "Definitely on the spectrum. I know *exactly* where that kid's at. I remember I used to talk like that. I even used to walk like that." Then he added in a more musing sort of way, "You know, he and I have enough in common that we might very well belong in the same box. It almost gives credence to this whole Asperger's thing. Most of my supposed *fellow sufferers* (he air-quoted the term to make sure I didn't miss the sarcasm) don't give me any sense of kinship, but Eddie does. It's a box of two, mind you, but still ... it could be a box."

I chimed in. "A box of *three*, you mean. Don't forget Glenn Gould. He was a fellow traveller, right?"

"Right, right, of course! And Robison too. I felt the same way when I read Robison." In 2007 John Elder Robison, who was diagnosed with Asperger syndrome when he was forty, wrote a *New York Times* bestselling memoir called *Look Me in the Eye*.[26] After a rough start as a social outcast and a high school dropout, he found success as, among other things, a restorer of luxury European automobiles, an author and lecturer, and a photographer—and now as an adjunct professor involved in autism research. His experiences growing up undiagnosed in the '60s had resonated deeply with Ray.

So now there were four people in the box. I thought Temple Grandin had earned a place in it too, but I knew better than to push. "How was Eddie's game, anyway?"

"He shows promise, but he'll need a lot of practice."

I hoped Eddie would come back—and not only to improve his chess strategy. But six weeks after the game, his mother gave birth to a baby boy, and life got too complicated at their house. He has never come back for a rematch despite repeated invitations from both Ray and me.

"Pity," I said to Ray in an email. "I'm sure it would have done you good to stumble across a wise and war-weary old man like yourself when you were fifteen."

Ray answered, "You can't imagine how true that is."

SHE ISN'T BROKEN

Our niece Emily's laundry list of learning disabilities had followed her all through high school. Her teachers described her as "hypersensitive" and said that she had difficulty reading nonverbal cues.

These are troubles Ray is well acquainted with, even though he is her opposite in temperament: she is, if anything, overly demonstrative—a hug from this six-foot-tall girl can engulf you—where he is physically aloof. She sometimes mistakes simple politeness for overtures of friendship. Her heart rules her head. You'd think Ray would run from this boiling cauldron of emotion—they wouldn't even know what to *do* with her on his planet—but he is her biggest advocate. Hurt Emily and you will deal with him.

I've always thought it strange that Ray would have so much time for someone situated on any spectrum of human behaviour as far from himself as it is possible to be. Emily's whole identity is anchored in the type of emotional drama to which he appears to be a baffled bystander, and yet there is no question that he loves her. Is it simply that Ray doesn't have to be on his guard around her? She has never, after all, been able to master the guile required to thrive as a neurotypical.

Emily has always loved to sing. Ray encourages her in this, and he went out of his way to attend school musical productions in which she played even bit parts. A family member once wondered aloud whether she might have Williams syndrome, which is characterized by developmental delays, learning disabilities, highly social personalities and an affinity for music. Though she can tick all of these boxes, Emily does not meet the criteria for Williams syndrome. But when it was being bandied about as a possibility, Ray got wind of it and stepped in:

> We have too many syndromes already. I'd bet a beer that she does not have Williams syndrome or any other syndrome for that matter. I think most of these

things are imaginary. Em has Em's syndrome and that's that. What comfort do these phony diagnoses really give us anyway? We can't "fix" Em, and I'd not even want to try since it would do more harm than good. She is an exotic, rare and lovely flower, and we should care for her as she needs to be cared for and stop asking pointless questions about syndromes.

The idea was never broached again, and the exotic, rare and lovely flower that is Emily went on trying with all her might to bloom without the sunlight of inclusion and acceptance by her peers. But despite her megawatt smile, she was recently diagnosed with depression. Another label to add to her collection.

"My fear," writes her father, "is that once she's told these labels (disabled, depressed) apply to her, she will give up on herself. It's true she has challenges, but she also has big ambitions, big emotions and a big heart that keeps getting pierced by the realization that for some reason it's hard for her to achieve things that come easily to everyone else."

Her mother echoes these concerns:

"Until very recently, despite being subject to cruelty and teasing and torment most of her life, Emily wore a big bright smile that could not be snuffed out. But she is now taking on those labels to find some way to make herself feel okay about being different from everyone else because it is totally apparent to her that she is."

Emily was put on antidepressants. While she was buckling under the weight of her labels, her Uncle Ray fought them off—his *and* hers.

Ray and I were at our local movie theatre for the screening of a new documentary. Waiting for the show to begin, we were discussing Emily's situation.

"Of bleeding *course* she's depressed!" Ray was riled up. "How could a sane person *not* be depressed in her situation? She doesn't need a doctor; she needs a friend."

"I know," I replied. "Too bad there's no drug for loneliness ..."

"If only we could find a safe place for her." Ray whispered those words as though in prayer. "She doesn't belong on this planet any more than I do. I can take it—at least on some level—but she can't."

His empathy for our niece was an almost physical presence in that theatre. What he was saying revealed as much about him as it did about her. But dare I risk being seen as "studying" him again?

I took the gamble. "I love how much you care for Em," I said, "but you're really worked up over this, Ray. Of all our nieces and nephews, why is this one so special to you?"

"You don't know anything at all about me if you need to ask," he replied. "Em is the opposite of Goongbalong. What she *has* is a lack of reptilian survival instincts. She is genuine. She doesn't manipulate people or use them. She would not step on your face to advance her status. Em is a candle in the wind."

I persisted. "But she's so steeped in pop culture. I mean, if some little starlet breaks up with her boyfriend, Emily will throw herself on her bed and cry for days. When Leonard Cohen died, she posted a gushing tribute on Facebook—and she had never even heard of him until that morning. She's living vicariously through social media. I thought you'd disdain all that."

"For the lack of anything *better*!" came his impassioned reply. "The veneer is so thin! Can you not see through it? She wants to belong to something, and if the only thing available is some celebutante's fan club, then she will try to belong to that. She's not shallow; she's deep, but she sometimes sees depth in things where there is none. She doesn't realize that she lives in a tinsel world of phony, plastic, posturing vampires. She thinks they are as real as she is. One could almost wish she *was* a plastic doll for her sake—she'd feel less pain. She isn't broken; the world is."

He sat back in his seat as though spent. Then he leaned forward again, reanimated.

"When she was little, I could sustain myself just thinking about her smile. She is simple and pure, and I hope she remains so. I never have to worry when I'm with her. She's the light of my life, actually. There is no one on this earth I love more."

The house lights dimmed, and the opening credits began to roll. But Ray had one more thing to add.

"And I *hate* your planet," he said with uncharacteristic vehemence, "because it is mean to Emily."

When we experience true empathy, the line between "self" and "other" is blurred. The DSM-5 lists "lack of emotional reciprocity" as a defining feature of Autism Spectrum Disorder—which means Ray will have trouble feeling the pain of another person as though it is his own. Right?

Wrong.

The problem, according to him, is not that he lacks empathy; the problem is that it is not always triggered when we neurotypicals think it should be, nor is it revealed in the manner and with the speed that we expect it. He explains:

> I am profoundly empathetic—*if* I get the signals
> right.

That's a big "if," and he's placed it between his trademark asterisks to acknowledge that it's by no means a given that he will get the signals right. But when he does—as he demonstrated in the case of his beautifully crafted emails to our depressed cousin Don—his empathy knows no bounds. He explains:

> It's just that I don't have this instantaneous empathy
> for the other guy. The *mechanism* of empathy is
> certainly there, but the specific triggers seem to be
> different.

I tend to absorb and reflect the emotions of people I care about, registering their happiness and sadness as if they were my own. My mirror neurons will see to it, firing automatically, as I imagine myself in their place. It doesn't work that way for Ray.

It doesn't seem to work that way for young Eddie, either. I lent him my copy of John Elder Robison's second book, *Be Different: Adventures of a Free-Range Aspergian*.[27] It was not as bleak as *Look Me in the Eye*. By the time he wrote *Be Different*, Robison had embraced his autism and begun to move forward with confidence for the first time in his life, knowing he was "complete on the inside."[28] Ray had loved the book. I thought it might bolster Eddie's spirits too.

Robison acknowledges that his own response to other people's "unspoken conversations" is different from the "normal" response. He writes: "An angry person looks at them, and they get angry too. It's a gut thing, instinctive. An angry person looks at me and I say to myself, *Hmm, he looks angry*. It's more of an intellectual process for me."

Eddie is dumbfounded at the notion that most people mirror the emotions of others, and he loses his Vulcan cool:

> *People react to others' emotions with emotional mimicry!!????* Whaaat?!?!?! How do people function!?! It is incomprehensible that people would respond to the emotions of others with emotions of their own. I ... I just can't understand it. If people are constantly mirroring other people's emotions, it seems to me almost like a loss of individuality. Why should the emotions of other individuals—with completely different histories, motivations, ideas and preferences—affect you in any way? All I can say is MIND BLOW!!!

Several months go by before I see Eddie's name in my inbox again. He is apologetic. He's been up to his eyeballs in schoolwork, he tells me. He's having trouble coping. The pressure is pushing him to the breaking point. But when he's had more than he can take, he knows he can "flip a switch" and shut down his emotions. He explains:

> I often "turn off" strong emotions just as one turns off a light because it is momentarily too bright.

Just like that.

Some researchers believe that the basis of autism is a hyperfunctioning of the neural circuitry of the brain. They see it not as a disability so much as an overability: hyper-perception, hyper-attention, hyper-memory and hyper-emotionality.[29] Early studies concluded that the lack of social intelligence in autism was due to a lack of activity in the amygdala—but the opposite could be true: the amygdala could be overly reactive in autism, leading to symptoms that look quite similar to underactivity, namely "withdrawal and decreased social interaction due to enhanced stress-response and socio-emotional overflow."[30]

Neuroscientists Henry and Kamila Markram have coined an expression to capture what they believe is the reality of the autistic experience: the Intense World Theory. In a 2012 interview on WrongPlanet. net, they describe their hypothesis for the layman:

> The Intense World theory states that autism is the consequence of a supercharged brain that makes the world painfully intense and that the symptoms are largely because autistics are forced to develop strategies to actively avoid the intensity and pain. Autistics see, hear, feel, think, and remember too much, too deep, and process information too completely.

I asked Ray what he thought of the "supercharged brain" theory. It's not theory, he replied; it's reality:

> This "Intense World" concept seems absolutely correct in my experience, and I can certainly sympathize with the idea that what is going on with autistics— insofar as they are on any "spectrum" with me—is a huge need to protect the self from overwhelming intensities of all kinds. This, paradoxically, produces the appearance of a sort of deadness, when in fact what is going on is a hyper-aliveness.

Sensory overload is part of the diagnostic criteria for autism—and we're not just talking about scratchy sweater labels and loud noises. In Ray's case, "overwhelming intensities of all kinds" must surely have included those strap-happy teachers in the Caribbean, angry householders on his mail route, confrontational colleagues, stern judges and weeping women. "Too much," the Markrams say. "*Too much*," Ray has said to me countless times. "I feel too much, hear too much, see too much."

Sure enough, when I look back over our correspondence, I can see that he has been patiently explaining it to me for years, but it's as though I'm hearing him for the first time. I admit this to him and brace myself for a scathing reproach, but his reply is only mildly patronizing:

> No, none of this should be new to you, but you only see what your own model lets you see. You are to be praised for admitting your ignorance and for letting the light shine in when it finally does.

Grateful to have dodged a bullet for once, I turn my thoughts back to Eddie. His ability to switch off his emotions, I see now, is not a cold, calculated decision to turn off his heart. It's a way to protect it—a circuit breaker of sorts. A safety mechanism designed to shut this sensitive boy down before he spontaneously combusts.

Eddie's a little sorry for me that I don't have a shut-off valve of my own. He writes:

> Indeed, I believe this is the best way to cope with most disasters, internal and external. Emotion is irrational in the face of a crisis. It can make you rush into a burning fire to save someone—and end up getting killed yourself—instead of calling the fire department or looking for a garden hose. I think it is far better to rely on logic and intelligence.

Eddie's reasoning is flawless. I'm afraid the best I can do is try to wrestle my own emotions to the ground when they threaten to hijack my good judgment. Eddie finds this really disturbing:

> But the two are completely different! They even *feel* different. Logic presents me with a problem to be solved. My mind continues to grope for the answer with the utmost concentration until I find it, whereas emotion is this enormous compelling surge I feel throughout my body that seems to want to direct my thoughts in a certain way without any consideration for the circumstances. How can people *not* separate the two? I hypothesize that those people have never really placed all their concentration into thinking something through.

I find myself smiling. In writing, Eddie plays a passable game of Goongbalong. With a growing sense of affection for this extraordinary young man, I read on:

> Quite frankly, I think that's a terribly volatile and dangerous way to live—but maybe that's because my emotions are stronger than most people's.

Ray agrees:

> I *know* that my thoughts and my emotions are different things. Lots of folks—particularly women—seem to believe that their thoughts are their feelings and their feelings are their thoughts. I think that Ed and I would agree that we are very clear on the difference. This does not minimize the emotions in any way; it just makes an important distinction. It might look cold and unfeeling, but it isn't. It's not that Spock doesn't *have* emotions; it's that he doesn't let them control him and prefers to keep them private.

Again echoing Ray's sentiments, Eddie writes:

> I certainly do have a very real and very strong self-preservation instinct that makes me want to cross the highest mountains to shield myself from hurtful or emotionally damaging situations.

By his own account, he is one big exposed nerve:

> My emotions are not "dampened" but excessively strong. When I am hit with an emotion, it feels like a MagLev train has sideswiped me at maximum speed.

If you're about to be hit by a train, what difference does it make what kind it is? But the second I looked up MagLev, I understood why he had chosen that specific train. A Magnetic Levitation—or MagLev—train doesn't thunder along a track on steel wheels. It floats over a guideway, with powerful magnets creating lift and thrust. It moves at five hundred kilometres per hour. And you don't hear it coming.

"It's not chugga-chugga-chugga-*wham*," explains Eddie. "It's ... *WHAM!*" He slammed a closed fist into his open palm.

His baby brother, just a few months old, was diagnosed with a rare and invariably fatal genetic disorder. When Eddie and I next corresponded by email, the switch had been flipped, his emotions turned off.

> For some reason, I don't feel anything. Occasionally, I am aware of a bit of disappointment that my little brother will not be able to live out his natural life, but nothing more.

On some indefinable level, the activation of his own survival mechanism disturbed him deeply:

> I keep asking myself, "Why don't I feel anything?" It's almost as if I was not human.

The morning the baby died, Eddie left his inconsolable parents and went to school as though it were any other day. He showed nothing. Maybe he felt nothing, but I hear he intends to go to university to become a molecular biologist so he can find out what killed his brother. If necessary, he will spend the rest of his life looking for a cure. And that's not nothing.

The Markrams believe that "runaway information processing"[31] can cause autistic children to develop excessive fear memories that are difficult to undo. These fears can cascade, taking on a life of their own. The Markrams say that great care is needed when exposing them to an often-chaotic world and that parents and teachers must exercise extreme caution in administering discipline. "They will never forget the punishment and will generalize it quickly to a point where they will fear so many things that they might not be able to function normally."

Ray ardently agrees. Even the threat of punishment by caning in Barbados paralyzed him.

I keep hearing that we're on the cusp of a revolution in cognitive neuroscience, but it will come too late to undo the damage done to my brother—a self-described "neurotic ruin" from decades of running for his life on the Goongbalong killing fields.

Uncle Ray's Legacy

My daughter Lesley reminisces about growing up with an extraordinary uncle as a mentor and playmate. "What other grown-up would ever invest so much time, money and energy in little kids?" she wonders. "All those music and poetry nights, building forts and rafts, looking at the stars and planets, astronomy swims ..."

But she grew up and grew away from him. "Losing Lol," Ray says, "that was a slow death for me."

His other nieces and nephews have moved on too. They have relationships, mortgages, jobs, families. There is less time for taking a swig of grog, dressing up like pirates and swimming around the ferry in the dark of night with Uncle Ray leading the way, a plastic sabre clamped in his teeth. Less time to notice the westward drift of the constellations through the seasons, and no time at all for sitting around memorizing poetry. Ray is running out of playmates. But he keeps looking for a way to be useful. A way to matter.

Last fall he spent some chilly nights outside mapping the sky with our twenty-year-old niece, Jessica—he calls her Buff. He thought he had a keen new student at last, and he had declared his intention to "turn her into the hottest little astro-girl on the Coast."

> Buff talks about going back to school, and I've told her that if she wants to do that, she'll have to learn how to learn. I thought that mastering astronomy would be a fun way to "practise," if you get me. But 90 percent of the time when I phone her or text with something we might do together—go to astronomy club, collimate the scope, have a sky session, do some research—she just ignores me.

Ray was crushed. So certain had he been of Jessica's passion for astronomy that he had gifted her his meticulously restored telescope. Now he struggled to understand her behaviour. Had he done something wrong?

> Am I missing some sort of Goongbalong signal? On my planet, the worst insult you can offer someone is to ignore them. When I am expecting someone, I will stand there like the Steadfast Tin Soldier. I will not dishonour them by taking off, even if I *know* they are dishonouring me and have no intention of coming. On my planet, respect is by far the most important thing shared between people, yet it is of the kind that is never demanded and is meaningless unless freely offered.

"She's young, Ray," I explained, "and probably doesn't know quite how to say no—especially to someone as powerful and persuasive as you are." I gently suggested that he may have misjudged her enthusiasm for astronomy. "Ironically, she is probably avoiding you because she can't bear to disappoint you by telling you straight up that she'd rather do something else." This did nothing to salve his hurt:

> I'd put that as the leading popular theory—it has the virtue of trying to make rudeness look like misplaced kindness, but sometimes it just doesn't fly. Buff did it again yesterday. She said she'd be here in "an hour or two" but never showed up at all, nor texted to say she couldn't make it. This cannot be given any good spin IMHO [in my humble opinion].

Ray had so much to offer, and now yet another promising young pupil had turned her back on him. These kids were all so busy poking and swiping at their phones, he lamented, when all they had to do was look up, just *look up*, for God's sake, and the magnificence of heaven would be theirs.

Jessica would never have hurt her Uncle Ray's feelings on purpose—I knew that, but by standing him up, she had hurt him more

than she could know. He was ready to wash his hands of the whole
business:

> I've spent most of my adult life trying to prime
> pumps with little or nothing to show for it. Time to
> retire. Everything I know will die with me.

☙

Several months after Ray's heartrending email, Ian invited some kids
over to play cards. Lesley was already at the table, divvying out the
poker chips, and I was in my office around the corner when I heard the
front door open. It was Jessica coming in for the game, with Reid and
Seth in tow. Ray's forlorn words still hung in my mind, and a lingering disappointment clung to me as I thought again of our niece's lack
of common courtesy toward her uncle. But when she poked her head
into my office with a cheery "Hey, Aunty Claire!" I made an effort to
push the bad feelings away. Maybe she wasn't aware of how sad he was.
Maybe she could still make amends. So after some light conversation
I said, "You know, Jess, Uncle Ray says he called and texted, but you
ignored him."

Jessica's face flushed at my implicit accusation.

"He gave me a star chart to memorize," she began, "and tons of
old astronomy magazines. And he bought me all these used textbooks
from the Trading Post. Wait—I'm pretty sure they're still in my car."
She disappeared before I could stop her and came back lugging an
armload of library discards from the '70s and '80s.

"He was going to make me write an exam on what's in all these
books." She set the pile down on my desk. "And I had to understand
about mirrors and how light is backwards in the telescope. I think I
still have all my drawings too."

This time I stopped her before she could go back to her car for the
evidence. I was starting to get the picture.

"And he gave me his ancient puffy down jacket to keep me warm.
The one with the feathers sticking out of it? And Grampa's old binoc-
ulars from the war," Jessica continued, "and a flashlight with red tape
over the lens to preserve our night vision."

"Where did you set up the scope?"

"On Aunty Trish's deck mostly. I was babysitting Tessa a lot when Aunty Trish was away for work. You know Tessa's scared of the dark, right? But we weren't allowed to turn on any lights in the house, so I always had to find someone to stay inside with her so I could be out doing stars. They couldn't open the fridge. Once somebody turned on the microwave and Uncle Ray got mad because it was light pollution. They had to go to the bathroom in the dark. I wasn't even allowed to look at my phone."

She took a breath and continued. "Most of the time I loved it! And I did learn a lot. But we always had to go at his pace, not mine. And it always made my asthma worse in winter, but he never noticed. It just got to be too much. It was all too much."

I nodded. I know how all-consuming Ray's attentions can be. And it seemed Jessica had not only logged more star time with Ray than any of our other nieces and nephews, she'd logged more time in the water, too. And she wanted me to know it.

"I've spent hours and hours learning how to do the crawl—he's *still* teaching me how to do the crawl. But first I had to learn how to do the dead man's float for at least three minutes. I was practising by myself once and someone tried to rescue me. Oh, and speaking of embarrassing, I've swum to Keats with a garbage bag on my head."

"What?"

"Yeah, it was our 'Unofficial Keats Swim,'" she explained, smiling now at the memory of it, "from Armours Beach to Keats dock. It was just me and Lol and Uncle Ray that time. You had to pay money for the official swim, so we did our own a few yards down the beach. They had safety boats and whistles and stuff, and they were all in matching Speedo caps, so Uncle Ray made us pirate scarves from black garbage bags, and we had to tie them around our heads. It felt horrible dragging along my back as I was swimming. Totally slows you down, too."

"How long did it take to swim across?"

Jessica yelled to Lesley at the poker table. "Hey Lol, how long did our Keats swim take? About an hour?"

"Yeah, hour, maybe hour and a half," Lesley called back. She laughed. "My arms were sore for two days."

I was pondering the fact that I was finding out more than a decade too late that my daughter had swum to Keats Island with neither a life jacket nor my permission when Jessica brought my attention back to her own Uncle Ray–approved activities list.

"I love free diving even more than swimming," she said softly. "When Uncle Ray kissed the mermaid? That would be the highlight of my life too."

"Even if no one was there to see it?"

"Even if no one was there to see it. Two summers ago I made fifteen metres. I've gone down through the thermocline. It takes your breath away. If I could be good at just one thing for Uncle Ray, it would be free diving."

"Fifteen metres." I did a quick calculation. "That's almost fifty feet, Jess. Isn't that enough?"

"Uncle Ray says he's conquered his fear and I can conquer mine too. Some of the best times of my life have been with him. But I can't always do everything on his schedule, Aunty Claire. I just can't."

Here I had been thinking about chastising my niece for letting Ray down. Now I was ashamed of myself. This girl who had grown up without a father had fought off every fear to win her uncle's approval.

She told me about the poems she has memorized, counting them off on her fingers: "'Oh Captain, My Captain,' 'The Shooting of Dan McGrew,' 'The Road Not Taken,' 'Ozymandias' ... My proudest is 'Sam McGee,'" she said, and launched into the poem. "There are strange things done in the midnight sun / by the men who moil for gold; / the Arctic trails have their secret tales / that would make your blood run cold ..."

Her brothers, distracted from their card game, appeared in my office doorway, first Reid, then Seth, leaving Ian and Lesley sitting at the dining room table. The two boys joined in on McGee, helping Jessica when she faltered. Then Lesley was there too. Between them all, they were cobbling together a halting rendition of "The Cremation of Sam McGee," the sixty-eight-line poem none of them had recited since they were children.

"Okay, okay!" I smiled, cutting them off when it was obvious they intended to plough through the whole thing.

Uncle Ray's legacy. Right there in my office doorway.

A Different Drummer

Henry David Thoreau said, "Could a greater miracle take place than for us to look through each other's eyes for an instant?" Well, I have made some progress in that regard. That's no small thing, considering that, when I "discovered" Asperger syndrome, I thought the only one who needed to make any progress was Ray. I'm making fewer blanket statements, using fewer *theys*: "*They* love computers," "*They* hate social functions," and the like.

When I tell Ray I'm weeding those egregious stereotypes out of my vocabulary, I expect him to be pleased. But instead of commending me, he donates a few to bolster my dwindling collection:

> I do think "they" tend to find all social functions a bit trying—though "hate" might be too strong a word. A good Dead Poet's or music night is food for my soul. Or a deep discussion of almost any subject. But it does seem to be a useful and accurate thing to say that "they" are intense about everything, as I am. It's *one* area where I think I fit the Aspie bill.

And that's how it goes. I have suffered many uncomfortable paradigm shifts and endured endless admonitions and corrections. I have become used to being humbled every time I think I've got the gist of it.

He tells me:

> You get closer to wisdom—rather than paternalism—when you try to understand that you *can't* understand what it's like for me.

He's right. I can't. I don't think he'll contradict me on that one.

But Ray lives on *my* planet, where he is hopelessly outnumbered and where just being himself is always risky.

It has been eight years since I read that book about Glenn Gould and thought, "Good Lord, it's my brother!" Now, thanks to Writing Man, I have been given a backstage pass to his most intimate thoughts and feelings, and permission to share them with the world.

Writing Man and I get on like a house on fire—even when we're fighting, we're having fun—but Ray and I still see almost everything from different angles. If I try to school him, he schools me right back. Most of the time, we still think it's the *other* guy who's got it all wrong, and we must still retreat to our computers to work things out.

Does Ray want to be understood? Sometimes he seems to plead for it. "You see?" he wrote to me once when we had arrived at some rare patch of common ground. "Our minds are not that different, really, are they? Inside I'm actually a human being."

But for every time he invites me in, there's another where he holds me off as though I am trying to steal something from him. Will he see what I have written here as a fair and balanced portrait of a complex man or as another cruel put-down? If I have attempted the former, is he guaranteed to conclude I've achieved the latter?

I remember the day I realized our correspondence could easily fill a book. I told Ray I was thinking of writing one with him as my collaborator. I expected him to be flattered—and he was. "Shucks," he said, suddenly bashful, "if I'd known I was being quoted, I'd have polished my prose!"

Only later did he reveal deep misgivings:

> I feel a mixture of anticipation and dread at the thought of reading this book. What are you telling people about me? Am I being caricatured? Suppose I denounce the whole thing? Then what you have is fiction at best, slander at worst—unless of course you feel that you are better qualified than I am to describe my inner life.

I was taken aback and I told him so. He immediately dropped his dukes:

Well, not "slander"—that's the wrong word. "Grossly misunderstand" would be better. If you are going to "explain" me, I hope you get it right.

I've questioned both my motives and my qualifications, reminding Ray at one point that I'm not a scientist or a shrink, not an expert on autism—I'm not even an expert at being his sister. I figured I had left myself wide open to accusations of arrogance and waited for him to come back with a stinging rejoinder, so of course he didn't. Instead he told me that my lack of qualifications was the perfect qualification:

Because you are *not* a scientist or a shrink, it is possible for you to see things with fresh eyes, as yet undimmed by the strictures and dogmas of the "learned."

Heartened, I said, "I want the world to know Writing Man."

And Ray's reply was, "Well, he could use an advocate, that's for sure."

Ray is still an Extreme Male, and I am still the scariest thing on this planet—an Extreme Female. But I am no longer exhausting myself trying to refashion him into a neurotypical. It can't be done, and he can only be asked to go so far in impersonating one. He could try a little harder to help himself, though. I still scold him when I see him tucking into a stack of brain-fogging pre-fab waffles doused with high-fructose corn syrup. I still want to burn those damn sweatpants, and I will never, *ever* be okay with his long fingernails, no matter how useful they are. And I still feel the need to vet my guest list for music nights. But I realize that, in all those years of trying to teach him how to do things my way, I was the one who learned the most. Still, I have misgivings of my own, and I express them to Ray:

I've worked hard to represent you fairly, but the book is written from my vantage point, and we look at things differently. I have my own "mix of anticipation and dread" at the thought of you tearing the whole thing to shreds.

After that, Ray's tone seemed more relaxed, but he wasn't letting me entirely off the hook.

> Well, of course if it's "observational," you have almost free rein. If you attempt any sort of insights, you should be a bit more restrained—but of course the thing would be far less juicy without some attempts to look under the hood, right?

He's not quite sure if I'm some sort of tabloid reporter digging for salacious details for the enjoyment of the neurotypical public or if I am the voiceless Writing Man's big break.

He's taking his chances. We both are.

Stargazing

Remember to look up at the stars and not down at your feet. ... Be curious. And however difficult life may seem, there is always something you can do and succeed at. It matters that you don't just give up.
— Stephen Hawking

It is nine o'clock in the evening when Ray calls me. "Hey, wanna do stars?"

It is the middle of March, and Mount Elphinstone is wearing a cap of new snow. My house is warm and cozy, and Ian and I are in the middle of a good Netflix series. I want to say no. The idea of going outside to stand and freeze in the dark does not appeal to me, but I might be his last resort for the evening. I will myself to say yes. He offers to come and get me, but I decide to take my own car, so I can make my escape when I've had enough. I get dressed in my warmest coat, gloves and scarf and drive down to Soames Beach to meet him.

He is waiting on the deck of our sister Trish's waterfront cottage. Keats Island, just four kilometres across Shoal Channel, is a featureless black shape, its silhouette barely discernible against the faint glow of Vancouver's lights behind it. The sea is calm, and we can hear the rhythmic sighs of little waves lapping at the high-tide line in the darkness below us. Ray shoves Trish's carefully arranged patio furniture out of the way so he can plant his tripod in just the right spot to orient the telescope to the North Star. Shells collected by her children tumble off the coffee table onto the weathered deck.

"See the Big Dipper?" Ray asks me, his foot crunching a shell. "The front edge points the way to Polaris, the North Star. Right ... there." When I don't see it immediately, he grabs the back of my head with one hand and swivels me until I am pointed in the right direction.

Got it.

He makes fine adjustments to the knobs and dials on his tele-scope, explaining things to me as he works. "To get the scope to track a celestial object," he says, "it has to be polar-aligned. This adjustment here sets the declination, which stays fixed for that object. However, all objects rise in the east and set in the west"—here he sweeps both arms in a great arc across the sky as though he's performing some sort of tai chi move—"and that motion is followed by adjusting this screw right here. For this to work, the movement must pivot around an axis that points directly toward the North Pole. If it doesn't, you get the same sort of error you get when you're trying to redraw a circle with a compass and you're not sure where the centre point is."

He squints into the telescope a while longer. Once he has his bear-ings, he straightens up and turns his face to the night.

"Hmm," he says, more to himself than to me, "what can I learn tonight?" He rubs his cold hands together and scans the sky hungrily, the way another man might scrutinize the offerings on a buffet table. A half-moon has risen over Keats, providing a little more ambient light than he'd like, but he says that if we wait for a cloudless night and a new moon occurring together on the west coast of British Columbia, we might wait forever.

"Right," I say, smiling. "Carpe diem."

"Carpe noctem," he corrects me. Seize the night.

Ray bends to the telescope again, fixes the moon in his sights, and steps aside, inviting me to take a look. "Careful, don't touch the scope," he cautions. "Even the vibrations from our footsteps can throw it off."

I step to the telescope, trying not to bump it or trip over the splayed legs of the tripod—an easy enough mistake to make in the dark. When I put my eye to the eyepiece, I gasp. The moon fills the circle of the telescope. Pinnacles and pockmarks on the illuminated portion of the sphere are revealed in stark relief, fading into the deep shadow of the dark side. If I stretched out my hand, I swear I could run my fingers over these contours.

The moon slides out of the viewfinder before I am finished mar-velling at it.

Ray has been standing back patiently, but he's anxious to move on. The moon's just a warm-up act. We have a whole sky to cover.

"There's Betelgeuse," he says, pointing, "just above Orion's Belt.

See how it glows reddish? It's a red supergiant. It's so big that if it was where the sun is, we would be inside it. It would encompass Mercury, Venus, us and Mars—maybe all the way out to Jupiter. And you thought the sun was big!"

"Wow," I say stupidly.

"And over there are Castor and Pollux, the twins, from the constellation Gemini. See them?"

We locate Procyon, Sirius, Rigel and Aldebaran. Despite half a century of looking at the sky, all are new to me. I'm pretty sure Ray knows it, too, but tonight he is gentle with me because I'm taking steps to dispel my ignorance.

"The sky is more beautiful when you know how it works," he says. "Can you imagine having friends and not knowing their names? Ah, there's Capella, right up there!" He points to a winking yellow light. "My favourite star, third brightest in our hemisphere." There is a warmth in his voice, as though he has spotted an old friend waving to him in a crowd.

"You have a favourite star?"

"Yes, Capella. Em's star. It's blonde and bright like her. 'It is an ever-fixed mark / That looks on tempests and is never shaken,'" he says, quoting his favourite Shakespearean sonnet.

Next he focuses his telescope on what looks to me like another star, but I soon learn that it is the planet Jupiter, part of our own solar system. Not only can we make out the streaky rings girdling its middle, but we see three tiny pinpoints of light, two above and one below the planet.

"Those are three of the four main moons of Jupiter: Ganymede, Io, Europa and Callisto, but I believe there are over sixty of them altogether. Did you know that Ganymede is bigger than the planet Mercury? It was Galileo who first observed those four moons through his telescope. Sometimes he saw four, and sometimes there were only three, so he concluded that when one of them disappeared, it must be hiding behind Jupiter. Up until Galileo, everybody thought the Earth was the centre of everything. He got into a lot of trouble for daring to suggest otherwise. After all, we don't feel ourselves hurtling through space—the very notion was preposterous in his day! The sun and the stars and the moon and the planets all *look* like they revolve around us, don't they? We talk about 'sunrise' and 'sunset,' but of course it's really *us* rising and setting." Ray is just getting warmed up. "My goal," he tells me, his voice animated, "is to be able to identify every major constellation that appears in the northern hemisphere."

He *will* learn them, of course, and I know he would love it if someone—anyone—would learn alongside him. But my nose is running, my fingertips are stinging, and I can't feel my feet. I make my excuses and drive away with the car heater blasting, leaving him there alone, peering into the cosmos.

For a moment I feel guilty, but then I realize there's no need to worry. With mountains at his back, the sea at his feet and a sky of stars overhead, he's among friends.

Endnotes

1. Peter F. Ostwald, *Glenn Gould: The Ecstasy and Tragedy of Genius*, (New York: W.W. Norton & Company, 1998), 27.

2. Ibid., 22.

3. Ibid., 109.

4. Ibid., 32.

5. Ibid., 131.

6. Temple Grandin, *Thinking in Pictures and Other Reports from My Life with Autism*, (New York: First Vintage Books, 1996), 31.

7. Temple Grandin and Richard Panek, *The Autistic Brain: Helping Different Kinds of Minds Succeed*, (Boston: Houghton Mifflin Harcourt, 2014).

8. Max Wertheimer, *Productive Thinking*, (New York: Harper and Brothers, 1959), 213–228.

9. Allan and Barbara Pease, *The Definitive Book of Body Language*, (New York: Bantam Dell, 2006), 9.

10. Natalie Stechyson, Postmedia News, "Top Court Splits on Witness Niqab," as quoted in the *Vancouver Sun*, December 21, 2012.

11. Allison Jones, "Woman Ordered to Remove Face Veil to Testify," *Vancouver Sun*, April 25, 2013.

12. Christine Hsu, "You Can Judge 90 Percent of a Stranger's Personal Characteristics Just by Looking at Their Shoes," Medical Daily, June 12, 2012, https://www.medicaldaily.com/you-can-judge-90-percent-strangers-personal-characteristics-just-looking-their-shoes-240793.

13. Oliver Sacks, *An Anthropologist on Mars: Seven Paradoxical Tales*, (New York: First Vintage Books, 1996), 257.

14. Ibid., 263.

15. Ibid., 275.

16. Leo Kanner, "Autistic Disturbances of Affective Contact," *Nervous Child: Journal of Psychopathology, Psychotherapy, Mental Hygiene, and Guidance of the Child*, no. 2, (1943): 217–250, https://simonsfoundation.s3.amazonaws.com/share/071207-leo-kanner-autistic-affective-contact.pdf.

17. Bruno Bettelheim, *The Empty Fortress: Infantile Autism and the Birth of Self*, (New York: Free Press, 1967).

18. NIH/National Institute of Environmental Health Sciences, "Prental inflammation linked to autism risk," ScienceDaily, January 24, 2013, www.sciencedaily.com/releases/2013/01/130124140725.htm.

19. Simon Baron-Cohen, "The Extreme Male Brain Theory of Autism," National Library of Medicine, PubMed, June 1, 2002, https://www.ncbi.nlm.nih.gov/pubmed/12039606.

20. Leo Kanner, "Autistic Disturbances of Affective Contact."

21. Tony Attwood, *The Complete Guide to Asperger's Syndrome*, (London, UK, 2007), 9.

22. Dr. Hans Asperger, as quoted in *The Complete Guide to Asperger's Syndrome*, 26.

23. Tony Attwood, *The Complete Guide to Asperger's Syndrome*.

24. Liane Holliday Willey review of Attwood, *The Complete Guide to Asperger's Syndrome*.

25. Associated Press, "'So Cruel': Cuckoo's Nest Villain Now Finds Scenes Too Agonizing to Watch," as quoted in the *Vancouver Sun*, October 5, 2012, D6.

26. John Elder Robison, *Look Me in the Eye: My Life with Asperger's*, (New York: Broadway Paperbacks, 2008).

27. John Elder Robison, *Be Different: Adventures of a Free-Range Aspergian*, (Toronto: Doubleday Canada, 2011).

28. Ibid., 9.

29. Kamila Markram and Henry Markram, "The Intense World Theory: a unifying theory of the neurobiology of autism," Frontiers in Human Neuroscience, December 21, 2010, http://journal.frontiersin.org/article/10.3389/fnhum.2010.00224/full.

30. Ibid.

31. Ibid.

Acknowledgements

Thank you...

To Betty Keller for her peerless mentorship in the art, the craft and the discipline of writing, and to Kathryn the Beloved for her steadfast belief in this project and her ridiculously hard work on my behalf. I am forever indebted to you both.

To the people in my writing groups over the years who helped subtly shape the work-in-progress with your critiques, insightful questions and encouragements.

To my early readers: Rohanna, Christabel, Cathy, Nancy, Jacenta, Brett, Launie, Mike, Anita, Sheila, Dave R, David G, Lana, Maureen, Lesley, Eileen and Paul. Your feedback and unique perspectives were so valuable.

To Temple Grandin, my hero, for caring about the autistic adults like Ray, and for lending her mighty name to my efforts.

To my publisher and the team at Caitlin Press, who helped me deliver a book I'm proud of.

To web designers Jordan and Jasmine for my website and "on call" technical assistance.

To Ray, for the courage and the honesty.

To the rest of my vast and complicated family. Your shameless boosterism kept me going.

Lastly, to Ian Finlayson, for *everything*. During the seven years it took me to write this book, holed up alone in my little office for hours at a stretch, you never once complained. Just kept on bringing me tea and encouraging me to keep at it. Words fail me now, and that's a first.

CLAIRE FINLAYSON

After a twenty-five-year career as a jewellery designer, running a business and raising a family, Claire Finlayson now writes full time. She has always been an essay writer, and occasionally a journalist, but her passion is creative non-fiction. *Dispatches from Ray's Planet*, seven years in the making, is Finlayson's first book, written under the mentorship of Betty Keller.

Finlayson lives in Gibsons, BC, and currently serves as vice president on the board of directors of the Sunshine Coast Festival of the Written Arts, Canada's longest running literary event celebrating Canadian writers.